Always By My Side:
Losing the love of my life and the fight to
honour his memory

Always
By
My Side

Christina Schmid

C

Century · London

Published by Century 2012

2 4 6 8 10 9 7 5 3 1

First published in Great Britain in 2012 by
Century
Random House, 20 Vauxhall Bridge Road,
London SW1V 2SA

www.randomhouse.co.uk

Addresses for companies within The Random House Group Limited can be found
at: www.randomhouse.co.uk

The Random House Group Limited Reg. No. 954009

A CIP catalogue record for this book is available from the British Library

ISBN 9781846059476

The Random House Group Limited supports The Forest Stewardship Council
(FSC®), the leading international forest certification organisation. Our books
carrying the FSC label are printed on FSC® certified paper. FSC is the only forest
certification scheme endorsed by the leading environmental organisations,
including Greenpeace. Our paper procurement policy can be found at:
www.randomhouse.co.uk/environment

Typeset by SX Composing DTP, Rayleigh, Essex
Printed and bound by CPI Group (UK) Ltd, Croydon, CR0 4YY

I would like to dedicate this book to my awesome husband and best friend, my 'hoofin" son Lairdster and my mother and Nanna for passing on to me the rare gift to be calm, unique, positive, principled, loyal and strong, and to overcome chaos and adversity even in the face of sheer hell.

QUIET HERO

by Kathleen Mills

She wakes very early, he's leaving today
She will stand tall and proud as he's walking away.
He glances back warmly at his children and wife,
Knowing they will bravely carry on with their life.
Her strength and her courage only one understands,
He is walking away with her heart in his hands.
For he knows that without it he would be lost,
But they both know freedom comes at a cost.
She walks away holding her children so close,
Swallowing tears for the one she loves most.
This quiet hero does not walk into war,
She soldiers on behind her front door.
She will move through her life the wind at her back,
Determined to keep her family on track.
Her tears fall in silence while she lies in her bed,
Her fear is right there but nothing is said.
She will ask that no medals be pinned to her chest,
Her husband's safe return her only request.
Few understand her commitment, her life,
She is the quiet hero, the brave Soldier's wife.

INTRODUCTION

Saturday 31 October 2009, 9pm

I opened the fridge and got out the bottle of wine.

Oz had put it in there the week before he was suddenly sent to Afghanistan. It hadn't felt right to enjoy it by myself, especially when he often didn't have enough to drink whilst he was working – he often went out with less than two litres of water a day as they had so much kit to carry and water was heavy – so I'd saved it. It was after midnight in Afghanistan by then and Oz would have finished for the day; he'd be on his way to Camp Bastion to catch a flight home for his break. It would be his first day off in just shy of six months. Only hours to go and he'd be back with us, safe in our arms.

Yet all day I'd had an uneasy, heavy feeling that I'd never had before. I'd woken early after dreaming about a colleague of Oz's, Gaz O'Donnell, who'd died in an explosion a year earlier. Oz had been so cut up about it; he adored Gaz, looked up to him. In the dream Gaz was looking at me, smiling. 'Don't worry, Chris, I'm here to get him when he comes over,' he'd said, 'I'll hold him. I won't let go.'

I'd woken early, gripped by confusion and dread.

I'd spoken to Oz two days earlier, on the Thursday evening. He was exhausted after months working in blistering fifty-degree heat, defusing one IED – Improvised Explosive Device – after another. Bomb after bomb after bomb. Oz had told me once that there were too many to accurately record so they were classed loosely as 'jobs'. Vehicles were few and far between or simply couldn't be used as the terrain was unsuitable.

Oz was almost always upbeat, despite the fear and the fatigue and the constant pressure. But this time he sounded different, low. 'I'm hammered, honey, I'm hanging out,' he said. It was the expression he used when he was at rock bottom, drained, wasted. 'The lads need to see I'm strong, they trust me and I won't let them down, but I've been away too long, worked too much, and if it's too much for me, it's too much for anyone.' He was mentally and physically drained. 'Come and get me. I just want to be home,' he was saying to me.

The hours had ticked by slowly that last day. 'Just let him come home safe today,' I whispered. 'Let him come home.' But the heavy, odd feeling wouldn't go away, despite the fact I was trying to be positive as I had been on the phone, joking with him that he was probably worried over nothing and was most likely just to stub his toe getting the hell out of there.

Laird was so excited, his dad was coming back, it was a Saturday, Halloween. He couldn't wait to go trick-or-treating with his friends. I didn't take him swimming that morning, but let him get dressed as a little wizard. We went out to knock on the neighbours' doors, along with other mums and children from the married quarters in Winchester that we had just moved into a couple of weeks before. By eight we were home, Laird with a bag full of sweets and cakes. I bathed him, put him to bed and read him a story. With every hour that passed, I felt a little better. Surely if anything had happened, I'd have heard? Oz, my beloved Oz, would be home soon. The heartache of months without seeing him would soon be over.

By nine Laird was asleep and I was in the kitchen, getting out the wine and a plate for the Chinese food I'd ordered in. I was marking the last day on the ground for him. We loved Chinese, it was a treat; it was what Oz chose to eat the evening before he left. Afghanistan was a few hours ahead so it would be gone midnight there. I was so proud of Oz, and chuffed that he'd soon be home with us, but was also annoyed with myself that after months of him being on tour I had allowed myself to feel wobbly and silly that day. I was going to eat, and have a glass of wine, and think of him on the plane home. Life had been suspended while he'd been away, but once Oz was back we could move forward with our plans and live out his dreams of a simple family life in Cornwall.

Laird's voice called down the stairs. 'I can't sleep, Mummy.'

I went back up. He was too excited to sleep. I looked beside his bed at the chart Oz had sent him; he'd carefully ticked off the days his dad had been gone. To a five-year-old, five and a half months had been a long time. He'd put a tick next to the last one that evening.

'Why don't you get into my bed, Lairdy, and I'll read you another story.' He loved that, it was a treat. He scrambled out of his bed and went into my room, while I picked up his favourite book and followed. He snuggled down and I sat beside him and started to read. Still excited after trick-or-treating and all those sweets!

A knock at the door.

I looked at the clock. 9.20. I wasn't expecting anyone.

Laird's face lit up. 'It's Daddy,' he said. 'He's come early as a surprise.'

It would have been just like him. Oz loved surprising us. But not this time.

'He's not coming till tomorrow, Lairdy.'

Our bed was under the window. I leaned over, pulled the curtain back and looked outside. The front door was directly below. Two men in Army uniform. I saw their hats – green lids, they call them. But they weren't Commando green lids like Oz's, they were just officers – clerks from the local camp.

I suddenly felt frozen in time – please, no.

I opened the window. They looked up and one spoke.

'Can you confirm that you are the wife of Staff Sergeant Olaf Schmid?'

'No,' I said. 'I won't. Can I talk to him?'

'Can you please come down and open the door and confirm that you are—'

'No.'

I felt dizzy now. 'Tell me I can still talk to him. I don't care if he's lost his arms and his legs, just tell me he's not dead.'

'I'm sorry, but you need to come down and let us in.'

'Tell me I can talk to him. Get him on the phone for me.'

'Please come down and let us in.'

I shut the window and drew the curtain. But there was no denying the truth or the gut feeling that I had had all day. I knew.

Laird looked at me.

'Mummy, they've got green lids. Daddy's home?'

'Yes, but they're not the same. That's not Daddy's green lid, his is Commando, and theirs is a different kind.'

He was silent for a moment. Then he looked at me, and I could see from his small, solemn face, and the pain in his eyes, that he knew, too.

'I think we should let them in, Mummy.'

CHAPTER ONE

June 2003

'Where are you? How are you getting on? I've been here for ten minutes.'

'I'm on the way. And you're early. We said two o'clock, Lofty!'

I was smiling to myself at the silly names we called each other. I parked in the centre of Winchester by the cathedral and walked hurriedly towards the Market Inn, trying to avoid getting my work heels caught in the gaps in the stone cobbles.

That's military training for you, I thought. Always bloody early and then wondering why the other person isn't there yet.

I'd slipped away from work to meet Oz for a coffee. He'd called that morning to say he'd be passing through. Despite gassing on the phone regularly and emailing, we hadn't seen each other for ages and I'd thought, why not? It would be good to catch up with him.

He'd been texting me through the day. 'Are you coming? Cause you always cancel.' It was true. He'd suggested meeting a few times whilst he was nearby, based at Tidworth. I was working in the same area, but we'd never managed it. I was always too busy working, at the gym, or spending evenings with family and girl-friends. And if I had any time left over, he was on courses or mucking about seeing mates or off seeing girls.

This time, though, it was good to have an excuse to escape. I had a stand at a pharmaceutical sales con-ference in the science museum just outside Winchester. As always at these events, there were endless meetings, sales pitches and talks, and after a few hours like that it was good to get some fresh air. So when the GP delegates went in to an after-lunch training session, I whispered to a friend to mind my stall and promised I'd be back in an hour.

As I walked up the path beside the cathedral, wearing a smart black shift dress and jacket, I was thinking, this is nutty, what am I doing? Why am I meeting this man? I haven't got time to sit around in the day having coffee. I had a list of customers I had to record, sales to confirm and then the stand to pack up. With that thought, I stopped and phoned my colleague, a friend who was also working that day with a stand, albeit from a rival pharmaceutical company, to let her know I had gone off site and into town.

*

I stepped into the Market Inn. The place was quiet. I saw Oz immediately in front of me and he turned around, grinned, bounded over and grabbed a kiss on my cheek. His face was warm. 'About time, chick. What were you doing, sightseeing on the way?'

I laughed. 'I'm two minutes late – give me a break.'

We ordered drinks and sat beside the open doors to the terrace. The waitress told Oz he could smoke, as there was almost no one else there. He reached into the pocket of his battered green gilet, got out a pack of liquorice Rizla papers, baccy and a menthol tip and rolled himself a ciggie. He looked up at me and smiled and I smiled back. Same old Oz, I thought. Except that he wasn't. Something had changed.

I first met Oz in Cornwall when we were teenagers, mucking about on boats. My family had sailed down from Southampton on *Avocet*, Dad's boat. Oz's parents kept a boat at Mylor on the Roseland Peninsula, where we and many others moored, especially during holidays. There was a crowd of kids down there, all of us hanging around the boats and the water. I was thinking about school and exams – about growing up. Oz was just a big kid, around thirteen, but I liked him. He was funny, made everyone laugh. He was a local. He asked for my number and I gave it to him. I didn't think that much about it at the time: teenagers always meet other teenagers when they're away, but few keep in touch.

But he'd called me a few weeks later, to see if I'd got home all right and if I was OK. I'd been surprised, but I didn't mind. We had a chat, swapped news. After that we'd meet up from time to time, or talk on the phone. I had a friend, Nicky, who moved to the West Country, and I used to drive across to see her and sometimes we'd end up Cornwall way, so we often went down there for weekends. She pretended she was at my house, and I told my parents I was at hers, and we took off. Typical teenagers. I told her I knew someone in Cornwall, and I used to call Oz when we got there, and he would come and meet us for a pasty and a Coke in Truro. He was younger and a bit goofy, but he was always easy-going and made me laugh.

Over the years our lives had taken us in different directions. Months would go by without either of us getting in touch, but then I would email, or he'd phone, out of the blue, and we'd talk for ages.

I thought he was mad when he called to say he'd joined the Army, at just sixteen. No thanks, I thought. He's going to be one of those fighting, drinking squaddies. Not my thing at all. However, looking back I can see there was nothing keeping him in Cornwall – he was bigger than that. There was very little work and the recession had hit. It had been great to have been brought up there and would be brilliant to retire to, but the pace was too slow and quiet for him. I was at university in Portsmouth by then, studying policy and economics and nursing three nights a week to pay the rent on my shared house. Studying and working hard, but still sailing at the weekends and going out clubbing too. But Oz and I found a rhythm despite our different lives, and he went on calling. He was always interested in what I was doing, he loved hearing about university, he'd ask lots of questions, sound wistful, say it must be great being with other students; then he'd crack a joke and make me laugh. When I graduated he called to congratulate me. He was always good at remembering milestones or important dates.

I liked him, we got on, but I was never interested in being more than friends at that point. I still thought of him as the gangly kid he'd been when we first met. He was quite lost and chaotic, drinking a lot, mucking about and dating girls who had a thing for military blokes. I couldn't see the attraction.

Now, though, sitting opposite him that day at the Market Inn, sipping my drink, I realised that Oz had changed. He had grown up. He was tanned, muscular; he looked older than me. He was wearing a white T-shirt and jeans with a rip in the back; the gilet, with its enamel poppy pin, was now slung over his chair-back. But it was more than that. I'd always thought of him as playful, but he was quiet and calm; there was a presence about him. He sat and smoked and asked me how life was, and I asked him what he was up to, and as we talked, both of us became aware that something extraordinary was happening between us.

I breathed in sharply, thinking I suddenly felt tired. A

bit of a chill came over me, despite the sun. Oz leaned over and took my hands between his and held them instinctively. 'Cold.'

I looked at his hands. They were perfect. Tanned, square fingers, clean but very masculine. The veins on the backs stood out and I could see he was tired.

He asked where I was in my life. I said I was moving nearer my parents and wanted to settle down a little. He said, 'That's great.' I told him Dad was still a regional manager of a large catering business and at the same time doing a lot more sailing, delivering boats to people all over the world. Mum was a manager at Winchester School of Art, but wasn't so well after a series of strokes and a heart attack. Dad ploughed himself into work, as we all did in our family.

'What about you?' I asked, changing the subject. It was clear from his body language that Oz didn't like the feeling of getting older and putting our childhoods firmly behind us. 'How's military life?'

Oz said very little about his work, just that he was doing lots of courses, as an ammunition technician. He was about to start another. 'Sorry if I'm a little edgy,' he said, 'got to be there in a couple of hours, so it's on my mind.'

'Ammunition technician? What's that?'

He was vague. 'Oh, boring stuff. Most of the time I'm just up and down the country, ticking boxes or blowing stuff up.'

He played it down so much that I didn't even twig, then, that it was about bombs. That was typical of him; he seldom talked about what he did in detail to anyone. Even people within the Forces found it hard to completely understand his work, so how could his family or a civvie he didn't really know? Plus when he was off duty he wanted to forget about it.

Every now and then we lapsed into silence, grinning at one another. We were playful and had lots of banter, both comfortable and happy in each other's company. We both had somewhere to be, but neither of us wanted to get up and go – it was as if there was a magnet connecting us, holding us there. I asked the time – he just laughed and looked at his watch. 'This is weird, look at us, what are we doing here? We should both be out of here.'

But we stalled for time. He had a pint, I had another drink, I told him a bit about work. But we didn't really want to chat about everyday things.

He turned his head, looking out of the windows. He had a small mole on his left cheek, a strong nose, a striking profile.

I didn't want to leave him.

'Do you want to go for a walk, get some air?'

He smiled. 'No, do you?'

I smiled back. 'No, not really.'

He got more drinks and sat down closer, next to me for another half-hour or so, before I reluctantly got up.

I was conscious that my phone had been ringing in my bag and knew I had to go. He grabbed his gilet from the back of the chair, kissed my cheek, held my hand for a moment, and then gave me a big bear hug when we stepped outside. We were parked in different directions. I noticed how dark blue and intense his eyes were as he held my gaze. He said he'd call me.

When I got back to my car it was after four. My phone was ringing. It was my friend at the conference. 'Where are you?'

'Sorry, got held up.' I raced back, switched into work mode, chased up the contacts I needed, sorted my sales and packed up my stand.

That evening I felt different. Seeing Oz had changed everything. It was as if the ground had shifted under me. Like going through the sound barrier. I hadn't expected it, hadn't looked for it, and now I didn't know what to do.

He called. It was five hours since I'd seen him, but we talked for an hour, maybe two. About anything and everything, just to stay on the end of the phone, hear one another's voices.

When I finally got to bed, I lay awake. What on earth was going on? I had loosely known a kid, a boy who joked around, played the fool. But this was someone else: a man, who was very independent, with a serious job and a big life of his own. And he'd touched something in me.

14

The timing was strange, because I was at a crossroads in my life. At twenty-eight I had been working in pharmaceuticals for a few years, doing well as a trainer and account manager, making good money, and putting in crazy hours, driving all over the south of England, selling to doctors, nurses and consultants in medical practices, hospitals, pharmacies and NHS Trusts. But I was weary of the shallowness of the corporate, competitive world I was in, and worn out by the busy social life I had with my old university friends and sailing crowd. It didn't seem to fit any more. Especially as Mum was ill. I decided to sell my flat in Southampton and move back to a village called Otterbourne in Winchester, to be close to her, so that I could help out.

I'd got a plan – I always had a plan. A quieter life, a home with a garden, more time in nature, walking in the woods, popping in to check on Mum, especially when Dad was away delivering boats.

The last thing I needed, or expected, was a man. I'd just finished a long relationship and I wanted a bit of space; time to think and take stock. Because there was something else – something I hadn't told Oz.

I was four months pregnant.

I had barely told anyone. I was still coming to terms with it myself. It had happened whilst on a holiday with Malc, the boyfriend I'd been seeing for several years. We'd headed off in February with a bunch of friends for a trip to the Dominican Republic – we both liked to travel and be outdoors. We'd decided to get a cheap deal and then kite- and windsurf for a week. Malc was a lovely guy, but it was never really serious between us; he was a surf dude, travelling the world in search of the next big wave, and I was a career girl, knuckling down to work, with a mortgage and a family to keep me rooted. We had friends in common and we got on well. We saw each other a fair bit, but it was never really going to go anywhere, like many relationships don't when you're in your early twenties, based as they often are on shared interests alone and not on the practical things that begin to matter as you get older.

It was just after my birthday, in early April, that I started to feel strange. I went off coffee and tea. It took a while for the penny to drop, and when I discovered I was pregnant, it was a shock.

Abortion was never an option. I absolutely understand why some women choose to go that route, but it just didn't feel right for me. I hadn't planned on being a single parent – who does? But I knew that's how it would be, because I wasn't about to get married just for the sake of convention either. I'd seen too many marriages that looked perfect to the outside world but were unhappy underneath. I preferred to cope alone than settle for that. Besides, my mum nearly dying after her strokes and a heart attack had made me realise that life was too short and precious to settle for something that wasn't perfect.

I knew my parents would be worried when I told

them – perhaps even a bit embarrassed by my single status – but I also knew that they would love having a grandchild and would help me in any way they could.

I was a little bit ashamed. It wasn't going to be easy telling all my friends, most of whom had married and settled down and were busy working at their careers or buying their first houses. I knew that eyebrows would be raised, that some people would think I was irresponsible or, God forbid, even pity me, but I hoped my real friends would be there for me.

When I told Malc he did offer to marry me and support me, as I knew he would. We cared about one another, but I wasn't tempted – we just didn't have enough in common any more, and were coming to the end of a stage in both our lives. I loved him, but I wasn't in love with him. He was a genuinely nice guy – friendly, kind, good-hearted – but he was the eternal boy; he lived for adventures on the waves. When I told him about the pregnancy he was warm and sincere, truly a salt-of-the-earth kind of guy. But he wasn't ready to settle down; our lives were at different stages. Malc accepted my decision, and if he was relieved, he didn't show it. He said he'd like to see the baby and support me. But I made it clear to him that keeping our baby was my decision and I would be responsible – financially and otherwise. However, Malc did help with some practicalities, even signing as guarantor for my bigger mortgage on a Victorian two-up two-down cottage I wanted to buy within walking distance of Mum and Dad's place.

So I was on my own. I knew it would mean huge changes in my lifestyle and there were times when I felt scared and lonely, but I was convinced I could do it. I had to do it.

I started to change my work habits. It was going to be difficult to be on the road all the time and making trips up to the head office in Leicester for training with a new baby. So I told my boss I'd like to concentrate on marketing just one or two products instead of four or five, and work a smaller territory. David, my boss at the time, had agreed and made it happen for me. He'd been really supportive – his wife worked in nursing and they had two young children also, so he knew how important it was for me to be able to work from home a bit more.

The cottage I'd moved to from my flat was a sweet little place: turn of the century, old and lovely, looking out over the village green and a big old oak tree in Otterbourne, just outside the city and less than a mile from my parents' home. The owner had recently renovated it. My offer had been accepted quickly and it was ready around September for me to move into. My baby was due in mid-November. Malc and I had grown to be good friends and accepted the idea of being parents, and Mum was thrilled to have me nearby, despite the challenge of me being a single parent, so all the pieces were in place.

Until Oz came along.

I told myself I was crazy to even think of another relationship at this stage. Especially with a man whose job took him away for weeks, sometimes months at a time. My life had become about serious responsibility. Was he ready for it? He had just turned twenty-four. He had no mortgage, lots of different girlfriends and no really strong roots anywhere. I got the impression that the life he'd lived up until this point was hard living, hard drinking, partying and racking up debts, like a typical bloke in his twenties. Despite the seriousness of the conflict he had seen, the travelling he had done and the promotions he had been given, he was shocking with money and making long-term plans.

And yet I couldn't stop thinking about him. He'd shaken my world to its foundations. Because from the moment I set eyes on him again in the Market Inn, I adored him. The connection between us was so strong that it went beyond everything else. His job, my job, his lifestyle, my lifestyle. All that fell away in the hours we spent together and on the phone.

Did he feel the same? I wondered. Would the strength of his feelings survive the differences between us? And how would a baby fit into things? I wasn't looking for a father for my child, far from it – I had Malc, my dad (granddad) and my brother around. But whatever happened, my baby was now part of the story. And some men would run a mile at the prospect of getting

19

involved with a woman who was about to have a baby. I had to tell him the truth, before we went any further.

We had arranged to meet at the Market Inn a few days later, when Oz came through town on his way back to base. This time we met after I finished work, so I'd swapped the black suit I associated with work for a yellow dress. But Oz looked exactly the same – T-shirt, jeans, brown hiking boots and the green gilet.

'Out of your work boots for a change then?' I joked.

'Yup, pretty much,' he said. 'I change the T-shirt sometimes.'

He giggled and asked me what I wanted to drink.

'I'll have an orange juice.'

'Really? You're not working now – let's get on it!' as he ordered a pint and some food.

'No, but I am pregnant.'

He looked at me, looked at his pint and took a sip as he took the change from the barman, shrugged and said, 'Cool, I love kids. It is what it is, I love you and how you make me feel – I've not felt that before and I am not going to walk away from that, or listen to people who say things should be this way or that.'

And that was it. I realised then, Oz was unflappable. Nothing was ever a problem to him. His attitude was, 'It's a child, we can deal with that.'

Later he used to say, 'If you wake up in the morning with your health, and money in your pocket, then life is good.' It was that simple – you're alive, so you're lucky. He had already seen conflict in Northern Ireland, uprisings in Sierra Leone and unimaginable death and destruction in the Kosovo war, all by his mid-twenties. All he wanted in life was peace and to be loved. The Army had become his family since he joined straight after school, but he said something was missing. He'd already decided that he wanted to be with me. If that meant a baby was part of the deal, it was fine with him.

'I know it's surreal, Chrissy, but I want us to be together,' he said. 'I don't know how it's all going to work, but let's just do it. If you want it too, we can make it work. Do you?'

I did, deep down, I really did. But I was cautious. 'Give me time,' I said. I had lots on with family and work and I was aware that I was settled financially and he wasn't. I also knew my friends wouldn't approve.

'Fine,' he smiled. 'I can deal with that.'

CHAPTER TWO

For a long time I kept Oz at arm's length. Especially with a new baby, I wasn't about to let anyone just walk into my life. If he wanted to be with me, and around my child, he had to be someone I could totally trust. For me that meant going slowly, one step at a time.

'Love's not enough,' I told him. 'There's more to being together than that.'

Oz was patient and understanding. He would have hurled himself into the relationship, body and soul, because that's how he did things, but I was a bit freaked out.

So we stayed just friends. I dated people casually during that time, but no one stuck like my best pal and soulmate, so I mainly concentrated on my house and work. Mostly Oz and I would talk on the phone, but sometimes we would meet up during the day when I was working. Winchester was our special place. Oz would meet me there, as it was the place where I liked to go and light a candle for my mum and wish for her health.

I knew Oz wasn't a saint and that he'd been partying, drinking, dating girls and spending his money as fast as he earned it. And even though he swore he was, I still wasn't sure he was ready to give all that up for family life. So I told him to get it all out of his system first, and if that meant waiting to be together properly, then we would wait. He had seen women with children before and it had always been complicated, so he agreed to take my lead this time. Like any bloke in his twenties, he had typically laddish friends who he felt didn't understand him at the best of times, let alone why he was making a decision like this, to be with me and Laird.

So we continued to spend hours on our mobiles to each other, often two or three hours at a time, sometimes not even talking much. We'd be in front of the TV, him at his end, me at mine. He'd be saying, 'Did you see that?' and I'd be saying, 'Yeah, funny wasn't it?' We'd comment, chat, swap stories, laugh. He'd tell me he was in his pit (bed) in his grot (room), and he'd describe it – small, basic, kit all around, just a bed, chair, wardrobe and TV. He would tell me about all the antics he and his mates would get up to. I would advise him about sensible things, like cars and finances.

Sometimes we'd talk about places and people we'd known in Cornwall, and we filled each other in on our roots, our families, and where we'd been in our lives so far. I told him about growing up with my brother Jamie, who is two years older, my mum Gill and my dad, John; how they had met and their history. Oz wanted to know everything – he asked a lot of questions and wanted all the stories. So I told him.

Dad grew up in Windsor and went to a good school. He always said he used to deliver newspapers to Windsor Castle when he was a child. He loved the Great Park and I remember walking through it with him when I was small – he knew all the gates and where they led, and all the best hiding places. He used to find me antlers which had been shed by the deer, and I'd take them home and hang them everywhere. Oz thought that was really cool; he loved nature, and his Scandinavian roots meant he loved the autumn and winters, as I did.

Dad had been a bit of a rebellious teenager, playing truant to bike-ride all the way to Heathrow and watch the planes taking off and landing. Later, he graduated from bikes to scooters and being a mod. Dad was full of energy and ambition, a real fighter. He was born only four pounds in weight after his mum had struggled to have children. When he was still quite young he started a catering company and deli with his friend George Halliday. They did well, branching out to cater for businesses in London. That's where Dad met Mum. She had grown up in Manchester and had been to catering college, then later she moved to London. She went on to cook for the London Clinic, the Royal Garden Hotel and the BBC.

When Jamie and I were born, Mum always made sure we ate incredibly healthy food. It was a bit of a thing with her: she always said that all you needed in life was good food, good shoes and something to read. She believed in the power of food so much that she made her own cosmetics and hand-scrubs with ingredients like honey, salt, lemon juice, cucumber and yoghurt.

As for me, I was a tiny kid with blonde ringlets, but the girly look was deceptive. I was definitely a tomboy, always climbing trees or racing around on my bike. My brother Jamie and I were incredibly close. I felt very protective of him, because at times he found life quite overwhelming and struggled to fit in with the world around him. He is a talented artist and, like many gifted people, he found a lot of situations in life daunting. The family always kept him close and looked out for him.

We had moved a number of times when Jamie and I were young. We moved from Tilehurst, Reading, to Winchester for our teenage years. Dad wanted to build a yacht in his spare time, and our family boat, *Avocet*, the place we often retreated to, was moored in Southampton Water. But we stayed in contact with friends from Berkshire. It was originally only meant to be a temporary move – Dad's company had won a big catering contract with Esso, the refinery on the coast near the New Forest, and Dad had loved the idea of moving near the sea. He thought we'd only be there for a year or two at most, but then George died of a heart attack and everything changed. Dad missed George terribly and he no longer had his heart in the business, so he scaled it down and we stayed in Winchester. Dad semi-retired and spent the majority of his time commissioning, delivering and maintaining yachts.

Dad's passion in life had always been boats, and so, after George passed away, he realised his dream and built his own, in the back garden. It was a big boat, a forty-eight-foot steel-hulled cutter, and he put his heart and soul into it, spending every spare hour on it. He called it *Magari*. The project took him ten years to finish and I was seventeen by the time he launched it in the Solent. That was a proud day for all of us.

His business ticked over while he took off for days, sometimes weeks at a time, flying out to some far-flung destination to collect a boat or do a course, or spending time pottering about with his like-minded friends at the boat club.

We had always spent a lot of our time sailing; as kids, Jamie and I had sailed all Easter and summer long. Dad taught us to handle boats, kayaks and canoes. He used to get cross because I wasn't competitive enough about it – I just liked messing about and capsizing. But Dad and I adored each other. He and Mum called me Swissy as a nickname. The whole family call me Swiss.

Oz loved that – he started calling me Swiss too. He told me his own nickname came from a rugby master at his school who used his initials – OS – and it evolved into Oz.

He had grown up in Cornwall, where his German mother, Barbara, and Swedish father, Hans, settled after they met in Germany. Hans already had a son, Greg, from an earlier marriage, who was fifteen when Oz was born. A year later Oz's younger brother, Torben, arrived.

Barbara and Hans ran a hotel, The Peacock, just outside Truro. It was an excellent hotel and they worked long hours. The food was lovingly home-cooked by Barbara, and Hans did front of house and took care of the guests. So from the start Oz was used to mucking in and was very self-sufficient due to his parents working long hours and being busy managing the hotel. He went to a private prep school in Truro, Polwhele House, where he made friends with Andrew Stevens, whose family ran The Old Ship Hotel at Padstow and who remained a friend throughout his life. 'He stood out,' Andrew said. 'Not just because his name was different, but because he was so full of energy and always trying something new.

'I used to get fish fingers at home,' Andrew said, 'but when I went home with Oz we'd get Wiener schnitzel or, on one occasion, steak tartare. I remember looking at this raw meat and whispering to Oz, "Your mum's forgotten to cook it," and he said, "I know, but we'd better just eat it."'

Oz even became a chorister at Truro Cathedral – something he got a lot of ribbing about from his mates – and was eventually made head chorister. He was also a good rugby player.

'I was team captain,' Andrew says, 'so when we had the official team photo taken, I was holding the ball. But a second before the camera clicked, Oz slipped his hand across and rested it on the ball. I used to say to him, "You couldn't even let me have the ball for the photo, could you?"'

In the summers Oz and Torben used to go and stay with Hans's brother Nicolai in Stockholm. Oz liked his uncle and had such happy memories of those visits and of Sweden, where there's a small population and a lot of the great outdoors, which Oz loved.

When he was thirteen, things changed for his family. It was the recession of the early nineties, their business was under pressure, and eventually they had to let it go, so Oz was sent to the local comprehensive, Penair. It was a good school but still quite a change for a prep-school kid who had been used to private education. His friend Andrew went off to boarding school, so for the next three years they saw less of one another, though they always stayed in touch.

Oz made a new crowd of friends at Penair, and became wild. He started smoking and was always oversleeping and having to be shaken to get out of bed for school. He was always a clown, the one who made the others laugh, the life and soul of any crowd, and he and his mates would spend their time on their skateboards or bikes, or camping on the beach. He was good friends with three boys whose mother, Margaret, ran the post office in Veryan, a village on the Roseland Peninsula. Oz would sometimes stay the night there. Later I met Margaret, and she told me that, though Oz could be exuberant, he was always polite; he would ask before taking something from the fridge, and offer to wash up. He was part of the furniture and was a bit of a kindred spirit, she said. Like another son.

Our families, though different in many ways, had big things in common – home cooking, working and boats. My parents had made their living feeding other people good food, and his did the same. And, like me, Oz had worked from the age of thirteen. I used to help out in a care home, first in the laundry, then as an auxiliary nurse, working long hours for the British Nursing Agency. Oz did all kinds of jobs – delivering papers and washing up, or waiting tables in local cafés. By the age of fifteen he was working several evenings a week helping out in The Nare Hotel in Veryan, a beautiful hotel overlooking a beach, where his mum also worked.

Though Oz loved Cornwall, he had itchy feet and couldn't wait to leave and see more of the world. He didn't want to stay on at school and there weren't many jobs open to sixteen-year-olds. He had a friend, Tim Willetts, who was a few years older and who was in the Territorial Army. Oz saw Tim going off on exercises in his kit and liked the sound of what he was doing. So one day, in January 1996, he walked into the Army recruiting office and signed up with the Royal Logistics Corps as a chef – an obvious choice, given his background.

In other circumstances Oz might have gone to Sandhurst and trained as an officer. He certainly had everything it took and he would have made a great commissioned officer. But Oz was never bothered about rank. He was a strong individual and wasn't afraid of hard work. He was keen to get going with his life and was never one for convention.

In the early days of our relationship, I used to hide Oz away. My dad would never have approved of him. When I was younger, Dad used to vet any boys who came near me, and I think he saw me with a city financier rather than a soldier. Oz was indignant and funny about it, but as it turned out I needn't have worried. When they eventually got to know him as I did, both my parents adored him.

So although we talked almost every day, for a long time I didn't tell anyone about Oz – and especially not my dad. It felt too early and I wasn't sure it would come to anything. I felt confused; I just couldn't see how two such different lives would fit together.

He'd call and say he'd been to the races with a crowd of friends, or up to London or to a big party, and I didn't want to be the reason he stopped all that. But he'd say he was only going because I was too busy and wouldn't commit to him. But over time Oz proved himself as my best friend and we carved out a relationship despite everything: his army life, my career, and the commitments I had nursing my mum, who had become blind in one eye and lost her ability to drive due to the strokes and hypertension. His commitment touched me; his persistence and loyalty struck me – it was a side to Oz that others rarely saw or appreciated fully.

In September, two months before my baby was due, I moved into the cottage in Otterbourne. I planted evergreen jasmine outside the front door and called it Jasmine Cottage. Inside I painted it in ice-cream colours, light and fresh. It had an open fireplace in the front room, overlooking the green, and a little kitchen behind, leading into a bright, roomy conservatory and out into a traditional garden. Up the narrow stairs there were two double bedrooms and a bathroom. I settled into one of the bedrooms, and began preparing the other for my baby. I painted everything blue and friends laughed and said I couldn't be that sure it would be a boy, but I was, I just knew it would be a boy. And I had fun doing it. For the first time in my life I wanted to build a home, a nest, and be earthy. For me it was a step into the unknown.

I wouldn't let Oz come to the house in those first weeks. I wanted to make it mine and to make a home for my child. I wasn't going to let him come and stay there until I knew we had something more than just an attraction for each other. So when we met I'd go and see him in Winchester, for a drink.

Oz never pushed me, and I was grateful. He made it clear he wanted to be with me, but I'd tell him we had a way to go before it could work. For a start he was terrible with money. It didn't take me long to realise that he was so institutionalised he had little idea of what life was like – or what things cost – in the world outside the Army. He had never paid his own gas and electricity bills, furnished a home, got a mortgage, had to budget or get insurance, and he certainly hadn't saved. He would get paid, and then go and spend it all – drinking, partying, buying his friends presents, buying cars he couldn't afford or maintain, or putting money behind the bar so that everyone in the pub could have a drink. Generous, yes, but irresponsible too.

And he hadn't just spent his salary, he had run up debts. He owed thousands of pounds on credit cards; he'd spend without thinking about it or planning and with no idea what he was getting into.

I told him he'd have to start paying off his debts – and stop running up any more – before I would get into anything with him that involved us both financially. I had been brought up to be an independent woman and not to rely on a man. I'd gone out and bought my flat when I was in my second year at university. I'd saved the deposit from the jobs I'd done before university. After my A levels I started training as a nurse, before deciding it wasn't for me. Then I worked part-time for pharmaceutical companies. The work was well paid and, because I'd done some nursing, I got the good jobs. I worked for the rest of the year, until I went to university, and even while I was there I did some weekend and evening work, so I built up good savings. Once I'd bought the flat I rented it out and used the rent to pay the mortgage. I was on the property ladder at twenty, I was financially stable, and even had some money in a slush fund for a rainy day.

I showed Oz how to budget, to have structure and begin to plan, and he reminded me how to live, be playful and value life. I was sometimes so busy planning that I forgot to enjoy the moment. I sometimes felt tied by mortgage, job, impending parenthood. Oz had a sense of joy that was infectious; he had a lightness of touch that defied the darkest moments. It was impossible not to laugh when you were around him.

When we met as kids I thought Oz was devil-may-care, daring and naughty. He tried smoking, which I thought was shocking. I was Miss Bossy, and a total goody-goody.

In so many ways we were opposites, yet in others we were kindred spirits. We both loved nature, beauty, woods, water, being out in the open. Not just on boats, but walking for miles, in all weathers. And we were both very spiritual.

Oz loved hearing tales about my grandmother, my mother's mother, who was deeply spiritual and had an enormous influence on me.

Nan lived in Rochdale, she was widowed with three children, and as a child I often went to stay with her. She also had an old crofter's cottage in Wales, near Llanberis Pass in Snowdonia, which the whole family would visit a couple of times a year. It was a very simple stone cottage, with slate doors, an inglenook and a pigpen at the back. From it you could see Snowdon and Anglesey. Nan and I would sit out at the back in all weathers. It was often blowy and cold up there, but we didn't mind, we loved the place. It had a stream and a standing stone and was so high up that the air was incredibly clear.

Nan was a remarkable woman, strong and inde-pendent. She would read to me a lot and we'd stay up late, buzzing around in her warm kitchen, with Radio Four on in the background. She was always cooking something. Her husband, who was an engineer in the war, had died, leaving her to bring up three teenage children – my mum and her two older brothers – alone. Nan was part of a line of strong women – her own mother had been the first girl to go to university in London, and a suffragette – and she passed that strength on to my mum and then me. She even managed to buy herself a Jaguar and put aside what she called her 'slush fund'. 'Women must have a good car, and a slush fund,' she used to say to me. 'Never, ever depend on a man. They haven't evolved, bless them.'

Nan was a health visitor in Moss Side at one point. She was articulate and loving and always dressed in an incredibly classy way, wearing gorgeous coats, shoes and handbags. Very couture!

I used to read her diaries and watch her intently as she pottered away. I loved hearing about her latest exploits – she was always writing to an MP or chatting to someone at university. Yes, at her age she still attended Open University, more because of her thirst for learning than for the social side. To me she was astonishingly unique. Nan was the person who taught me that women could and should be strong without the need to look sexual or aggressive; she was my rock. She'd always say to me, 'Keep your own identity. You know what's right in your gut, you don't need telling. People who have agendas are troublemakers or are precious.'

She had always had a thirst for life and loved to travel, was always writing us beautiful letters and postcards from wherever she went. When she was in her eighties she spent a few months going around Russia. 'Haven't you heard? I am going now to see the real Russia before the Mafia take hold and try turning it into rubbish!' she used to say.

She was incredibly passionate about books and always had a book on her and she would talk to me about literature and read to me. At night in the cottage she would light candles and we would sit together on the windowsill in the moonlight and read Chekhov, or Brecht.

Mum was very down-to-earth, but she wasn't as keen on the cottage as we were, because it was so chilly and muddy. When we were sitting outside or reading by moonlight, she'd be in the kitchen, busy making sandwiches for the next day. But while she didn't join in, Mum never resented how close I was to Nan, she felt there was enough love to go round, and she was right.

It was being around Nan that caused my love of all things to do with to nature grow. She believed in natural remedies and cures, and in trusting the ways of nature. She went to a spiritualist church and believed in hands-on healing. If we were hurt she'd use a natural witch hazel compress and she had little bags of lavender all over the place. Her cottage had a stream running past it, and beside it there was a standing stone – a large vertical stone like the ones at Avebury and Stonehenge, which were used in ancient religious ceremonies and which often indicate ley lines, those invisible lines that connect places of spiritual significance.

Through Nan, I became fascinated by the traditions of ancient Britain, including the use of natural remedies, as well as with little rituals: using natural objects like stones, feathers and flowers to bring about the things you wish for. Nan taught me that we are all in charge of our own destiny; opportunities will come along and we must make firm and wise decisions as they arise. The best way to achieve what you want is to focus on it with all your energy and intention. She also taught me to question everything, and never to accept just one point of view. Things always have grey areas, flip sides to them: life isn't black and white. Only to those who don't feel anything.

Nan died when I was sixteen and I was devastated. I missed her terribly, but I still find myself thinking, What would Nan say? Before she died she told me to look after my mum, 'because she looks after all of you', and she left me some little gifts, like her pillbox, diary and rings, which I still carry and treasure.

I had hardly ever spoken about the things Nan taught me, especially the connection between nature and spirituality. I thought people would think me odd if I mentioned believing in the power of nature, and self-determination. But it all made sense to Oz, perhaps because he loved nature so much himself. He used to say that the only real strength is inner strength.

That didn't stop him teasing me, though. 'You're spooky,' he'd say. 'I don't get it but I love it and I love you.'

Not long before my baby was born, I sat in my new

garden, in the warm September air, and thought of Nan.

'What do you think of Oz?' I asked her. 'Is he the one for me?'

The answer rang out like the chime of sweet bells, all around me.

Yes. Yes. Yes.

CHAPTER

CHAPTER THREE

Two weeks later, Mum had a stroke. It was Jamie who found her in her favourite chair in the garden. Dad was away sailing, so Jamie called me. I was in the car, miles away, on the way to see a client.

Jamie was frantic. 'She's not moving, Swiss. She's being odd and isn't making any sense.'

I told him to call an ambulance, not to give her anything, just to wait with her until help came.

Afterwards, going over what had happened, I regretted that. I knew that action in the first three hours after a stroke is vital to try to avoid long-term damage. Strokes are blood clots which travel to the heart or brain, so after her earlier strokes, Mum was already on daily aspirin, which has a natural blood-thinning effect. Jamie told me that she'd obviously forgotten to take her tablets that morning as they were on the side and she had been feeling funny all day. Perhaps if he'd given her the aspirin, it might have helped. But I wasn't there, and I was so afraid of making the situation worse.

By the time I got to the hospital, a doctor had seen her. 'She'll be fine,' he said. 'There is likely to be some long-term damage and we want to keep her under observation for a short while, but then she can go home.'

But when I saw Mum I was worried. She didn't seem herself at all and I felt certain she shouldn't go home anytime soon. I had a feeling something more was going to happen. I asked them to keep her in for twenty four hours and they agreed. That night she had a heart attack.

It was a terribly worrying time. Jamie and I were with her most of the time, and Dad had made his way home. She was only fifty-eight, which seemed too young for either a major stroke or a heart attack. It seemed cruel that she had always eaten so healthily, and taken so much care over food. But in the end, nothing she did could have helped: she suffered from genetically bad hypertension. In other words, her blood pressure was sky-high, it was an inherited condition, and no amount of clean living would have changed that. Strokes and heart attacks were inevitable. I cried myself to sleep that night.

Mum was in hospital for several weeks after her heart attack, and when she came home, she was a changed woman.

Her confidence was knocked terribly. She felt frustrated at not working or driving, and she no longer trusted herself to manage things alone. Just grating cheese for a jacket potato would feel like an epic battle, leaving her frustrated and in tears, as things that needed hand–eye co-ordination and two hands were tough for her. She became very low, and had to take anti-depressants for a while. It was the first time I had ever seen her in bed during the day.

The timing was heartbreaking. I was about to have her first grandchild, a baby I knew she would dote on, and she was in no position to help care for him or enjoy this new step in our lives. I felt so sad for her, and worried too – I had been so looking forward to Mum helping me through the early days of becoming a parent. All I could hope was that she would slowly grow stronger and more confident. Perhaps, I thought, having a grandchild would help her recovery.

By mid-November the weather was very cold, but the day before my baby was due I went out and planted honeysuckle in my garden, bulbs in the pots, and laid some slabs for the patio.

Even though my bag for the hospital wasn't yet packed, I felt ready. The house was sorted and the baby's room was done, but what I wasn't prepared for was just how hard the birth would be. I had been hoping for a simple, natural birth. I knew I didn't want an epidural or a

Caesarean, because of the effects on the baby of the drugs involved, but other than that I hadn't got a checklist for the midwives or a birth plan, and I hadn't asked anyone to be there with me. I wanted Mum, but she hadn't been out of hospital for long and was still very weak and there was no one I wanted in her place. I always preferred to be alone if I was ill, and I felt it would be the same with giving birth. So when I went into labour I set off on my own in the car I used for work. I parked in the hospital car park and wondered how long I should get a ticket for.

One of my best friends, Tina, was adamant I shouldn't have the baby alone. She'd said, 'Oh Chrissy, let me be there.' I loved Tina. She was a feisty woman, a former ballet dancer and air stewardess whom I'd met when we were both pharmaceutical reps. She owned a farm and had raised her own two gorgeous children pretty much single-handedly in Wimbledon. Since then she'd married a surgeon from Mauritius and had a smallholding to look after in the Cotswolds. I loved going up there to visit because it was so welcoming and warm. But while I appreciated her kindness and didn't want to upset Tina, I honestly felt better being on my own. I suggested she come and see me after the birth, and reluctantly she agreed to wait until then.

I dreaded giving birth in hospital, despite being in Winchester Hospital, which has a wonderfully intimate maternity ward. I hated hospitals, bright lights, all the things that would inevitably be part of it. I wished I could curl up in a warm, dark place. I'd have loved to do it on my own, at home, but I had a feeling it wasn't going to be straightforward and I knew I needed to be in hospital. As I checked myself in, I wished I could just be the other side of the whole thing. I felt anxious, afraid I wouldn't be a good mother, and worried that the birth would be difficult.

It was. In fact it ended up being more surreal than anything I could have imagined. It went on for many, many hours and I was in a huge amount of pain and lost a lot of blood. At one point one side of my face appeared to drop and the medical staff were saying that I'd suffered a stroke.

I'm normally very tough when it comes to pain. 'Nails,' as Oz later put it. I can put up with anything. But this was different. I couldn't get the baby out – my pelvis was too small. They decided to do a Caesarean, and gave me an epidural for it, but it didn't take on one side and the Caesarean had to be abandoned.

When my son was eventually born, on Sunday 16 November, just before four in the morning, I was utterly exhausted. My body had been ripped apart, and I was very weak. But when my baby boy was put into my arms and I looked down at his button nose, smiling, knowing face, and fluff of white-blond hair, I felt the most extraordinary love.

He was absolutely beautiful. So gorgeous that the

midwives were calling one another over to look at him. They put me in my own room and I just stared at him in silence for hours, quiet and calm, breastfeeding and happy.

Tina arrived the following day and I was so glad of her warm, reassuring presence. I wanted to go home as soon as possible, so I discharged myself and Tina took me home and then went back to get my car.

When I saw Malc after the birth he was horrified by how ill I looked, but Tina promised she would look after me. Malc thought the baby was beautiful and we named him after the longboard surfer Laird Hamilton, and rugby player Jonny Wilkinson. I hadn't thought about a name, I just wanted him to be well physically and strong in spirit, so I agreed, because Jonny was for my dad too. So my son became Laird Johnny Avis, keeping my surname. Malc gave him a cuddle, gave me a kiss on the cheek, announced he had to go back to work and left us to it.

In the days that followed, as I gradually healed and got to know Laird, I was so content. I felt a deep connection with him, and I knew that for the rest of my life I would be protecting him, fighting for him and encouraging him to be strong, courageous and good-hearted.

Mum, Dad and Jamie had come to see him as soon as he was home, and they all loved him from the moment they set eyes on him, passing him from one to the other and staring down at him with faces filled with tenderness and amazement. Jamie took loads of photos as he always did.

Any disapproval that Dad might have felt about the circumstances melted away when he held his grandson. The two of them were to form a close bond, with Laird spending long, happy hours fixing and making things with his 'Gandalf', as he called Dad.

When Laird was seven weeks old I started work again. I was very lucky to be able to do most of my work at home. Managing the accounts for the company meant I was out on the road a lot less, so I could breastfeed Laird, put him down to sleep and then get my work done. It was tough and could feel overwhelming, because there wasn't a lot of time to rest, but it was also a lovely time, just me and my baby, getting to know one another. Mum would come over to the house and would sit and have Laird. We also had fab neighbours who helped out too.

Throughout those early weeks I was in touch with Oz. We met once or twice, for a drink, and I showed him photos of Laird, but I still kept him at arm's length, because I saw him as a risk. It was a vulnerable time in my life, and I didn't want to get involved with someone who might disappear. Nor did I want anyone thinking I'd rushed into the first relationship that came along, just so that I could have a man in my life – and Laird's. I was quite prepared to go it alone, in fact that's what I had expected, and as far as I was concerned that wouldn't change until I was really sure.

So he came and went in my life over the next few months. He would disappear for a month, and then rock up again.

I kept saying, 'You're not ready, you haven't got all that crazy stuff out of your system.' He'd have racked up another debt, and I'd say, 'How many times are you going to put your hand in a blender? Debt is not sexy, go away.'

He'd go off again, see his mates, spend his money and then come back and say, 'I'm not giving up, Chrissy, I want to be with you.'

So we were together, but not together. I wasn't going to be officially with him until it felt right. I knew my dad would say, 'No man's good enough, they are all liars or no-goods nowadays.' I wasn't about to get seriously involved with someone who would turn out to be flaky or cause trouble.

'Make sure it's what you want,' I told Oz, 'because this is really adult. It means shaping up, not going out on the lash all the time, getting your finances in order, looking after a child. I love you being around, but we need to see how it goes over the next couple of years. We've got time.'

Oz would laugh. 'Bloody independent women, always laying down the law.' But he understood. 'I'm bored with going out all the time, having crappy relationships, wasting my time and my money,' he'd say. 'I'm ready, bring it on, I want responsibility. I want a family – you and Laird. I can be myself around you. I don't know how we're going to manage things, with your life and mine. But somehow we'll make it work.'

Oz liked the fact that I had a business brain and promised me he would sort himself out. And he did. It didn't happen instantly, but over the next few months he took out a loan to cover all his debts and started paying it off, and he calmed down a lot.

After Laird was born I wanted every minute with him, just me and my child, but bit by bit I let down my defences. In time I invited Oz to come and meet Laird, and he was wonderful with him from the start. We'd go for walks with Laird strapped to Oz in a sling. Oz wanted Laird to get to know the great outdoors and I felt the same way. Oz had done a lot of survival exercises as part of his Army training, and he knew his plants. He'd stride along, pointing them out to Laird, who dozed happily, wrapped in warm layers, in his sling. 'See that one?' Oz would say, peering down at the bundle on his chest. 'Three of those berries will keep you going for days. Remember that.' Or, 'That's wild garlic, it adds a hit to bland food! When you're out camping.'

Once he began visiting us at the cottage and I was beginning to get comfortable with it, Oz came more often. But I was still nervous, and I told him, 'Stop making it a routine, I don't want to play at happy families. If you want to be around us, you've got to prove you're serious.'

Oz said, 'Fine, I will, because I am and I'll prove it to you. I'll be there regularly, as much as I can. It's not just that I fancy you, it's about you and me and our connection, because we've got something I haven't ever had with anyone else.'

He came whenever he could, rolling up on a Thursday or Friday night for the weekend and slinging his work bag into the corner, which he christened 'the admin area', before insisting I put my work phone and files away, kick off my shoes and relax. 'It's the weekend,' he'd say, producing a bottle of wine for us and a cuddly toy for Laird. 'Now go and get that baby so I can cuddle him and then I'm going to make you my killer tempura prawns.'

Oz was the only man, other than my dad and my brother, who was consistently there. And because he was, and he never faltered or gave up in his determination that we would be together, I began to trust him.

Sometimes Mum and Dad would take Laird for a few hours so that Oz and I could go out for the evening, but after a while we'd both start to miss him and we'd pick him up, go back to the cottage and curl up by the fire without the TV on.

I never announced to Mum and Dad that I was with Oz. They just knew. We were more than a couple – we were best friends, soulmates – and I think they were glad I had someone around who cared so deeply for me and Laird.

Oz would have liked to move in, but I wasn't ready for that. He even said he wanted to marry me, tomorrow, if I agreed, but I told him we needed more time. 'Think it through,' I said. 'I'll commit to it, and we'll be a family, when you can be here, but I'm not going to marry you and live in married quarters in the middle of some Army base miles from anywhere and have a heap of kids.'

He was indignant. 'Why not? What's wrong with that? Don't be a snob.'

'I'm not being a snob. I wouldn't be fulfilled,' I told him. 'I like my cottage and my career, and my freedom. I want to grow herbs and vegetables in my own garden, one that I won't have to leave. I want to raise my son in the best environment for him.'

Oz smiled. 'Yeah, I get that,' he said. 'But I'm telling you now, we're going to be together. And even though you don't think so, we do want a lot of the same things. Our lives are going to be mad for a bit. I know no one understands or would choose our life, and that our families and civvie friends don't even get it. But in a few years I'll come out of the Army at a decent rank and get most of my pension. I won't be in the Army forever, you know that. I'll have another forty years of my life to enjoy. And then we'll get a house in the woods in

Cornwall, and watch the seasons, and grow food, and sit outside, in front of a fire, and finally do what we want.' He grinned. 'I might even like being a kept man.'

I threw a cushion at him. 'You can forget that,' I said. 'We're both working.'

But I did see, then, that he was right. We did want a lot of the same things. We weren't so different. Perhaps we just might be able to make it work.

CHAPTER FOUR

Six months after Laird was born, in May 2004, Oz was sent to the Falklands, the tiny islands off the coast of Argentina that no one had ever heard of until the conflict in 1982, when British Forces went to wrest them back from invading Argentina.

Britain has always kept a military presence there, and since the conflict it's been stronger. Oz had already been once before, in 2002, for four months, so this was his second tour of duty. It wasn't a dangerous posting, as there was no active conflict, but it meant our first real separation.

I knew from the start that Oz would have to go away, sometimes for months at a time, but dealing with the reality wasn't easy. We had been together properly for a few short months, we were just getting to know each other, and he was about to vanish to the other side of the world.

'I'll be back before you know it,' he said, holding

me tight and kissing the top of Laird's head.

I had my baby, career and my parents – especially Mum, who was still recovering – and Jamie to think about. I didn't have time to worry about pining for Oz.

Whilst he was away he would phone, and we'd chat. I'd tell him the news, send him the odd photo of Laird, but that was it. It must have been hard for him, so far away, but he always sounded cheerful and told me he was busy and the time was passing. And Oz being Oz, with energy to spare, he decided to pass the time even faster by doing a sponsored walk around East Falkland island, where the Army is based, to raise money for a local school. It was a long walk – East Falkland is about half the size of Wales – and by the end Oz's feet were in shreds; he sent the photos back to prove it!

When he left, Laird was six months old and sitting up. By the time Oz got back in the autumn, Laird was pulling himself to his feet, clinging on to the nearest piece of furniture and swaying precariously as he beamed at us. Oz was thrilled and swung Laird up into his arms. 'Top man, Laird. This calls for a celebration.'

Oz celebrated everything; not just anniversaries and promotions, but the little things – a good day for me at work, a tiny windfall, even the sun shining. He'd get out a bottle of wine for us and apple juice for Laird and the party would begin. He had a natural sense of fun, and he had already seen so much of tragedy and its after-math that he had come to value every moment of life.

As for birthdays, they were huge for him, involving celebrations that went on for at least two weeks, as he would always make the weekend or week running up to the day part of it. There would be piles of presents, balloons, all your favourite foods, seeing every friend you had and being spoiled rotten. Birthdays had been a relatively quiet affair in our family until Oz came along. Of course we had presents, a cake and so on, but that was it. So Oz-style celebrations came as something of a shock. But it was impossible not to be swept up in his enthusiasm.

As for Christmas, to him it was an excuse for the biggest nonstop party of all. By the time he got back from the Falklands our first Christmas together was only a few weeks away, and Oz was already excited and making plans.

But sadly, just before Christmas, Mum had another stroke. She had already lost the sight in one eye, and this time it weakened the sight in her other eye and her hearing. We were all devastated, including Oz. He and Mum got on incredibly well, right from the start, and had already formed a bond all of their own – they loved to drink red wine together and chat – so he was dreadfully upset. She wasn't home in time for Christmas, and Oz said to me, 'Let's give your mum as much happiness as we can.' He showered her with presents, and on Christmas Day he cooked her favourite foods, which we ate at her bedside in hospital, alongside the traditional roast that Dad had cooked us all. Mum loved that, she thought it was hilarious, and Oz, whom she called Ozzy, sealed his place in her heart.

It affected him deeply, seeing Mum, who wasn't yet sixty, so affected by the strokes.

After that he would say to me, 'Come on, let's go for it, let's be a family and do the whole thing. Life's just too short to hang about.'

I loved him, but I was still afraid. And perhaps, if I'm honest, I was a little afraid that it would be too hard for me being with someone who was so often absent. So I continued to put the idea of marriage on hold.

Oz was posted to the Royal Marine Barracks at Stonehouse in Plymouth. This was because only the Army trains ammunition technicians and 'high threat' bomb disposal; the senior ones get posted to different regiments and are able to offer that capability and expertise to the Armed Forces. For a number of years he worked with the corps as their resident expert. He had his own office and autonomy, and was based back home in the West Country where he had spent his child-hood. He said he felt at home by the sea and was delighted. He had wanted to join the Marines when he was a kid, but the Army had been right there and he'd gone for that. So now he was going to fulfil his next career benchmark, to work alongside and offer something specialist to one of his most respected groups of individuals, those with a 'green lid', a Green Beret. He couldn't have been more pleased. He would join them for their yearly training session in Norway, and would be working closely with them on all issues relating to bomb disposal.

Once Oz was settled in Plymouth we fell into a routine, of sorts. He was always subject to last-minute changes, being sent on courses or 'pinged' (sent) abroad, with cancellation of leave, but for the most part his life was stable, and he determined his own diary. He had a lot of independence, and thrived in that specialist environment, proving himself time and time again as a team player. He epitomised their core values: cheerfulness in the face of adversity, integrity, teamwork. It came so naturally to him. He said that even though they were seen by the wider forces as physical and tough, he found their team ethic and warmth, especially amongst mid- to higher ranks, where there was no place for big personalities, was different.

As soon as he was off duty for a day or more, he would get in his car and come the scenic couple of hours from Plymouth to Otterbourne to be with us. Traffic was usually heavy, but Oz always said he didn't mind – he'd listen to music and look forward to a weekend relaxing in the cottage with Laird and me.

Sometimes, if he'd done a lot of miles that week, Mum and Dad would offer to have Laird and I'd drive the other way and go down to Stonehouse to see Oz. I'd stay in his room with him and we'd go out walking on Dartmoor, or see friends.

Oz loved walking, he walked absolutely everywhere, including the two miles or so from the barracks into town to go shopping. I loved walking, too, but I'd get a bit fed up with going backwards and forwards into town. 'Let's get the bus,' I'd suggest. Oz would look amazed. 'Why? It's only down the road.'

Sometimes on a Sunday we'd go into The Artillery Arms, the pub outside the gatehouse at Stonehouse. The landlady there, Belinda, was a strong yet motherly woman who loved Oz and always welcomed him with open arms. He used to go behind the bar and help himself to a drink and Belinda would roar with laughter and pat him on the back. She had enough on her plate with the amount of people in and out all day needing feeding, without Oz mucking about.

Everyone loved Oz, perhaps because, although he joked that he didn't like people, he actually loved them. He had a way of connecting with absolutely anyone, and within minutes of meeting him they'd think of him as an old friend.

I need never have worried about my parents taking to Oz – they absolutely adored him. Mum thought he was good for me and gave us all the support she could. In the early days she couldn't look after Laird alone, but she'd have him if Dad was there; later, as she grew stronger and Laird got a little older, she could manage him alone.

It was a two-way thing with Mum and Oz. We'd be out shopping in Winchester and he'd say, 'Let's pop in for that cuppa with your mum.' We'd go over and Mum would be delighted, rushing to the kitchen saying, 'Crikey, quick, get that cake out.' Oz would laugh and tell her not to worry, a cup of tea would be enough, but she loved to spoil him.

Mum's ill-health hadn't stopped her cooking. It was her passion and joy in life; she always made us beautiful, fresh food. And Oz loved cooking too – it was his way of relaxing. So he'd join her in the kitchen. Sometimes Dad, who was also a chef by trade, would be in there too, the three of them chatting as they concocted some glorious meal. But mostly it was Mum and Oz who took over the kitchen.

The two of them used to conspire against me. I've always been into healthy eating. I don't eat much wheat or dairy and I try to avoid salt and to keep my food low fat.

Oz and Mum would be in the kitchen, singing along to Rod Stewart and drinking wine. I'd stick my head in and Oz would say, 'Yes, it's low fat, no we're not using loads of salt, now get out.'

They'd make wonderful food: a tomato salad with beef tomatoes, basil, mint, lots of herbs and a bit of mozzarella. Oz would sprinkle a bit of rock salt on the top and I'd say, 'It didn't need that', and he'd say, 'Stop, just enjoy it, leave it alone for once.'

The two of them could be irritatingly conspiratorial; they were constantly teasing me. After Mum's strokes I was very bossy and always checking on her: where's your paperwork, your prescription? Right, put your feet up, you shouldn't be doing this or that, what's your blood pressure today, have you had your cuff on? and so on. I had a reasonable amount of medical knowledge, from my brief nurse training and my job in pharmaceuticals, so I tried to make sure she had the latest treatments and was doing all she could to stay well.

Oz would come in and say, 'Oh, here she is, Gill, gobbing off again. She's terrible, isn't she? Swissy, leave your poor mum alone,' and they'd both roar with laughter.

When Mum and Dad came to us, Oz would usually cook. He liked to make slow-cooked stews, soups or big roast dinners with mashed root veg like sweet potatoes. Dad wouldn't drink much because he was driving, and I wouldn't drink much because I'd be working the next morning, so Oz and Mum would enjoy the wine together, though she'd have a glass or two and he'd have the rest of the bottle.

Oz's bond with Dad was centred around the boat. He loved *Magari* almost as much as Dad did. In spring Oz helped Dad get it into the water, and over the summer the two of them would go down and potter around on it. It was a big, heavy boat, but they'd sail it up the Beaulieu River and out into the Solent. Sometimes we'd all go, and Mum would cook us roast lamb Sunday lunch on board. Oz hadn't had time for a lot of sailing, so it was a joy for him to get back to it.

Oz and Jamie liked one another too. I initially thought Jamie would be a bit arty for Oz's liking, but that was just one of his many interests.

Jamie cycled twenty or thirty miles a day, did yoga, meditated, ate well and didn't smoke or drink. He was a quirky, eccentric, sensitive and lovely man. And he was a fantastic artist. One of those people who can look at something and then draw or paint it perfectly, his ability was at times uncanny. He also painted beautiful portraits and would occasionally sell them to make himself a modest income.

So when Oz treated Jamie with warmth and respect, it meant a lot to me. Jamie, in return, thought Oz was magic, and the two of them would enjoy a joke and a mountain-bike ride together. Oz would go on Salisbury Plain and take his map and navigate all the best tracks for mountain biking – they shared the same love of fitness. It was important to me that they got on together.

As Oz was now spending most of his free time with us, he became very hands-on with Laird. At times he was around a lot, between training courses or when waiting to go on operations, and he'd look after Laird while I worked. I was going out on the road more again, and Oz would tell me to go off and work, or go for my runs or walks along the river, or see my friends, as he knew I needed the change of scenery every now and then.

Oz would take Laird to the woods for a walk, or round to see Mum. They often went over to Mum's when I was working. Oz would chat to Mum over a cup of tea while they looked after Laird together. They would pop into town to do the shopping and some weeks he saw a lot more of my mum than I did.

When Oz was with us he liked to slow down, walking down to the village pub, which was only yards from the cottage, where he'd sit on the bench out in the front, smoking his liquorice Rizla roll-ups and enjoying a glass of whisky, looking out over the green. And he loved to relax after work in the evening with a gin and tonic. Or he'd have a Glenmorangie whisky, neat – he said I spoiled it when I insisted on mixing mine with lemonade.

One of the things he enjoyed was mixing cocktails. He'd go out and shop for all the ingredients, using organic lime, fresh herbs and so on, and then play the barman, whipping up mojitos with fresh mint or margaritas with lime, handing the cocktail over with a flourish to wait for my verdict. We'd have barbecues at home and he loved having family or friends over.

We were incredibly close. I found Oz amazingly sexy,

but our relationship wasn't based on just physical attraction – we had a real intimacy, in which we could tell each other anything. We talked for hours, after Laird was in bed, often in the garden where Oz loved to sit in front of a little chiminea or, when it was really cold, in front of the fire inside. He was mad about real fires; he wanted one all the time and could sit for hours, looking into the flames or the glowing coals, nursing his drink, deep in thought.

In the cottage, with the rest of the world shut out, we would truly relax. We laughed together a lot. Oz would tease me, or fool around, and it was impossible not to laugh with him. But he would be serious too, and we talked a lot about how we saw the future, and what we both wanted – a cottage in the country, more kids, dogs, a vegetable garden, time together away from demanding jobs, and his past. He had experienced Sierra Leone and the former Yugoslavia and had said that they had been more shocking than any conflict he had ever seen. He was affected by the ethnic cleansing that went on and baffled at how foreign policy could orchestrate such evil on women and children. Oz was frustrated that we couldn't reach our future sooner, but we both felt we had plenty of time. He talked about leaving the Army, but he wanted to stay in long enough to get a good pension, and that meant waiting until his fifteen-year point – just a couple more years. However, he had decided that Army life wasn't always going to be for him, and that was the turning point in my head – that I knew he wanted out at some point.

When the three of us were together we lived life at our own pace. Our jobs were very rule-bound, so it was good to get away from that. We'd eat when we felt like it, and have what we fancied. We'd go round Waitrose looking for nice food and then go home and prepare it together, enjoying a glass of wine, music and plenty of time. It didn't matter whether we ate at three in the afternoon or nine at night, we'd just cook when we wanted to.

It was a while before we met one another's friends outside of work, as it was hard to find the time. I would see mine during the week when Oz was away, or I'd see them out and about with the children. But Oz wanted me to know the people who mattered most to him. First among them were Andrew Stevens and Mark Hayes. Andrew was a childhood friend. He and Oz had met at the age of five and had been close friends ever since. Mark Hayes – Hazey – was a sergeant in the Royal Marines. He had been based at Stonehouse. They had clicked the moment they'd met and had spent a lot of time mucking about together. I liked both Andrew and Hazey straight away. Both of them were like Oz: bright, funny, thoughtful and loyal.

As luck would have it, Hazey fell in love with a girl called Sam, who was an old acquaintance of mine. She had actually attended the local village primary school in Otterbourne, and we'd been on nodding terms because she grew up in Chandler's Ford and the surrounding area. She was a stunning, clever legal assistant. We soon became the best of friends, as we were both high achievers and had other halves in the forces. Sam was savvy, wise, supportive and great fun. We'd joke about their ways as boys, like when they got their phys kits on to play Nintendo Wii, and laugh at the sayings they'd use when we were out drinking and partying.

They met when Hazey was security officer and driver for the Navy's Commander-in-Chief Fleet (CINCFLEET), and was accompanying Admiral Sir Jonathon Band through the VIP section of Southampton Airport on their way to the Naval Base at Portsmouth. Sam had left her legal career behind because she wanted to pursue a career in film production, but as a stopgap she was working at the airport in the Signature VIP Handling Area, where her job was to meet and escort all the VIP flights and passengers. As fate would have it, Hazey and Sam met only three weeks before she was due to leave the company and depart for California. Hazey, in typical bootneck style, asked Sam for her number, saying she couldn't possibly depart for the USA without a toast. A week later they went for that farewell drink and have been inseparable ever since! Sam's brother 'Sucky' had joined the British Army for a short period and served in

Northern Ireland, so she understood the military, but neither she nor I could have predicted our futures as military wives.

Hazey was drafted to London when Admiral Sir Jonathon Band became First Sea Lord, the head of the Navy, and was based in the Ministry of Defence in Whitehall. Hazey lived in an MoD house in central London. Oz and I would go up and stay with them if Sam was visiting, and the four of us became incredibly close. Just as Hazey and Oz were alike, so were Sam and I, both of us career women who had to find a way to fit our own lives together with the complex life patterns of military men, all the while keeping up with our family commitments. I found a kindred spirit in Sam, who did go on to start a film production company. Hazey, who was seven years older than Oz, was a guide and mentor as well as a friend to him. If Oz was worried about something, or uncertain, I would say, 'Call Hazey, talk it over with him.' Hazey was much better with money than Oz was and had always advised him to stop throwing his money around and invest in property, so I trusted Hazey's judgement as much as Oz did. He was the first male friend to see potential in Oz and really help sort him out. Sam was there for both of us. She liked Oz from the moment he turned up at their house and gave her a tight hug. That first weekend became legendary as the next morning, Oz, having assured Sam he'd been a chef when he first joined the Army, offered to cook breakfast and then made the worst fry-up they'd ever had. 'He was hungover but I adored him,' Sam told me later.

They were fantastic friends, and we had many good times together. Hazey and Sam's wedding, the week before Oz went to Afghanistan for the last time, was one of the happiest days of our lives, and later they were to be an enormous source of comfort and support to me.

CHAPTER FIVE

O z had joined the Army at the tender age of sixteen as a chef, just 'for something to do', as he put it. He'd got reasonable GCSE results and could have gone on to take A levels, but he was eager to get going in life, to do something that would give him tangible skills and involve travel. He was a boy with vast amounts of energy, talent and enthusiasm, and growing up in relatively sleepy Cornwall had left him longing for adventure, sports and an identity after school.

The Royal Logistics Corps is the biggest corps in the Army, and provides the services required by wider forces. It offers training in all kinds of different trades, from chef to driver to railway operator or communications specialists. Oz had loved the idea of going in and being able to chop and change. He felt that although he was hard-working, he wasn't yet sure that he wanted a career in anything in particular. But learning to cook anything, anywhere – on the move, in snow or in the desert, in battle and in training – had appealed to him. Soldiers need to eat, so Army chefs have to be adaptable and resourceful, and for a while Oz really enjoyed it.

A few years later, one of Oz's colleagues on an early fitness-training course told me he had been a real friend to her then. When she had struggled with some of the physical demands of the assault courses, he encouraged her on, saying, 'Dig deep, suck it up, come on, get oxygen into you, I'm not leaving you.' She made it, and never forgot that he had pulled her up when the others went on ahead. Oz was always a friend to anyone who needed help, and he showed leadership qualities from the start.

Later she showed me a photo of the troop passing out, with a ridiculously young-looking Oz grinning in the middle. It reminded me of how he looked when we first got together.

While being a chef was fun, it wasn't a challenge, so it wasn't long before he was drawn by another of the trades the RLC offers – ammunition technician. Oz told me he'd seen the bomb team at work in Northern Ireland and thought, that looks different, I think I can do that. That was typical Oz, confident he would do anything he set his mind to.

Andrew Stevens told me that Oz had phoned him one night from Northern Ireland. They were both eighteen or nineteen at the time. Andrew was helping to run his family's hotel, The Old Ship in Padstow, and Oz was on guard duty in Northern Ireland and very bored.

'I'm thinking about a change of trade,' Oz had told him.

'Oh yeah, what are you thinking of?'

'Don't know,' Oz replied. 'I'm looking around.'

The next night, back on guard duty, Oz phoned again.

'I've just put my name down for bomb disposal,' he said.

Andrew was horrified. 'You what? Do you know what you've done?' he said.

In some ways Andrew wasn't surprised. Oz had always loved playing with firecrackers and bangers. The two of them went to France on a school rugby tour and brought back a load of French bangers. Oz used them to see how big a hole he could blow in the beach.

It was a strange irony that Oz often seemed to be around explosions which weren't of his making. Once, in Northern Ireland, the catering truck he was working on blew up, when a gas canister exploded. Not Oz's fault, and he wasn't hurt, but it was the first of several near misses he had and it was odd how explosions seemed to follow him around.

Not that it put him off working with explosives. He loved the idea.

The pull of bomb disposal was strong. The top ammunition technicians were, as Oz put it, 'like

well-respected football superstars' to the rest of the
Army. Their motto was to preserve life, civilian or
otherwise. 'Felix' became the call sign of the AT or ATO
(ammunition technical officer), which many believe to
be a nod to the cat with nine lives.

To a keen, bright young soldier who was feeling
restless, they were the pinnacle of success, doing an
exciting job which was well paid and earned the respect
and admiration of their peers. It was unique, which
appealed to Oz.

The job has always carried risks, but at that time ATOs
were very rarely killed or injured. There was no major
war going on and it didn't seem anything like as high-
risk as it does now.

The ammunition technicians learn about all aspects
of the Army's use of ammunition, including management, storage, handling, inspection and so on. And if
they show an aptitude for it, they may go on to train in
bomb disposal for the best part of a decade, and then
take possibly the hardest course in all our Armed Forces:
the 'high threat' bomb-disposal course.

The Royal Legistics Corps website says: 'Being an
ammunition technician calls for intelligence, clear
thinking, a calm outlook and excellent attention to
detail. You'll also need good people skills, because
when it comes to handling ammunition, you need to be
heard and understood. This job is about safety and
protection. People's lives will depend on you.

'As a trained soldier you'll develop specialist skills to test, inspect, maintain and dispose of all sorts of ammunition, from bullet clips to anti-aircraft guided weapon systems and Improvised Explosive Devices (IED). You'll become a technical expert and gain skills that will be valuable for the rest of your life.

'If you think you've got what it takes, we'll unleash your talent and train you to the highest standards of combat, scientific and technical excellence.'

This was what drew Oz. And very early on it became clear that he showed a remarkable natural aptitude for the job.

It's hard to quantify the characteristics and ability that are needed to deal with a job as potentially dangerous and demanding as bomb disposal. An ability to stay cool and calm under immense pressure, to think clearly, make decisions, take charge of those around you, be adaptable and apply complex knowledge. All of these qualities are vital. But there's more to it than the sum of these parts. Men and women who can handle high-threat bomb disposal are extraordinary people who deal over and over again with extreme risks that most people would do anything to avoid. They put others before themselves, time after time.

They're also modest. Oz, like every other person I've ever come across who is doing a similar job, seldom talked about it. And though he took his job deadly seriously, when he was away from work he treated it lightly, dismissing what he did as just another job.

Oz wasn't yet a high-threat operator – the highest of the high in bomb disposal – when I met him, but he was working towards that rare achievement, and was already a respected and experienced ATO. He had also been picked out early on as officer material, and promoted to the rank of junior, then senior NCO, or noncommissioned officer.

In the field of combat, the ATOs wear badges marking them out, so that other soldiers know who they are, and who to turn to in the event a bomb or explosives are discovered. Oz called it the flaming arsehole. Ever the clown.

There's a huge amount of training involved in being an ATO, so Oz was constantly off on courses, at the time usually held at the Army School of Ammunition at Kineton, in Warwickshire, which has since been renamed the Defence Explosive Ordnance Disposal, Munitions and Search School, or DEMSS Kineton. Oz did his basic nine-month training there, and was back there almost every year after that, sometimes more than once, as he took on increasingly specialised courses, or relicensed.

On training exercises the instructors would stand behind with a brown paper bag, ready to burst it with a bang if he cut the wrong wire on the imitation bomb. And the tensions and pressures were always there. He told me, 'You do the same with a training bomb as with a live IED. If you make the wrong cut, then you're in trouble. It doesn't matter that they're not real when you train. You know when you've messed up and you feel terrible.'

All the ammunition technicians move up the ranks at a different pace, so Oz would be on courses with different people each time. But as only a handful of men and women choose, or are able, to train to a senior level in this skill, he inevitably got to know most of the others heading towards being high-threat operators. There were those ahead of him that he admired and respected, and those coming up behind who looked up to Oz.

Oz had been sent to all kinds of places throughout his career. A lot of his training had been done in Cyprus, where he'd been several times, and as well as the Falkland Islands he'd been posted to Northern Ireland, Sierra Leone, Germany and Kosovo.

There had been a conflict in Kosovo, in 1999, between the Kosovo Liberation Army and Serbia, of which Kosovo was a part. The Kosovans broke free and the British Army sent troops, as part of a NATO intervention force, to help stop the 'ethnic cleansing', as Kosovo made the transition to becoming a new state, with its own majority government. The Army's role was a peacekeeping one, but they also had to deal with the aftermath of appalling slaughter and destruction.

After the worst of the conflict it was discovered that

thousands of ethnic Albanians had been killed. Mass graves were found and the bodies had to be exhumed. And the killings were still going on.

Oz was part of a force dealing with this aftermath and it had a huge impact on him. He said very little about it, but when he did talk he told me that he'd had to shovel scores of bodies from flat-bed trucks, dripping with blood. Children. Beautiful, awesome women and children. Body after body, still warm. People who looked just like us and our family. There's no doubt in my mind that it left him with some form of post-traumatic stress disorder (PTSD), though he never complained as he preferred to be in denial. PTSD is a condition that results from trauma and it can show itself in so many different ways, and sometimes up to fourteen years or more after the events that caused it. For Oz it revealed itself in the little things. He hated anything dripping. And he couldn't pick up a sleeping child. Small children often fall asleep on warm evenings during family gatherings and usually a dad will pick them up and carry them off to bed. If Oz did that with Laird he would be up all night afterwards, talking and drinking. He told me that he'd had to carry the warm body of a small girl who had just been shot. She had been blonde, like Laird, with the same brown eyes and fair, tanned skin. Carrying Laird off to bed, a hot, dead-weight, unconscious child, triggered terrible memories for Oz. I would protect him, rushing to pick Laird up and take him off to bed before anyone could suggest Oz do it.

He used to say, 'I've got a little black box for all those bad memories, so they don't affect me much.' But I saw his denial. He had horrible dreams and would cry out and I'd wake and try to shut him up before Laird or the dog kicked off. We'd talk about it. I'd suggest he go and talk to someone, a counsellor, but he'd say, 'No amount of counselling is going to get me through it.' He said there was no point. 'What do civvies know?' I said, 'I have heard enough. My mum would understand, why don't you talk to her? I won't listen to any more – we have a life. For us it won't end tomorrow, we can't live life like it's the last day, we need to crack on.'

Sometimes he did talk to Mum. When I was away at a conference and he and Laird stayed at their house, he'd occasionally wake in the night and come down to find Mum pottering around with the radio on. Ever since the stroke she'd had trouble sleeping. They'd sit in the kitchen at three in the morning, and talk.

There was a physical legacy he carried too. Oz suffered from acute colitis, a particularly bad type of Irritable Bowel Syndrome (IBS). On top of dealing with mass-scale slaughter, he'd had an emergency appendix operation while he was in the field, after his appendix became infected. He said he'd been operated on in a field hospital and that he thought it had gone wrong, as he'd had gut problems ever since. 'I was butchered,' he'd say.

I learned to deal with the reality of Oz's 'gut problems' early on, as it affected him every single day. He had to go to the loo several times a day, often in a rush. Out on a walk he'd disappear into the bushes, or in town he'd race into the nearest pub to find a toilet. At night he was often kept awake by severe cramps, his bowel in spasm. I had to go to friends and doctors to ask for help.

Oz tried to make light of it, laughed it off at work, but it was a serious condition and at times he did get very down about it. It compromised his energy levels, and was worse if he ate wheat or drank coffee or tea. He saw doctors, and tried various treatments, but nothing came close to curing it. Everyone who knew Oz knew about it. His colleagues would rally round and protect him – if he needed the loo when he was out in the field, or on a training run, they'd just let him find the nearest clump of trees or stone wall to crouch behind. They were a team, and whoever was in charge would understand. He would use leaves and also pages from his notebooks.

I told him it didn't faze me. I had nursed old people and looked after a baby – to me bodily functions were just part of life, and you coped with them. I didn't see it as a problem between us. In fact, the opposite was true: dealing with it brought us together; it was very intimate and we were closer because Oz knew he could trust me.

To me, coping with it was just a part of loving him. I wanted to help and I would have done anything to make it more bearable for him.

As well as certain foods, undoubtedly stress of any kind made it worse. When he was with me I fed him a very healthy diet, and his guts would improve. He'd be more relaxed, need the loo less frequently, and sleep better. I was certain he was wheat and dairy intolerant, because when I took all wheat and dairy foods out of his diet he improved dramatically. Because he had to do a lot of physical exercise, he was always hungry, so I'd fill him up on a high-protein diet with lots of nuts and fish, potatoes and vegetables. I'd give him double portions, so that he didn't need to top up with bread. We found snacks that he could eat on the go – smoked salmon, handfuls of walnuts, cold meats, wheat-free pasta, flasks of soup. I'd make him drink lots of water, cut back the alcohol, and after a week of that Oz would be much better. The pain would have gone, he could sleep and he was going to the loo only a couple of times a day. But as soon as he got back to the Army, all the problems would escalate again. The diet, which inevitably included lots of bread and cheap rations, didn't help him. He'd be eating toast for breakfast, packs of sandwiches at lunch and more bread with dinner and within a couple of days he'd be in a chronic state again and in crippling pain.

He'd laugh it off most of the time, but it did truly trouble him and it was a bone of contention between us that Oz wouldn't tell anyone senior about his problems. His mates at work knew and I felt he should tell his bosses, but he was afraid he would be seen as weak and that it would go on his record. He knew that if he had health problems it would affect his chances of getting a job in security or some related field after he left the Army. And that was his plan: to leave healthy for a new life.

'Chrissy, stop,' he'd say. 'I don't want to tell people. I'm not some Fat Rupert, complaining about everything, looking for a claim on it and a desk jockey job. I'd rather grizz it. It won't be long and I don't think they will send me out again.'

Grizzing it was a very Oz expression. It meant facing it head-on, toughing it out, getting through. Something he did a lot.

Fat Rupert was the term he and many others in the Army used to refer to officers who'd never seen any active service, who sat behind desks ordering everyone else around, or those who had cut short a posting or mission because of a health complaint, playing the system. War-dodgers, as Oz called them. If Oz heard of someone coming back early from a posting because of a stress complaint like an ulcer or headaches or stomach problems he'd mutter, 'Cheeky fucker.'

As far as Oz was concerned, you just had to get on with it, pain or no pain, and if you needed a crap once an hour, well, you just found a way to cope with that.

But he did feel angry and irritated with the way his body let him down; it was embarrassing and emasculating. After a sleepless night of pain and constant trips to the loo, I hated seeing him go off to work looking exhausted, but he would never take time off or stop. He drove himself on like a machine.

I did a lot of research into IBS, looking for natural cures, anything that might help. Cumin is anti-inflammatory, so I'd put that in his food. He'd laugh and say, 'You're spooky, why don't you do me a potion?' If only I could have. As it was I tried to help, and Oz was grateful, but over time the condition got worse, not better, as his stress levels were one thing I sadly could never control.

In addition, Oz suffered from damaged hearing and bad tinnitus – ringing in the ears – as a result of being around one too many explosions. Being in AT inevitably involves blowing things up, as you learn to handle explosives. Oz said that on one practice he was detonating an old car, as part of his training. Being the clown that he was, he got a friend to take a rear-view picture of him – in full uniform to the waist and naked from the waist down – with the explosion going on in the background. Unfortunately Oz had used too much explosive – the resulting bang was massive and left him with damaged hearing.

His bizarre knack of being around explosions, whether he was working or not, hadn't diminished.

Around Easter 2006 he and Hazey went to Egypt for a week. Hazey, who was an experienced windsurfer, had promised to teach Oz, and they decided to do it somewhere warm, where they could be in the water a lot without freezing.

Hazey was also keen on waterskiing, so one afternoon, when the wind had dropped and there wasn't much chance of going out windsurfing, Hazey got out on the waterskis and Oz followed behind in the boat, filming the action on Hazey's camcorder. Suddenly, with no warning at all, the boat blew up. Oz was thrown into the water, along with the camcorder, despite his attempts to hold it clear, and Hazey (with typical bootneck humour) shouted, 'Save the camera.' He was left with nasty burns down his leg, but it could have been so much worse. He and Hazey – who had watched in astonishment from where he'd ditched in the sea – had absolutely no idea why the boat blew up. Oz enjoyed retelling the story during his best man's speech at Sam and Hazey's wedding!

On that same holiday, they used to eat every night in a nice little restaurant they'd found, where they'd enjoy steak, chips and a beer. The day after they returned to the UK, the restaurant was blown up by terrorists. Oz and Hazey were stunned – and grateful for the narrow escape.

I'm sure Oz wasn't the only AT to have hearing problems, it's a hazard of the job, but like IBS it's a condition that's very hard to cure. Oz had to live with it. He'd say, 'When I want to retire there's a claim, honey,' but he wouldn't tell anyone. He was so deaf, and he used to really annoy me by putting the TV on ridiculously loud and then falling asleep in front of it.

None of this sounds particularly romantic, and it wasn't. Everyday issues seldom are. But Oz was a romantic through and through, and he showed it every day. He loved flowers, candles, champagne, spontaneous gestures, little presents. There was a particular kind of jelly sweet that I loved, a Haribo mix that had lovely flavours like apple and melon, but you couldn't often find them. I'd keep them in the car, for fuel and a pick-me-up on long journeys to see clients. Oz rolled up one day, triumphant, with ten bags that he'd found in a little corner shop in Plymouth.

Another time he rolled up with a T-shirt with 'Witches are so sexy' printed on the front. 'I can just see me wearing that to work,' I told him.

He used to buy me gifts of black or white natural beeswax candles, which I loved. I would put our names on, white candles for good, black to absorb any negativity. And he would buy me all kinds of things to do with angels – cards and figurines, as well as hearts made out of rose quartz, a stone I thought especially beautiful.

He was such a romantic about togetherness that at times he would drive me mad. I'd leave the house to go shopping and before I was in the car he'd be phoning me. 'I miss you, Swiss, can I come too? When are you coming home?' I'd be saying, 'For goodness' sake, I'm only going to Tesco, I'll be an hour.'

The first time we spent my birthday together, Oz bought me a gold and diamond necklace. It was beautiful, but it had cost £700 and I was horrified. I couldn't bear for him to spend that on me when he had debts to pay, so I took it back to the shop for a refund. He was upset and offended, but he said, 'I want to be happy, not right. I'm not going to argue about it, it's your decision, but I do take issue with it.' I felt bad, but I was doing it for us, so that we could be together, debt-free.

That certainly wasn't the last expensive present Oz bought me, and it wasn't the last one I took back, but I did keep, and treasure, some of them. He was incredibly generous, not just with me but with everyone he loved. He'd say to me, 'Honey, get yourself something nice,' and I'd say, 'No, I'm waiting for the sales.'

I never bought him presents that cost a fortune, but I did help him pay off his debts. We did it together. I was earning good money, and when I knew he was serious about us being together, and having a clean slate, I wanted to help. We agreed to put everything we could into the debts, and after that we'd pay off the mortgage on Jasmine Cottage as fast as we could, so that we'd eventually have enough to get the home we dreamed of.

Some of the happiest times we had together were in places that were special to us. I took him to Cowley Manor, an absolutely beautiful country-house hotel and spa set in fifty acres of meadows, lakes and parklands in the Cotswolds. I had always gone to Cowley when I needed a couple of days' peace and quiet, to restore my spirit and my energy. It was a very spiritual, nurturing, cleansing place, where you could come and go as you wanted. I went there with Oz and he loved it – we used to stay in the stable block and just do our own thing. We'd keep our boots outside the door and go for long walks, eat when we wanted to and go out to 'moonbathe' down by the lake.

Both of us needed to unwind regularly. Oz's job was full-on and hugely demanding and, in its own way, so was mine. I was back on the road, attending conferences, seeing clients and working long hours. I had enormous stamina – Oz used to call me 'the machine' and say to me, 'You're Ninja, woman.' He'd get quite annoyed sometimes and say accusingly, 'I'm knackered, why are you not knackered?' But I'd keep going, just knowing that at some point we'd get some time off and go for a break to one of our special places.

If we had enough time, we'd go to Nan's cottage, which was still in the family. It was usually freezing when we went, but Oz adored the place. We'd walk for hours, then come back and he'd build a massive fire. He loved the stream and the standing stone. 'Let's make sure we have one of those beside our house when we find it,' he'd say.

Oz was a single-minded, private man. Much soppier than I was! Whatever he did, he did to the full. So when he relaxed, he really relaxed. He didn't tend to let things stay on his mind. If we were on a break, he might start by having a moan about his mates or work, but then throw himself into enjoying it.

Our shared passion for nature gave us both a lot of joy. We were both at our happiest in open spaces, around plants, trees and water. At Christmas we'd go and walk under pine trees, or have chestnuts around the Christmas tree that was put up in the centre of Winchester. In spring we'd go and walk along the River Itchen, through Winchester and out into the countryside.

And just as I introduced Oz to my favourite places, he took me to his – Cornwall. Oz loved his birthplace, and he still had a lot of good friends there.

He loved his family dearly, but their lives were so different and seemingly much more simplistic than ours or his. He was almost envious that they were so cocooned and lived a more sheltered life in Cornwall. Greg, Oz's brother, was a builder by trade and loved his boats, and he was married to Lindsay. Torben worked in bathroom sales; he was married to Debbie and they had a little boy, Arthur, and went on to have a baby girl, Agnes, sadly only a few weeks before Oz was killed. I've often heard of that happening, a baby being born around the same time someone dies.

One of his favourite pubs was The New Inn at Veryan, which was run by Jack and Penny. Oz would phone ahead to let them know we were on our way down and to hang out the bunting, get the whisky in.

After making merry in The New Inn, we would hare over to Padstow, to The Old Ship, run by Andrew Stevens and his family. We'd have a warm welcome from Andrew and his then girlfriend Amanda. She was lovely, and they were so close we used to call them Amandrew. We'd often stay with them, they were a great couple, and the four of us became good friends. Oz and Andrew loved to go for a run together, or sit on the quay at Padstow and chew the fat, reminiscing about their childhood and old friends. Oz had spent a few Christmases with them and, more than once, after tanking up on a few drinks and in a wild and merry mood, he'd stripped to the buff on Christmas Day to run down to the harbour at Padstow and jump into the icy water.

Andrew's parents owned and ran the hotel; after finishing their education, he and his sister joined the business as partners. They were a lovely family who got on with one another well, but inevitably in a close-knit family business there are moments when it all feels like hard work. If Andrew was stressed Oz would say to him, 'It's not too late to join up, you know.' But Andrew would grin and say, 'Thanks, mate, but it's not for me.'

When Andrew's dad, who everyone knew as Pop, turned sixty, he decided to step back from the day-to-day running of things a bit and spend more time in his garden. Oz was really fond of him and we went down for his sixtieth birthday party. Oz gave him a very posh trowel which he'd had engraved with 'digging for glory' and said to Pop, 'You've done your bit for humanity, now go and have fun with this.' Not that Pop ever did – the trowel was so nice that he kept it, afraid that if he used it in the garden it would disappear.

We did plenty of partying in Cornwall, but we spent a lot of time in the open air too, walking on the cliff paths or on the wide, beautiful beaches. Oz loved Nare Head, and Carne and Pendower beaches. We would take a picnic down to the beach and spend all day there, playing games and running along the sand, Laird squealing with excitement as Oz chased him and then swept him up into the air.

One day, sitting on the beach looking out to sea, Oz turned to me. 'Let's live here. Let's have a house in Cornwall and send Laird to a good school and have a boat, and spend all our time out in the open.'

I laughed. 'Sounds like a plan to me.'

CHAPTER SIX

Oz was thrilled when Laird called him Daddy. He looked on Laird as his son, loved him with all his heart, and the two of them were incredibly close. They would lie on the sofa watching TV together, Laird on top of Oz, or with their legs entwined. Often Oz would trim his toenails. They shared food at the table, walks, jokes, tussles on the floor and tender moments, when Laird had hurt himself and Oz would cuddle him.

Oz was immensely proud of Laird and made a big deal of every milestone and success. 'Look at that,' he'd say. 'He knows fifty words. Did Einstein know fifty words by the time he was two?'

Malc rarely saw Laird, who called him Malc or Daddy Malchie. Victoria, Malc's younger sister, whom I had got to know well, has three children. Both Victoria and I felt strongly that the children should know each other, so we stayed in regular contact and met up often.

As far as Laird was concerned, Oz was his dad. Laird viewed as dad whoever loved me and us, whoever was there for us year after year.

They were so contented in each other's company. Oz used to stride off into the woods with Laird on his shoulders. They'd sit together under a big old yew tree, where there was a hollow at the base of the trunk, looking out on a little valley that spread out below them within the wood. Oz would start a fire and build a look-out. They'd spend hours there before wandering home, their pockets full of Laird's finds.

Although Oz was around a lot at this stage, he knew it was only a matter of time before he was sent overseas again, and he wanted to be sure we knew he was genuine about our identity, who we were, and what we were going to be and do when he was away and beyond. So he decided we should have a dog.

We decided on a lovely white Boxer puppy, and both Oz and Laird adored him. We didn't get round to naming him for a while, but then Oz called him Bo – for BO, body odour, because he said he smelled that bad! Poor Bo, he didn't really smell worse than any other dog, and he was a lovely, affectionate dog. Oz felt happier when we had him with us and he trained Bo to bark at strangers.

Every morning Oz would go out running with Bo. It gave them both the exercise they needed, and it became a routine that Oz always kept up when he was at home.

Oz took to calling Laird and Bo 'the kids'.

As for me, he let me know every day that he loved me. I would often come home to find little notes – written in capitals, because that's how he always wrote – like this from him when he'd gone back to Plymouth:

MORNING GORGEOUS,

JUST A QUICK NOTE TO TELL YOU HOW HAPPY I AM NOW. I LOVE YOU WITH ALL MY HEART. NOT SELFISHLY JUST FULL-ON. NO BACK-UP PLANS. LOVE YOU ALL. WOULD FILL THIS PAGE, BUT I'VE GOT TO GO.

LOVE YOU SO MUCH

OZ XXXXX

It wasn't all hearts and roses. I still had doubts and fears, and there were times when we rowed and I'd tell him I didn't think he was right for me. He wanted us to marry, and I still didn't see myself as an Army wife in married quarters, waiting for months while he was away. I clung to my independence because it made me feel safer; if I didn't need him or rely on him, then I wouldn't miss him so much when he was away. I know that hurt him, because he was so single-minded about us being together. And it was crazy, because I already loved him. But somehow, by refusing to let Oz fully into my life and my heart, I felt I was protecting myself and protecting Laird. A lesser man might have given up, but

Oz never did. He would come back, time and time again, to claim us as the future he wanted.

But if we did row from time to time, we soon stopped. On the occasions that we had a disagreement, if either of us was getting worked up, we'd use a code word to shut it down. We chose our code word because it was a word I hated so much! When we used that word, it meant, 'Stop right now, take stock, it's not worth a row.'

I know I could be difficult to be around – I could be bossy, critical and distant – and perhaps inevitably there were times when Oz was not easy to be around either. One of those times was the anniversary of the ending of the Falklands conflict on 14 June. It fell just three days after Oz's birthday, which was on 11 June. He would spend his birthday partying, and then slump into a brooding despondency as the anniversary came. He would close the curtains and sit, silent and alone, drinking heavily for at least twenty-four hours. When I asked him about it he'd say, 'Someone ought to remember the men and boys who died then. That could have been me. I'd want somebody to take a day out of their year to remember me.'

Oz valued honour and integrity and loyalty above all things, and he was right to want to remember the 255 members of the Armed Forces who died in that conflict. He had been to the islands twice and had seen the scenes of battle, so it was very real to him. But when he drank steadily and became distant and morose, it was hard to carry on with normal life around him, especially with a small child.

Oz was never violent, or even aggressive. He was the gentlest of men. But I did find these episodes, when he became so withdrawn, difficult to handle. It wasn't often, and I understood that the effects of what he had seen in Kosovo were undoubtedly a big part of it. I would take Laird out and leave him to it, but if it went on for too long, I'd go and talk to him, and tell him it was time to get back to the land of the living.

Life can be sad and tragic, and it can be funny and lovely. That's what Oz was – two faces, poles apart, and yet all part of the same entity. Grief and humour went hand in hand. After grieving for a day, or sometimes a whole weekend, he would get himself together and get on with life.

At that time, in the first half of 2006, he was training with the Marines.

Marine training is some of the most arduous and demanding training in the world. It was rigorous, tough and pushed him to the limit. Oz had to keep himself at a peak of physical fitness and, despite his health problems, he did.

He passed the course in the summer of 2006. It involved four tests, all of which had to be taken within a seven-day period. These four tests were:

- A nine-mile speed march, carrying full fighting order (kit), to be completed in ninety minutes, meaning they had to cover a mile every ten minutes.
- A six-mile endurance course across rough moorland and woodland terrain at Woodbury Common near Lympstone, which included tunnels, pipes, wading pools and an underwater culvert. The course ended with a four-mile run, followed by a marksmanship test, where the recruit must hit six out of ten shots at a 25-m target simulating 200 m.
- Next came the Tarzan Assault Course, an assault course combined with an aerial confidence test. It started with a death slide and ended with a rope climb up a thirty-foot near-vertical wall. It had to be completed with full fighting order in twelve minutes.
- Finally there was the thirty-miler. A thirty-mile march across upland Dartmoor, wearing full fighting order, and additional safety equipment carried in a daysack, to be completed in seven hours.

Hazey, who, being a Marine, had already completed his commando training some time before, drove down from London on the day Oz did the thirty-miler. He took a bottle of Moët et Chandon champagne and waited on the finishing line for Oz who, as tradition dictates, sprinted the last few yards, before being sprayed with fizz – Oz finished looking as fresh as a daisy. They drank a toast and Hazey watched as Oz, along with the others who had made it, was presented with his green beret.

Oz was extremely proud when he passed the Commando training, and he kept the handwritten letter of congratulations sent to him in August 2006 by one of his commanding officers, Major Iain Bayliss of the Royal Logistics Corps.

This is an extract from the letter, which was three pages long.

Dear Sgt Schmid,

Firstly, huge congratulations on passing the Commando Course. I must admit that I am as chuffed as you are and you can now feel rightly proud to wear the coveted 'Green Beret' and Commando dagger. I am sure that these prized possessions felt at times out of reach, but you have demonstrated the exact qualities required of a Commando soldier. These qualities of physical strength, mental robustness and high standards of soldiering skills, have no doubt been tested to the extreme limits. Just as important however, will have been your outstanding sense of humour and positive attitude, which I hope does not diminish . . .

The day that I received my beret and dagger is

permanently ingrained in my memory, as no doubt it is with you . . .

Always remember the history of the Army Commando and the standard and traditions that we, the current Commandos, must protect so that they endure long after we have gone.

Once again my sincerest congratulations and I wish you the very best for the future.

Yours Aye,

Iain Bayliss

Oz went on to add parachute training to his qualifications. Those who have passed the Marine Commando training, or other equivalent training, can take an RAF parachute course, which qualifies them to wear the British Military Parachute Wings flash on the shoulder of their uniform. To qualify they have to do seven parachute drops, at heights from 1,000 feet to 600 feet. Six of these drops are with full equipment, and two of them are at night.

Oz faced every test with courage and determination, and he was hugely proud of his Commando beret and dagger insignia, and the Para wings.

Soon after Oz completed his Commando training, he heard that he was to be sent to Afghanistan for a six-month tour. Oz wasn't unduly worried about the idea of going, and neither was I. The situation in Afghanistan was very different then to the situation he faced when he went for the second time three years later.

Like so many people, at that time I didn't know a great deal about what was happening in Afghanistan. I knew our troops were there, and I'd read the official line, that they were trying to keep the terrorist organisation al-Qaeda, headed by Osama bin Laden, out of Afghanistan, and to help the country become more stable. But it was only when Oz was sent there that I learned more about it. Oz and I both wanted to understand what was going on, what the war was about and why he had to go. So we read up on it.

The conflict in Afghanistan began after 9/11, the twin towers tragedy in America, in which planes were flown into both towers of the World Trade Center, and into the Pentagon. A fourth plane, headed for Washington, crashed after passengers overwhelmed the terrorists on board. In all nearly 3,000 people were killed. These four suicide missions were part of a coordinated attack by al-Qaeda; the deadliest attack on the United States in its history.

Al-Qaeda was – and is – a terrorist organisation. At that time it was led by Osama bin Laden, who planned the attacks on the States because of objections to US foreign policy – in particular the US support of Israel, sanctions against Iraq and the presence of US soldiers in Saudi Arabia after the Gulf War.

Bin Laden was from Saudi Arabia. But he set up al-Qaeda from Afghanistan, a country then run by the

Taliban, an Islamist militia group which had taken over the government and which, with an ancient history of hospitality, gave sanctuary to bin Laden and his organisation.

The scene was set. Within weeks of 9/11, America launched air strikes against Afghanistan, backed by NATO (the North Atlantic Treaty Organisation), a military coalition that today has twenty-eight member states. The idea was to strike quickly, take out al-Qaeda, drive the Taliban out and replace it with a stable government that would no longer harbour terrorists. And so it appeared to go: al-Qaeda and the Taliban fled and a new, moderate leader, Hamid Karzai, was found.

Job done, or so it seemed. America and its ally, Britain, took their eyes off Afghanistan and turned their attention to Iraq, leaving only a modest number of troops to help keep law and order and bring about a transition to a more stable and peaceful society.

But Afghanistan is an ancient and complex country, twice the size of Britain and filled with warlords, warring tribes and opposing factions. It also has few modern facilities, little infrastructure and virtually no communications systems.

The Taliban rose from the ashes of defeat, licked their wounds, regrouped and fought back, determined to recapture the capital, Kabul, and to reinstall themselves in government. In response to this, increasing numbers of American and British troops were sent to Afghanistan in an attempt to oust the Taliban once and for all.

Much of the fighting centred on Helmand province, in the southwest of the country. Helmand borders Pakistan, where many of the members of al-Qaeda and the Taliban had fled. Helmand is a desert state, where the principal economy is drug production, and half the population are illiterate. The British troops were based there, and when they first arrived, the idea was to bring about a sustainable peace and win the hearts and minds of the Afghan people, in three years. A goal that most military leaders and politicians agreed was utterly impossible.

By September 2006, when Oz was sent there for the first time, Operation Mountain Thrust had been launched; a combined NATO–Afghan mission targeted at Taliban fighters in the south. British troop levels, alongside US troop levels, were increased.

Although the troops in Afghanistan were now engaged in combat, rather than in a peacekeeping role, it still didn't seem to me – or even to Oz – a particularly dangerous mission. During the first five years of British involvement, there had been only two British soldiers killed in action.

By the time Oz went, there had been ten more deaths in action that year. Desperately sad, but not enough to make us seriously worried. Oz was part of a highly trained team, and they were dealing with a limited number of Improvised Explosive Devices, or IEDs. He often reassured me that they knew what they were doing, and because of that, the risks weren't high. It wasn't until later, when Oz became head of his own team, and the dangers – and bombs – became increasingly complex, and multiplied by hundreds, that I became afraid for him.

Oz felt, like many others, that the British troops in Afghanistan were fighting a war that could go on for many years. The Taliban were angry and cunning. They knew the land so well, and they used guerrilla tactics – remaining in hiding and attacking with grenades, suicide bombers, stealth attacks and, increasingly, IEDs. These were home-made bombs, often planted just under the surface of roads and fields, difficult to detect, and intended to be triggered by the pressure of a vehicle driving over them, or a person stepping on them, or sometimes by remote control.

Oz operated as part of a team, detecting and defusing these devices. His boss, and good friend, was Dean Taylor – Deano – then a staff sergeant. Deano was a little older than Oz and always one step ahead in the training. Oz was his number two – there to give him back-up and support at all times.

After kissing Oz goodbye early in September, I did my best not to worry, and to get on with life. I was working hard, and when I got back from work I spent most of my time with Laird. We'd go over to the woods with Bo and sit by Oz's tree.

We missed him terribly, both of us. Laird was just over two and a half when Oz went – old enough to talk about his daddy every day, to wander around the house looking for him, and to ask me when he was coming back. I would reassure him, and when Oz phoned, he would ask me to pass the phone to Laird for a chat. Laird's face would light up and I'd have to prise the phone out of his small hands so that I could talk to Oz again.

He said very little about what he was doing. Just that everything was fine, his team were the best, not to worry and that he missed us. He was much more interested in hearing how we were doing. 'How's your mum?' he'd ask. 'And your dad, and Jamie? Are they OK? Give them my love.'

He came back briefly at Christmas for ten days, R&R – rest and recuperation – before going straight back. He went first to Padstow, to see Andrew, and then back to Stonehouse, where I joined him. No one knew until the last minute that he would be allowed home, so everyone had sent him Christmas boxes. You can send two kilos to someone in the Forces, free, and about a dozen boxes of goodies had been sent to Oz. Alcohol is not allowed, but his friends had thoughtfully sent him an extraordinary amount of 'mouthwash', which he no doubt shared with all his mates out there. Andrew, one of the friends who'd contributed to this quite astonishing level of oral hygiene, was delighted to see Oz turn up in the flesh just before Christmas.

It may sound strange that he didn't come to Winchester, but going from a war into civvie life is a huge transition and he had such a short time back in the UK. Not enough to get back into life here, especially in the middle of Christmas, then prepare for war again. He needed a few days, just to rest, with a supportive friend, and then for us to spend a few days quietly alone together. I couldn't leave Laird and my parents over Christmas, so I spent it with them and then went to be with Oz afterwards.

When I got to Stonehouse on Boxing Day, he looked tanned but tired, and a little older. He didn't want to talk about Afghanistan, which I understood. We walked, talked and holed up quietly, just watching TV and relaxing for a few days. And then he was gone again.

He was due back a month later, at the end of January 2007, and in that month I thought a lot about how things would be between us. Would we be able to pick up our life where we left off? Had he changed? He had seemed so quiet at Christmas, so withdrawn. Could we really have a future together?

This time he came straight home. He arrived at the cottage one freezing cold afternoon, dumped his bag on the floor and threw his arms around me and then around Laird, who ran around the room squealing, and Bo, who joined in the excitement, haring around the room, tail wagging.

It was good to have him home. More than that, it felt right, just completely right.

We spent the evening, all of us together in front of the fire, Oz just so happy to put the past few months – and all the long hours of hard, tense, difficult work – behind him.

I'd read about how native peoples around the world have cleansing rituals, to heal any negative energy and restore the person to harmony. Oz was up for it. 'I want to start healing, honey. Starting with a long, hot, soak in the bath,' he said. So I got handfuls of herbs, lit candles, ran him a deep bath and fixed him a drink and a good spread of fresh food and let him wash away all the energy of war.

I think it was then, after Oz returned from Afghanistan after that first tour, that I realised how deeply I loved him, and that whatever happened this was it; not just me and him, but us, together, loving each other and making it work. Our feelings hadn't changed and I knew, then, that I wasn't going to give in to doubts any longer. What would be, would be, but we wanted and needed to be together. I felt, at last, that it could really work. Oz had stood the test of time, he'd been consistent and proved himself, and he stood head and shoulders above any other man I had ever met.

And it was then, when Oz was back and we were truly happy, with so much strength and passion and laughter between us, that I discovered I was pregnant.

CHAPTER SEVEN

We had talked several times about one day having more children. Oz loved the idea of lots of kids, and while I was less sure about the 'lots', I had definitely come round to the idea of one or two. Laird was three by then, a lovely age; he was bright, curious, soaking up information like a little sponge and just lovely to be with. I'd forgotten the worst of childbirth and begun to think, yes, more kids should definitely be part of the plan.

So when I found I was pregnant, we were both incredibly happy. 'This is it,' Oz said. 'This is the start for us. We're going to have a big house in the country and a pack of kids, and muddy dogs, and take them all out hiking—'

'OK, OK,' I laughed. 'One step at a time.'

We didn't tell many people – just my parents and a few close friends. We wanted to wait until we'd had the first scans, and I was beginning to show. But we were excited. 'This is our year, honey,' he said.

We found a lovely nursery for Laird, Lanterns, where there was a big outdoor space, lots for an active little boy to do, friendly staff and a really good, warm feel about it. He settled in happily, made friends, and would come home chattering about his day.

Oz was still based with the Marines in Plymouth but, as he'd been away, he had quite a bit of time off due to him, and that was lovely for all of us. He'd take Laird to nursery and collect him, do the shopping, make a meal for when I got back from work. Ordinary, everyday things, but special to us because we hadn't had them for so long.

He didn't talk a lot about how things had been in Afghanistan, though I really wanted to know what the reality of being there was like.

'Hot, dusty, basic,' he'd say, and when I asked for more he'd smile. 'Very hot, very dusty, very basic.'

He did say that many of the Afghan people seemed shy, polite, kind. He said he felt desperately sorry for them, having to live with endless war and conflict going on around them, for decade after decade. 'This war is just the latest of so many. We've been there before,' he'd say, 'and it didn't work out then. Even the Russians couldn't win, back in the eighties. We're crazy if we think we can beat off the Taliban, or impose order in just a few years.'

Oz said that he'd felt all he could do was try to save

lives. That was always his purpose. Not to kill, but to preserve life. He and his team had defused devices that would have killed or injured not just British soldiers, but local Afghan people. 'If we saved a handful of people, then it was worth it,' he'd say.

The truth was that while Oz was on that tour another eleven men died, six of them Marines whom Oz would have known, and five of them killed by landmines or suicide bombs – the rest were shot or killed during attacks. Oz and his team would not only have defused landmines and IEDs but would have dealt with the aftermath of some of those devices that went off. This meant, among other things, examining the bodies of those killed to make sure that they didn't contain any residue of explosive. This is something that always has to be done before medics and other team members take over.

Deano would have been the key person doing this but, as his close support, Oz would have been involved too. He was having to deal with things that would leave a permanent, deep and traumatic impact; no one could ever forget having to pick up the pieces of friends who have been blown to bits.

I didn't know much of this at that stage, because Oz didn't talk about it. It was only later, further down the line, that he told me more, and I began to really understand what he and so many others went through.

It's hard to say, now, how much Oz had changed after that tour. There were times when he was quiet, and there was a distant look in his eyes. He had nightmares sometimes, and he could be cynical, joking about death and destruction. But that's how he and the others coped. If they hadn't joked they would have spiralled into despair.

I don't doubt that Oz had been deeply affected by what he had seen and done and that sometimes he felt very low. But when he came back, more than anything else, he just wanted to live. He sometimes hurled himself at life as though determination alone would keep him alive forever.

In February 2007 he went to Norway on an Arctic warfare training exercise with the Marines for a few weeks. The Marines went every year, and this was Oz's first time going along with them. He looked forward to it because he was half Swedish and he loved the Scandinavian connection and yomping about in all those pine forests and snowy landscapes. He'd always had a thing about the Norse gods Odin and Thor. He had a Viking tattoo on his chest and he often called Laird 'Thor'. It was during this Marine training that Oz really came into his own. He thrived in that environment and smashed their courses, especially the ice-breaking drills. He used to jump into the fjords and didn't mind the cold at all.

His emails and calls were cheerful, full of funny stories and hopes and dreams. He was training hard, but it was going well.

Then I woke up one day and knew something was wrong. I had had a miscarriage. I was four months pregnant and had been lifting the last of some boxes and some bits to go into storage. I had been working hard, putting in lots of miles in the car and running around after children. I was tired and a bit stressed, but none of that really explained what had happened. I hid it and cracked on, taking just one admin day off and calling my friend, who was a GP, for a private consultation to get a D&C. I had Laird and a career to hold down and I didn't want my mother to know or worry; she was getting older and was unwell herself.

I took a hit both emotionally and physically. It took more out of me than I realised and I was left exhausted, washed-out and weak. My doctor was worried and warned me to rest; he said that I was too unwell to cope on my own and that he was going to call Oz's superiors, but I didn't want to tell Oz until he came home. However, the descision was made for me when I developed an infection and was too ill to work or look after Laird, and it was requested that Oz be sent home ASAP.

He got back a few days later and I broke the news to him. Oz was angry that I hadn't told him earlier, but I didn't want to worry him out there. Partly because I knew he'd be upset and I wanted him to finish his training until we could deal with it together, and partly because I just wanted to move forward – it had happened, so onwards and upwards was the way I saw it. He said I should have told him straight away, he'd have got permission to come back. We were both gutted – I think Oz was even sadder than I was. He said it had broken him and made him realise what was important, and had made him keener to start to look at an exit plan and children.

For a while we both felt extremely low. The miscarriage had been a huge loss. Oz had given up smoking – my friend Tina, who had been there after Laird's birth, had helped him to give up when we had gone to stay with her the previous year. But now he started again. I was still tired and run-down and Oz was sad, because we'd had a dream and it hadn't come to fruition. He felt grief for both of us, and I think we both felt a little lost.

He was wonderful about looking after me, bringing me my favourite blueberries and blackberries – full of iron to build me up – and insisting I rest as much as possible.

It was then, in the aftermath of the miscarriage, when I felt weak and tired and fragile and Oz was there beside me, that I realised how much I needed him. He was my best friend, the person I could talk to about anything. Lying on the sofa one day, looking at his face, that strong profile, I realised I would be lost without him. He had proved himself to me over and over again, he had been there for me and for Laird, and he had kept all his promises.

'You know you go on about marrying me,' I said. 'Well, let's do it.'

'What?' Oz was startled. He'd got used to me saying, 'No, let's wait, let's be sure.' 'Do you mean it?'

I smiled. 'Yes.'

He'd already bought me an engagement ring, at least a year earlier. It was a beautiful art deco-style antique ring – he knew I always preferred the old to the new. It had a central diamond, an old-fashioned hand-cut imperfect stone, with three small diamonds set either side of it in platinum, and I thought it was utterly beautiful.

He'd bought it in a little shop near the waterfront.

'Come on, I'm going to buy you a ring. You *will* be my wife one day, I don't care when,' he'd said.

I had wanted diamonds to symbolise eternity, and when he put the ring on my finger he looked into my eyes and said, 'That's forever, honey. You and me.' After that, if I ever took the ring off, even to avoid damaging it when I was doing something like gardening, he would say, 'Where's your bling?' He liked me wearing it. 'You can have a "ring-off" with those cupcake-fetish women who power-walk their kids to school,' he used to joke.

After buying the ring we went back to The Artillery to celebrate. Belinda admired the ring and then beamed. 'I'm not worried about my Oz any more, not now he's got Chrissy to look after him.' Then she rummaged behind the bar and came out with some pink and white nougat and a Mars bar, handed them to me with a grin and said, 'Celebrate with these. It's about time you put some weight on.'

Belinda always wore flip-flops around the bar and had incredibly long toenails. Oz put his arm round her. 'Don't worry, Belinda, I'll still suck your toes. We can still do soft porn.' The place was full of ex-servicemen and they fell about laughing. Belinda cackled loudly. That night we celebrated and the men sang traditional Devon songs by the fire.

I'd worn the ring from that day on. We both knew we'd marry, when the time was right, and now it was. Excited and happy, we talked about when to do it, and what kind of wedding we would have. It was either going to be everyone we knew – and between us that would mean about five hundred people – or no one but our families.

In the end we decided against a big wedding. It would have cost a fortune! Plus we were so sociable that we could never have kept everyone happy. So in the end I felt the wedding was for us and for Mum, and a huge do with hundreds of people would be too much for her. Oz agreed, and said he'd be happy to keep it small. 'I don't want a huge party,' he said. 'I just want to be married to you.' I felt the same way – it was the marriage that mattered, not the wedding.

I never felt strongly about being formally married. For me it would just put the seal on us being together and it was the strength of our relationship that counted.

But being married mattered a great deal to Oz. He had said, more than once, that if anything happened to him and we weren't married, in the eyes of the law and the Army I wouldn't exist. He used to say, 'That's not right. You are my family and I want that recognised. It's not like a few years ago. I am your man; you and I are each other's family.'

We told my parents, who were delighted. Mum had felt heartbroken after I'd told her the news of my miscarriage; now she had tears in her eyes as she hugged us both. 'About time,' Dad said, wringing Oz's hand and beaming. And Oz's family were delighted for us too.

Oz couldn't wait to tell people. He'd say proudly, 'Chrissy just cares about the real things in life, that's why I love her and she's going to be my wife.' That was why I loved him too. Oz was all about real things – there was no pretence, no fakery, no hot air about him. He was straight, clear, honest and good to the core.

Oz had a break due in mid-May and decided to take off for Cornwall – I couldn't go as I had too much work on. He went to stay with Andrew and they spent a few days walking and talking. One day they drove to their old prep school, Polwhele House, which was close by, and went for a walk along the cross-country track and into the woods beside the school. When they emerged it was playtime and dozens of children stared at these two men appearing out of the woods as several teachers descended.

They explained that they were old boys and were welcomed with open arms, had a tour of the school and went to meet the head, who invited them both to come back and give talks – Oz about his work in the Army, and Andrew about his voluntary job as one of the team manning the Padstow lifeboat.

On the last morning, Oz got a message to say that his father, Hans, had been admitted to hospital. He had been a heavy smoker all his life and he had lung cancer. He had been into hospital several times before and Oz, who never liked hospitals, said, 'He'll be fine, Dad always comes through.' But Andrew insisted he was taking Oz to see his father. When they got to the hospital, Oz's mother was there, and they could see things were serious. Andrew told Oz to spend a bit of time with his dad, and said he would wait in the car park.

An hour later Oz came out and said, with typical understatement, 'He wasn't looking too good.'

Later that day, Oz set off back to Stonehouse, and work. Halfway there he sent Andrew a text. 'Dad didn't make it.'

Andrew sent a message back. 'I'm sorry. Do you want to come back?'

Oz said no, he had to sort out work stuff.

Oz called me.

I was out in Gunwharf Quays in Portsmouth; I didn't answer my phone as I was with my mates and he was supposed to be with his for a few days. Then a minute later I got a text from his work phone. 'Dad is dead. I am sorry but I need you, no one else, I have to see you. I am in Stonehouse. I will wait here.' I sent a text back saying that I was sorry and thinking of him and his mum and family. He then texted back, 'What about me?' and I saw him ringing my phone again, so I made my excuses and agreed to go and see Oz. When I spoke to him I told him, 'I get it, hun. I get that you marry your best friend for these reasons. To hold you through these times in life and remind you what you have – real family and future . . . come and get me? I will wait here.'

He said that he didn't want to see anyone else, only me. 'Only you,' he said. 'Only you understand. How quickly can you get here?' Baz, his mate, got on the phone. 'Hun, I can't tell you, you gotta get your ass down here. He is nothing without you – he needs you. We are in The Artillery. Hurry up. He is really low and can't do the whole Cornwall thing. He keeps asking for you, chick . . .'

I went straight there.

A few days later I drove Oz down for his father's funeral, which was in the church in Veryan and then at Truro Crematorium. After the service, a simple, family affair, Oz hugged his mum and brothers goodbye and we drove straight back to Stonehouse. Oz had a bit of time off and we spent it on Dartmoor, staying in bed and breakfasts and walking. That was how Oz dealt with the turmoil of feelings that his father's death triggered in him – out in the open, walking it off. The end of an era.

Soon afterwards he was back at Kineton, for more AT training. In April he had been promoted from sergeant to staff sergeant. He was proud of that. At twenty-seven he was a senior noncommissioned officer (NCO). He had worked his way up the enlisted ranks from private to lance corporal to corporal, sergeant and now staff sergeant. There was only one higher rank of NCO, the warrant officer – so called because they hold the royal warrant, which is signed by the Secretary of State for Defence. Oz hoped he would achieve that by the spring of 2010. Beyond that there would be two increasingly senior levels of warrant officer, but Oz didn't plan to stay in the Army long enough for that – he simply hoped to achieve warrant officer status before his planned exit at fifteen years' service, not least because, as well as the honour of achieving that rank, he would have more pay and a higher pension.

The NCOs are the backbone of the army. They are leaders, trainers, organisers, and the link between enlisted men and women and commissioned officers, most of whom start off in the Army with authority but little experience.

Oz never got hung up on rank; what mattered most to him was whether someone deserved respect. And with his Commando and Para training and his level of skill he had reached a point where he was respected by everyone, no matter what their rank.

Now that he was a staff sergeant it would mean taking on more responsibility and demonstrating increasing leadership. Oz was keenly aware of this, and he took it very seriously. He wanted, always, to be someone that others could lean on and look to for answers and encouragement – and he was, naturally. He was the kind of person who kept other people's spirits up. Whatever he was feeling, no matter how tired or unwell or uncertain, he never let it show.

And he did feel unwell, because he was still suffering from severe IBS. It troubled him so badly that at times it left him drained, anaemic and dehydrated. He was constantly seeing consultants because by this time he was bleeding frequently from the bowel.

He had to endure a lot of undignified procedures, and he did it with humour and not a shred of self-pity. He felt that, as a Commando, he should be able to put up with it. He even managed to make the consultant laugh by saying, 'Look mate, I just want to get to the bottom of this.'

I went with him to a lot of his hospital appointments. He'd insist on getting there twenty minutes early, even though we always had to wait well past his appointment time, then he'd pace around saying, 'Honestly, civvies.' On one occasion when he was having a colonoscopy, something Oz referred to as 'the snake', the consultant said, 'No man brings his partner in for this.' Oz said, 'I do.'

And I wanted to be there. To me it was something you do, part of loving each other. We wanted it sorted out and we were in it together.

Doctors found that his bowel was riddled with pre-cancerous polyps and decided to operate to remove them. But sadly the operation didn't seem to help him, and then things were further complicated when his notes were lost. He was suffering from chronic pain, which often kept him awake at night, and frequent painful spasms. It was a chronic condition, but he lived with it and tried to joke about it.

He'd say, 'It would be all right if I had a desk job.' I think it was part of his reason for wanting to come out of the Army, so that he could pick and choose what he did.

I would have given anything to help him. But not even the surgeons and consultants he saw could do that. The best we could manage was calming the condition through changing his diet, when he was at home.

In the summer of 2007, Oz took Laird and me down to Cornwall for a break. We saw his mum and brothers, caught up with friends, had barbecues on the beach, surfed, swam and played. When we got home I had to get straight back to work, but Oz had a few more days off, so he looked after Laird. When the two of them caught a flu bug and began to feel awful, they decamped to Mum and Dad's for a couple of days.

I was at a conference overnight, so I rang Mum. 'How are my boys?'

'Much better,' she told me. She took a picture of them, lying under the apple tree in the garden. Oz was lying on his stomach, and Laird was lounging on Oz's back, looking up at the sky, both of them so totally at ease. I smiled when I saw it. They were fine. More than fine, they were perfect. I couldn't wait to get home to them.

It was hard, at times like that, being away and working long hours. But I felt I was doing it for us, for our future. Oz had sorted his finances and was paying off his debts, and I was putting everything I could into the mortgage on Jasmine Cottage. We both felt that if we grafted for a few years we could pay everything off. Then we'd be in a position to buy a home in Cornwall and have more choice about what we did. Oz wanted to take a bit of time out when he left the Army, to think about what he would do next. And I wanted to slow down, have more time for us, for Laird, for more children. We didn't mind working flat out, because it was an investment in our future, a future we both felt excited about.

CHAPTER EIGHT

We chose the first of December 2007 as our wedding day. We both liked the idea of a winter wedding. We felt it would be good to have something to celebrate, bringing light and love into the darkest part of the year.

Oz chose the venue. We didn't want a church wedding, just somewhere that would feel intimate and peaceful and warm. I told Oz I would be happy with his choice, I wanted him to know that I trusted him to take the lead.

He chose Lainston House, a seventeenth-century country-house hotel set in beautiful grounds, just outside Winchester. Oz liked it because it had a lovely room with a roaring fire where we could eat after the ceremony. I liked it because it was small and pretty, and didn't remind me of the big, impersonal hotels that I had to go to for work conferences.

We invited Mum, Dad, Jamie, my aunt and uncle, Oz's mum, his younger brother Torben and his wife Debbie, and his older brother Greg and his wife Lindsay. Five people each. Laird went to stay with his cousins; we decided we would take him on a special trip to celebrate. There were no expensive, ostentatious hen nights, but Oz did have a run ashore stag night in Plymouth.

The wedding was late morning, so we had plenty of time to get ready. Mum liked me in a particularly old-fashioned ivory silk dress, which was fitted and knee-length. That was it, no veil or train, just a small bunch of white flowers I picked up from Sainsbury's that morning and lashed together myself.

As for Oz, I thought he'd look good in a proper suit, but in the end there seemed no point in buying one for just one day, so he wore his number two uniform, his 'ginger' suit. The number one uniform is full mess dress with all the regalia, red jacket, and so on. Hot, uncomfortable and far too smart. He called it his Buttons suit because it made him look a bit like Buttons in a Christmas pantomime. The ginger suit is actually a khaki green wool suit worn for less formal occasions. The guys joke about it – most of them hate it because it's scratchy and a bit cheap-looking. They're supposed to wear a proper shirt under it, with a white T-shirt underneath, for warmth and to stop the suit scratching, and a matching ginger wool tie.

Half an hour before the taxi was due to arrive to take us the four miles to the hotel, I came downstairs to find Oz sitting in a black North Face T-shirt, a towel around his waist, smoking a rollie.

'Are you ready?' Silly question really.

'Yeah, honey, just got to put on my trousers.'

Five minutes before we left he threw on the shirt, the trousers, tie and jacket.

Oz was always a bit of a rebel about clothes. He wasn't keen on dressing up for anything, and when he wasn't in his Army kit he wore a T-shirt, jeans, the boots and his green gilet. That went everywhere with him, because he kept his things, keys and so on, in the pocket. Same clothes, every day, everywhere.

Mum used to tease him, when we were going out and Oz would appear in the same old clothes. She'd say, 'Look at Oz, all dressed up for a change, love.' And Oz would grin.

Before the ceremony we went to the bar and had a quiet drink. Our families came and found us there. 'Er, hello, here we are at your wedding.' I think they were a bit surprised at finding the bride and groom relaxing in the bar with a drink.

The registrar was from Winchester and he was perfect because, by extraordinary coincidence, he was an ex-policeman who had serving friends in bomb disposal. Oz had liked him from the moment we met him, and insisted it had to be him to marry us.

The ceremony was simple and perfect. Love and honour, joined from this day forth.

Afterwards the registrar had a drink with us and said to Oz, 'I think you should seriously think about your job. I can't join a couple like you, so much in love, and then see you go and do that job.' He said he had married many people, but that none were as special. He could feel that we must be together and were insep- arable. It was a sobering moment. But Oz was feeling festive. The moment passed, and we went and ate a huge lunch of roast pork with our families, in the dining room with the blazing fire.

Afterwards we said goodbye to our families – Mum and Dad were off to collect Laird and look after him while we went to the New Forest for the rest of the weekend, to another hotel called Carey's Manor, which had a spa where we could chill. We didn't want to travel or go abroad – we both had enough of that through our work. That night we both had a massage and Oz fell asleep.

It was a simple wedding and a simple honeymoon, and that's the way we wanted it. A celebration that we'd made it this far, through so much. The calm start to our years ahead. After the miscarriage and the death of Oz's dad, it wouldn't have felt right to have a grand wedding. Apart from everything else, it wasn't us.

Some of our friends were upset that we'd married without them there, but the people closest to us, real friends like Sam and Hazey, understood and were fine about it. They respected it was about us, not others. They knew we'd had some rough things to deal with that year and needed the wedding to be a quiet affair.

We did give each other wedding presents, though, the night before the ceremony. He'd bought me two glasses, engraved with our names, and a silver kidney flask, engraved, 'To my wife, Oz and Swissy', with our wedding date, 1/12/07. He always loved getting things engraved. He said, 'Get some Glenmorangie in that and keep it near you. You'll need it, with all the shit I'm going to put you through in this marriage.'

I gave him a shot glass, a bottle of expensive whisky and a Zippo cigarette lighter, in a burnished, dark steel, engraved with his name, Ozzy. He loved that lighter, he never used anything else after that. The lid used to open and shut with a click and I still have to catch my breath whenever I hear anyone using one.

My wedding ring was simple, a platinum band with diamonds to match the engagement ring, and I bought Oz a ring with the same matt look as the lighter. He loved that ring, and wore it all the time, which wasn't practical with his job. He was always having to fit his hand into tight spaces or handle heavy things.

A couple of weeks after the wedding, we went on another little mini-honeymoon, this time with Laird, to Cowley Manor. We told him we were married and that it meant the three of us would always be a family. We visited Avebury, a magical place, where we all made wishes. Mine was that we would stay as happy as we were then.

I didn't think that being married would feel any different – I hadn't been bothered about it, except in a legal sense, but there was a subtle change afterwards. I felt a sense of completion, as if things were right. We were two individuals, but we were also now a unit, a whole, together.

I was apprehensive about marrying into the military and the life that brought with it. I found it an extra level of pressure. There's so much that goes with being an Army family – duties, expectations, lists of dos and don'ts, paperwork, formal events to attend. Mess events I was expected to attend, often on a Thursday or Friday, which were my busiest work days. However, I found it all made sense once I got the basics. Oz said to me, 'You're now in my institution, you'll have to stomach it for a couple of years. It's a bit like Marmite, you're either going to love it or hate it, and then we can leave it for the better.' We took on each other's way of life, and that meant we needed a huge amount of mutual respect, communication and hard work.

Oz absolutely revelled in being married, he thought it was wonderful. He took to calling me 'wife' or 'the boss' all the time.

He would leave me notes when he went back to Plymouth on a Monday morning.

LOVE YOU HONEY AND THINK YOU ARE DOING A HOOFIN JOB ON RAISING OUR SON. I KNOW 99% OF THE TIME IT FEELS LIKE YOU ARE DOING IT ON YOUR OWN BUT I DO TRY AND I RESPECT AND ADMIRE YOU SO MUCH FOR THAT. YOU ARE A SEXY WIFE FOR ME & I LOVE THAT SO LET'S THINK BIG PICTURE, HOUSE IN CORNWALL FOR ALL OF US. HAVE A GOOD WEEK + SPEAK TO YOU TONIGHT.
LOVE
HUSBAND XXX

Hoofin was one of Oz's favourite words – it meant awesome.

His notes, written hastily at the crack of dawn, always warmed my heart as I got Laird ready for nursery, and ran round the house organising my laptop and work things into my bag.

I had owned Jasmine Cottage for nearly five years by the time we married, and I was really happy there. Oz loved it, too; we'd become a family there and it was filled with memories for us. But he wanted us to move into married quarters as we needed more room for his kit, and financially it would make sense.

'I want to be the one who puts a roof over your head for once,' he told me. 'That's my job, I want to look after you and Laird and I can give you that now. Me man, you woman,' he joked. 'Let's work the system to our advantage now – we need to look ahead and be fit and stable and work smart, as I want to save and be able to be in the best position when I leave, for the future we want.'

I knew how important it was to him, so I swallowed my misgivings and we packed up Jasmine Cottage and moved into married quarters at Tidworth, just over the border from Hampshire into Wiltshire, where there is a large Army barracks. As Oz was pinged around to other regiments and forces quite a lot, plus the quarters in Didcot 11 Regiment were condemned and unavailable, we had a certain amount of choice about where we went. He wouldn't be at Plymouth for much longer, so it didn't make sense to go there. Tidworth is about thirty minutes' drive from Winchester, so it meant Laird could stay at his nursery, I could still work, and we were still within reach of my parents, the boat and the friends we had in the south.

I was grateful that we weren't too far away. However, the house was such a change from the character-filled cottage, which I really missed initially. It wasn't small – much bigger than the cottage, in fact, but it was a modern house in a row of similar houses, next to more rows of similar houses, and it was hard for me to imagine how I would make it feel like home. But Oz made it into a Gucci quarter, as he called it – it had new wood floors and he painted it throughout. It had a massive kitchen with a big table in there – we got my parents up for dinner the first Sunday after we'd moved in. It had a huge garden, too, and before long we were outside a lot with our fire pit, and Lairdster was enjoying the freedom of playing out on a secure estate. There was a park and lots of kids on bikes and scooters everywhere.

Browsing the internet I came across a description of it that just about summed it up:

The place is a bit of a dive. Imagine a large housing estate with poor corner shops and miles away from anywhere. Reasonable bus service and schools but very mediocre way of life.

Thankfully we had decided to let Jasmine Cottage to my brother, so that he could have his own place and we could still go back there at weekends if we wanted to. That worked really well. Jamie paid a bit of rent, which helped with the mortgage, and we still had the cottage to stay in if we were down sailing for the weekend.

In early February 2008, Oz went to Norway again for Arctic warfare training. The email below is typical of those he wrote home: warm, loving, full of hope for the future and energy and enthusiasm for his job.

Friday 29 Feb 2008 08:30

Hello gorgeous wife,

Eventually I have found a moment to get on a spare terminal and send you an email!!! Very hard being away from you all as I have found where I want to be in life and that is with you. So glad we have each other and even happier that we have built what we have together over the last few years and now fully share what we are. I love the fact that we are so close and that when with you I feel complete. I love laird and think he is the most beautiful thing and just want to get back and be a hoofin father figure for him which he so desperately needs.

Work is busy now and will be till I leave. Got a huge demolition package starting next week so plenty of planning is going in at the moment and coordinating all the assets required in order for it to be carried out. Bit of a nightmare when resources are strapped and the operating temp is between -20 and -40. I am sure it will go smooth. Deano is up here on sat with my replacement so that will be good to see him and then tues, weds, thurs, fri out on the range doing the large scale demolitions. Have tried to plan it to be as relaxed as poss with knowing how much Deano hates it. Got a range hut booked for staying up there and a couple of crates for the couple of nights. Should be a good letting off steam routine after the graft during the day. Got a chef going up as well so think i have covered all angles.

Normally when in field you're on field rations so hopefully the blokes will appreciate it and the remaining 2 tonnes of explosives to fight through. You're probably nodding off right now and i need to crack my demolition orders. So honey will see you soon.

Love everything about your stunning self and know you don't feel it but to me you are the most gorgeous thing on this planet.

Take one thing away and that is you are the best thing that has ever happened to me. I love the fact that we are now married and am very proud of you, Laird and of course the dog and the fact that you are all mine. I miss you all more than you could ever imagine and am really looking forward to seeing us all flourish as a family.

I Love you Mrs Schmid
All my love hugs and kisses
xxxxxxxx
HUSBAND

Oz was so full-on that even when we were apart it felt like he was with us all day every day. People say love isn't measured in the length of time you have known someone, it's how someone stays with you in the moments that matter. He was always looking forward. Always wound up when people misunderstood him, or how sensitive he was. He said he just switched off to them and carried on regardless. If something didn't go well at his or my work, he'd always say, 'You won't change people, Swiss, you can only control your reaction to them.' He would always say, 'Teflon shoulders people like that,' which meant just let them slide off you and not grip you.

I didn't keep all of his emails, letters and cards over the years that we were together, but those I did keep I treasure for their passion, their warmth and the sheer love that radiates from them.

Oz was particularly low going back to the Army and a regiment after being in a team environment in Norway and having autonomy with his job. He went through the options of transferring, but financially he would be better off staying where he was until pension time in a couple of years. He said he wanted to grizz it out until then and start looking and planning for civvie jobs outside in security contracts, etc.

Oz was in Alpha Troop, based with 11 EOD (Explosive Ordnance Disposal)Regiment at barracks in Didcot. He joked it was called Shitcot or Deadcat. He made me giggle, was always playful and cheerful in the face of anything negative. Eleven EOD Regiment was the bomb-disposal regiment and Didcot was only forty-five minutes away from Tidworth, which meant Oz could get home to us far more often. It made a huge difference to me having him around so much more. I had found

Tidworth very bleak on my own, not being part of a group and friends and family being so geographically far away, but with Oz there it wasn't so bad – even if he was on a pager and a phone with one hour's notice to move.

With Alpha Troop his job was to be on call wherever and whenever he was needed to provide a bomb-disposal capability to any specialist unit. Oz's job would be to deal with explosives. Only someone with Oz's specialist knowledge and physical training would be able to tick that box.

It was an incredibly demanding job, the effects of which came out through odd emotional triggers.

On a Friday evening we'd meet down at the cottage, Oz arriving after I'd picked Laird up and got there first.

Oz would come in, get his work bag and throw it into the 'admin area'. 'See that daysack?' he'd say. 'Goodbye until Sunday night. Laird, where's yours?' Laird would run and get his little bookbag and say, 'Hang on, Dad, I'll just get my books out, and my stone and my piece of wood I found. OK, Dad, now I can leave it,' and they would hurl it into the corner next to Oz's. Then they would go straight out with the dog.

I would often be trying to finish work calls, but if I was still on the phone when they got back, Oz would say, 'It's Friday night, switch your phone off.' He'd say it over and over again and I'd be hissing, 'Just let me finish my work calls.' He'd say, 'No, what's the rule? Shoes off, bag down, it's Friday.' We both hated the phone or distractions from the outside world in family time. In the end, if I didn't stop, he'd rugby-tackle me to get the phone. He was so strong, he'd have it off me in seconds and then he'd launch it across the room. Laird thought it was hilarious. Oz was always incredibly respectful to women. Even when he play-tackled, he was very gentle and made sure he never hurt me.

I'd start to cook and Oz would say to Laird, 'Look at my beautiful wife, look at your amazing mum. I am a lucky man, why you're with me I don't know. But I look at Hazey too and think why would Sam be with him? But I get it now, you marry and live with your best mate, regardless of everything else; everyone else has to butt out. Everything that I believed about when you love someone isn't true. It feels calm and relaxed when you're with them, and you don't feel right when you are away.' We lived in the kitchen when we were at home, as we always had friends coming in and out and Laird and Bo charging about in there. We didn't like to put the TV on – listening to the radio and sitting around talking at the kitchen table was the norm for us. We'd talk for hours.

Over the weekend we'd go down to see my parents. Mum in particular missed having us in walking distance up the lane, so we tried to go and see her as much as we could. She welcomed us with open arms, especially as Dad was so often away and Jamie was now in the cottage during the week, so she cherished the time she had helping us out as a family with a young child and demanding jobs. She got it. 'Your mum is hoofin.' He called her Mum too. 'She's easy-going and makes me feel comfortable.' She is a typical positive northerner. Hardened, strong moral codes.

Often I would phone Oz on the way home from work and see where he and Lairdster were and what they fancied for supper. But they'd be round at my mum's. I'd rush in, work mobile in one hand, personal phone in the other, briefcase over my shoulder, and Oz and Mum would giggle at me. He'd say, 'Oh, here she comes, I'd forgotten what you looked like, Napalm Schmid . . . Shall I divorce her now, Gill, as she is always working and never switches off? We'll split the money shall we? And just bugger off, me and you.'

He loved that I was a successful businesswoman with a life, income and career of my own, but he didn't understand half of it. Switches, PCOs, KOLs, dispensers, territories, brand messages, ABPI, field training, account management, conferences. However, it gave us lots to discuss. He always had questions and took it all in.

Once I'd put down my work stuff, I'd be all over Laird and Oz like a rash, asking what they'd eaten for lunch, had they drunk enough fluids that day? What was new? What needed washing or sorting out? They'd tut and ignore me fussing them, and just laze around whilst I was going into housework mode, as I couldn't settle unless all that was squared away. Oz would say, 'She can't stop, can she? Leave us alone. Laird, get your mother off you.'

We'd all wash our hands when we came in, it was just what we did, like washing off the world outside and all the things we'd done during the day. Laird and Oz used to wash their hands together, Oz holding him up to the sink. Then Oz would say, 'Olives and dips, Gill?' and they'd head off into the kitchen.

Dad wasn't always there, but if he was he would often take Laird off to the garage to do a bit of 'fixing'. Dad was brilliant at mending or making just about anything, and he enjoyed teaching Laird, but he was sometimes a bit enthusiastic about letting Laird loose with adult tools. Oz used to joke, 'That's fine, John, yeah, let him have a nail-gun and that electric drill to crack on with.' Eventually we got Laird some miniature tools – not toys, but proper working tools. Laird would say, 'Granddad can do anything,' and he could. They made a mini cricket bat together which Laird treasured. They would do simple electric circuit boards with light bulbs and switches and buzzers. Those hours in the garage gave them their own special bond. There was a lovely familiarity between them; we'd overhear the most bizarre conversations. Laird would pick his nose and Dad would be saying, 'Oh, you going to eat that? Let's put some salt and pepper on it. Give us one?' Mum and I would be cringing and saying, 'Oh disgusting,' but we let them do their thing.

On a Saturday morning I had my routine, which was to go out early for a run, walk the dog, do the washing and a bit of shopping and prepare for the following week. I loved to get fresh produce from the farm shop. Before I set off, Oz would be eating breakfast in bed and watching TV while Laird made hills and tunnels with the bedcovers – he'd have all his Playmobil people out and mocking up all sorts of scenarios – and Oz would say, 'Look, Mummy's going out – honey, don't go.' I'd say, 'Stop doing that in front of Laird. I'm only going to the shop. I don't want to sit in bed all morning with you lot. It's lazy!' Then I'd be in the shop and Oz would phone to tell me the landline had been ringing. 'I love you, wife, come back and answer the phone. You know I don't answer it.' I'd be laughing and saying, 'Stop texting me, I've only been out of the house ten minutes and I'm trying to get the shopping in.' He could be completely annoying and sometimes he drove me mad, but we were truly content and our life just seemed to work.

CHAPTER NINE

The next step of Oz's training was the high-threat bomb-disposal course. When he completed that, it would place him amongst a small band of elite bomb-disposal experts. It is reputedly one of the hardest courses in the Forces and only a handful pass. This is because it requires unique skills. You not only need to be physically fit, but also strong and calm mentally. It takes these skills and knowledge, but for the contemporary conflicts you definitely need a natural aptitude and a flair for it, and that is something you either have or don't have. The most difficult, challenging and dangerous of situations with IEDs had begun in Afghanistan and they were unlike anything that had ever come before. The numbers were growing and the types were rudimentary and home-made and increasingly dangerous.

Only the very best personnel got as far as the high-threat course, so a good high-threat ATO is one of the most respected people in the Forces. They're the ones who are called on whenever there is an explosive device to defuse, and their cool nerve, steady hand and calm leadership will mean the difference between life and death. Always harking back to their motto: to preserve lives at all costs, both civilian and those of their own team.

Oz was due to go to Kineton for his course in the autumn. He was immensely proud that he had been selected for such a high level of training, and it was a huge personal achievement for him. Oz was the sort of person who would always demand more of himself, want to be different, raise the bar in every way. He knew that from the moment he passed the course and his training was up to date and current that he would be going back to a very different Afghanistan. The situation was getting worse by the day, and this time when he went back, as he was certain to do, he would be leading a team as troop commander in the deadliest of environments.

In 2006 there had been 38 British deaths in Afghanistan, of which 19 had been as a result of hostile action – 14 of the remaining 19 had been in a tragic RAF Nimrod accident and the other five had consisted of 1 friendly fire death, 3 accidents and 1 as a result of a suicide attack.

The following year, 2007, there had been 42 deaths, 34 of them as a result of hostile action. And in 2008, in the first eight months up to the end of August, there had been 30 deaths, 29 of them as a result of hostile action and only 1 in an accident, when a vehicle overturned. During the remainder of the year there were to be another 20 deaths, all of them as a result of hostile action.

The rise in the Army death rate from hostile action over three years was extremely worrying. Especially as the majority of deaths in 2008 were as a result of explosions – landmines, suicide bombs and, increasingly, IEDs. Oz knew that the number of IEDs being laid by the Taliban was multiplying rapidly, and with it the risk to anyone doing his job. But no high-threat operator had been killed in Afghanistan, which was at least reassuring. These were people who knew what they were doing, and did it well.

All that changed on 10 September 2008 with the news of Gary 'Gaz' O'Donnell's death. Gaz was a high-threat operator, a member of 11 OED Regiment and a well-respected colleague of and mentor to Oz. He died when an IED exploded as he was defusing it.

Gaz had been a decade older than Oz and had achieved warrant officer second class. He was a big, jovial man, full of humour, highly skilled and hugely liked within the trade. He had won the George Medal in Iraq and a long service and good conduct medal a few months before he died; he was one of the superstars of the regiment and Oz looked up to him like a father.

The official notification said: 'It is with deep regret

that the Ministry of Defence must confirm the death of Warrant Officer Class 2 Gary "Gaz" O'Donnell GM, from 11 Explosive Ordnance Disposal Regiment Royal Logistic Corps, on Wednesday 10 September 2008, in Helmand province, southern Afghanistan.'

The report on his death said: 'WO2 O'Donnell, 40, died from injuries sustained from an Improvised Explosive Device (IED) in Musa Qaleh, Helmand province. At the time, he was commanding an Improvised Explosive Device Disposal (IEDD) team within the Joint Force Explosive Ordnance Disposal (EOD) Group who were dealing with a confirmed IED that had been detected by a high risk search team. Their task was to clear a route in a vulnerable area for 5 SCOTS Battlegroup, in and around the Western side of Musa Qaleh. Sadly, WO2 O'Donnell, who had completed almost 17 years of military service, died as a result of the explosion.'

His death was heartbreaking. He had four children, the youngest of them a son who was just nine weeks old. He was married to his second wife, Toni, they had Aiden, eight, and baby Ben, and he had two children from a previous marriage, Cayleigh, sixteen and Dylan, thirteen.

The whole of 11 OED were heartbroken. Tributes to Gaz poured in, but none of them was able properly to convey just what a well-liked man and outstanding soldier he was.

As one of the tributes said, he was the epitome of what the ammunition technician trade stands for, with his exemplary service, exceptional high standards and a humbling degree of courage and bravery.

Another said: 'WO2 O'Donnell was an amazing man. Hugely talented and unbelievably brave, he was at the very top of his extremely dangerous and difficult trade. It was a trade at which he excelled. It was his passion and he took immense pride in making places safer for other people, the danger to his own life rarely seemed to affect him. If it did, he kept it to himself. He was a real character and a natural leader of men, his big smile often giving reassurance to the less experienced or more anxious.'

Oz carried him during the repatriation ceremony at Wootton Bassett. Generally the regiment chose the pall-bearers, a team would be ready, and they would not be personal friends of the man who had died. But in a few rare instances – in pinch-point trades such as Oz's, where at that level it is a close-knit group – those going out to war nominated the people they wanted to carry their coffin.

For Oz, it was an enormous loss, and a terrible shock. He wept after he heard, then went to RAF Lyneham and, with the other bearers, carried Gaz's Union-flag-draped coffin from the plane that brought him back, into the waiting car, which would drive him first to the chapel and then, like all of the others who had died before him, through the small town of Wootton Bassett, on its way to the John Radcliffe Infirmary.

For all of those who are asked to do the job of carrying a friend or colleague's coffin, it is an immensely emotional and difficult thing, but it is a matter of pride to do it as efficiently and steadfastly as possible. No one, no matter how heartbroken, would allow themselves to break down while carrying out this duty. It is their way of showing love and respect to the fallen, to perform their roles with faultless military precision.

I went to Wootton Bassett for the repatriation to stand at the side of the high street, alongside the townspeople who always turned out to pay their respects, and watched the car bringing Gaz's coffin drive slowly past. It was a heart-rending moment. Gaz's family and friends, as tradition dictated, stood on the opposite side, and the hearse stopped in front of them, so that they could place flowers on it.

Oz felt strongly that it was important for as many people as possible to turn out and pay their respects, and if I possibly could I went to Wootton Bassett whenever there was a repatriation. The territory for my job was Wiltshire, Hampshire, Berkshire, Surrey and Sussex, and so I was able to get to them easily, as Wootton Bassett is just off the M4.

Each one was resonant with respect, pride, tenderness and heartbreak. It always left me feeling desperately sad. I agreed with Oz that it was important to go, but I often said to him, 'I'll go, every time, but don't you ever put me in a position where I stand on the opposite side of the street, honey, for you – not doing it.'

When we got home I got a text from Becky Phillips, one of the other ATOs who had helped to carry Gaz. Like the others, she had been up most of the night before the repatriation, drowning her sorrows and grieving for Gaz, and by morning she was exhausted and feeling rough. In the text she asked me, 'Did I look all right?' It wasn't vanity, she wanted to know whether she had done him proud. So I texted back to say, 'You looked fine, didn't look like you'd been up all night, and you were impeccable.' Many ATOs are renowned for being untidy and mavericks, always in a mess, clumsy, not the best turned-out or cleanest looking.

When I told Oz about the text conversation he snapped at me, 'Don't talk about her looking good, don't do that.' I was startled, it was so unlike him. He knew I was reassuring Becky, who was also deeply upset.

Gaz's funeral took place in Scotland. Later we heard that he had been awarded a second George Medal – the first person in twenty-six years to win it twice – for 'repeated and sustained acts of immense bravery' in Afghanistan. He had a wake at Kineton, the spiritual home of bomb disposal and where they trained.

There was a great deal written about Gaz in the weeks after he died. One of the warmest tributes was from 'Moxy' James, a good friend of Oz's and of Gaz. He said,

'Gaz loved what he did because of the people he worked with. The people he worked with loved Gaz because of the way he worked. He died doing the job he loved, surrounded by people who loved, admired and respected him.'

That struck a chord with me, because I knew how important the people he worked with were to Oz. The bond between them was powerful and a real source of strength and support.

One of the newspaper reports I read, written by a journalist who had interviewed Gaz in Afghanistan, said so much about the job that he and Oz and the others did:

A decorated hero, WO O'Donnell was a man with an easygoing manner towards anyone he met, a soldier who shrugged off compliments casually . . . the outrageously dangerous tasks he carried out unflinchingly in Afghanistan, spoke volumes about his humbling courage . . .

Amid a British army camp full of headquarters staff in neatly pressed uniforms, Gaz and his merry band of bomb disposal experts meandered about unshaven, their hair wildly unkempt, blatantly thumbing their noses at petty rules. Perhaps they had ignored pleas to smarten up or perhaps nobody had the nerve to challenge a group of men who had become so crucial to everyone's survival in Helmand.

In the past four months, the IED teams have defused 120 roadside bombs and dealt with the aftermath of 80 that had exploded.

Gaz was one of a select number, whose job it was to make the 'lonely walk' to defuse the bombs, leaving others at a safe distance.

When I read this I had to smile. Gaz was like Oz, who was forever forgetting to get a haircut, or leaving his socks off. They were much more focused on doing one of the toughest jobs any soldier can do.

After we got back from the repatriation, Oz drew the curtains, got out a bottle of whisky and dug in for days. He barely moved from the room, he hardly ate and he said almost nothing. He was broken, consumed by grief, and as the days passed I became increasingly worried. I kept Laird out of the way, telling him 'Daddy's really tired', and taking him to play with friends and for sleepovers round at my friends' and parents' houses, but when Oz showed no sign of coming out of his self-imposed wake the following weekend, I decided I had to say something.

I put Laird to bed then went into the room where Oz was slumped on the sofa, drinking again. I sat down opposite him, and switched off the TV, which was tuned to Sky News and reporting on the situation in Afghanistan. I took a deep breath.

'Wallow all you want, grieve all you want, but don't

take the piss. We have a life here, if you haven't noticed. We have both got careers and we have a son to raise. If you truly believe in love and life, and mean it when you say you would die for the friends you love and me and Laird tomorrow, then why don't you live for us today? We are married, and Lairdster is in this house, so if you want to be like that, go and do it, but not round us. I have to crack on and I can't keep fending off your calls and your life. This is not the husband I married, the Oz I know. And it sure as hell isn't sexy. Not communicating, lying here like a sack of whatever . . . if you want to carry on like this, fine, but the last time I looked you have got your arms and legs, you are alive. So man-up, it's time to get up and get on.'

Oz said he was sorry. He cried. Said he needed time, and suggested Laird and I go away somewhere for a few days, but I said no. I told him it was because it was our home, but the truth was, I wouldn't have left him alone in that state. 'We're not leaving, and I'm not taking Laird out of school or time off work. You think about it for a bit, have a little chat with yourself, then text me or phone me, I'll be upstairs.'

I went into the kitchen and made two smoked-salmon salads – some healthy, fresh food would help. I gave him one of the salads and went upstairs to eat the other in bed.

An hour later he came upstairs and asked to talk. He said, 'What's worrying me is that I didn't sign up for what we're dealing with now in Afghanistan. Our job's dangerous, but if we do it correctly and efficiently we should be safe. What's going on out there now is something I've not seen before. The number of IEDs is multiplying at an alarming rate every day. I don't mind the risk of death being part of my job, I know it is, but if a man like Gaz can't make it, I won't. I signed up, but not for this, but I am too loyal to the job not to go. I couldn't live with myself knowing that I am an operator on the ground who can save lives and have the skills to protect people but I wasn't out there doing the job.'

I could see the conflict going on in him. He was torn between wanting to do the job he was good at and save lives, and knowing that the risk to his own life was becoming greater every day. And of course he was right – this wasn't what he'd signed up for. When he'd started AT training a decade earlier, it was a good job, with real promotion prospects and very little chance of being killed. Now all that had changed.

I thanked him for telling me, said I understood and hugged him. He was very teary. And after that he did come out of his dark hole, literally, and get himself together. He said that if he got a high-threat tour under his belt, then he would have opportunities when he came out; also if he hurried and passed the training, the sooner he would be sent, as they were so short of operators to meet the growing need.

*

A couple of weeks later, Oz went to Kineton for his high-threat course. Only a handful of ATOs get as far as this, and even then most of those taking it fail the first time. The high-threat course involves being trained to deal with the very latest devices, because they're changing all the time. Those who make explosive devices for the Taliban, and for others elsewhere in the world, are constantly updating their lethal creations, in an effort to outwit bomb detectors and those whose job it is to defuse them.

The tests involve wearing a bomb suit for up to ten or twelve hours at a time. These suits are hot and heavy and almost impossible to wear in extreme heat and in a 'permissive' environment – that is, one involving being shot at, threatened and possibly captured. The high-threat operators in Afghanistan don't wear them as it can compromise their safety in more ways than one. It singles them out, for a start. Oz thought it was nuts people didn't understand why you can't operate in one. You can't defy biology and wear those suits in that heat and be effective. He felt so strongly about this, and about other details of his work, that he even stopped talking to people who didn't understand, because it wound him up. You were either in Oz's little clique of mates or not at this stage; he was a specialist in a high-pressure field and we had withdrawn ourselves and become a quiet, reclusive family. We both felt that because Oz's and my lives were so different it was easier to just not talk about it, as friends and family alike, old or new, trusted or not, just didn't seem to get our lives, our pressures. But how can they? I thought. Oz was more and more focused on his future than ever and was chewing through that year, and we both had an awful lot on our minds.

The devices Oz's team dealt with involve everything from large car bombs to smaller pressure plates and all the potential bombs in between. They had to understand not only the bombs but the scenarios and how they are handled. Sometimes this would involve blowing up entire areas. Other times they're broken down into their constituent parts, so that the operators become absolutely familiar with them and the delicate procedure involved in unpicking them and rendering them safe. They needed to be able to catch the archer, not just the arrows, so forensics and bagging and tagging were important in reducing the number of devices and in finding those making them.

Only the high-threat operator will actually defuse a bomb. He is the one who takes the 'lonely walk', while the rest of the team provide cover and back-up.

It takes a minimum of six years to train as a high-threat operator, and in practice it is often longer. And when Oz was training, there simply weren't enough of them being trained. Soldiers in Afghanistan were three times more likely to be killed by an IED than by gunfire, and yet they were woefully short of high-threat operators.

In 2002 there had been a decision by the Ministry of Defence to halt training for high-threat operators, as a cost-cutting measure. This lasted for eighteen months, until training was resumed. So there was a major shortage of trained ATs from then on. No one had anticipated that the Taliban would discover their most effective weapon by far was the IED, and that there would be a surge in their use.

It was against this background that Oz went forward into a job that, for all these reasons, was far more dangerous than it should have been.

The course lasted for several weeks, and he did fine until the final test, which he failed. He kept muttering, 'I can't believe it, I've never failed anything.' He knew that the pass rate first time was about fifteen per cent, but he still didn't like having failed, and that night he downed a fair amount of whisky.

A couple of weeks later he went back to take that final test again. For the final test the operator is faced with an unknown explosive device in a potential scenario and will have to make the decision about how to approach it and how to deal with the situation.

When Oz faced his test, he said, 'Right, I'm going to refer up, lads.' This is the phrase they all use, and it means, I need time to think and, in some cases, to go back to my notes so that I can decide what to do and then let my team know.

Oz went into the woods behind the centre, smoked a

(*Right*) A young Oz (back row, second from right). It was his rugby master at school who first used his initials – OS – and it evolved into Oz.

(*Above*) Me, Jamie and Mum (Dad behind the camera) on holiday. This is typical of the holidays we would take to the West Country.

(*Right*) Us aboard *Avocet*, Dad's boat, just off Brownsea Island in Poole Harbour.

(*Left*) My wonderful Nan. Sitting in the garden of her cottage in Wales, near Llanberis Pass in Snowdonia. Oz and I loved it here.

(*Above left*) Laird at four months. The tallest and happiest baby in my baby group.
(*Above right*) Laird and me at Stone Terrace, just after his bath.

(*Left*) In 2004 Oz spent time in the Falklands where this picture was taken, after a 15-mile yomp.

(*Right*) A proud day. Oz fresh as a daisy after completing his 30-miler and getting the coveted green lid.

(*Left*) Oz at Cowley Manor in the Cotswolds. We'd often go there when we needed a couple of days peace and quiet.

(*Above*) Our family. Me, Oz, Laird and Bo at the 'Gucci' quarters in Tidworth.

(*Right*) This picture is how I most remember Oz and how I know he saw himself.

(*Above*) A picture of Oz and Laird taken by my mum. I was away and had called to ask how my boys were; this was the picture she sent me to show me, and it really shows just how intimate and comfortable Oz and Laird were in each other's company.

(*Left*) A Christmas mess do with some of the other ATO wives. There was and still is a great camaraderie between us.

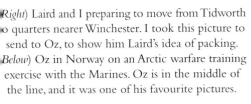

Right) Laird and I preparing to move from Tidworth o quarters nearer Winchester. I took this picture to send to Oz, to show him Laird's idea of packing.
Below) Oz in Norway on an Arctic warfare training exercise with the Marines. Oz is in the middle of the line, and it was one of his favourite pictures.

(*Left*) Taken just after
my miscarriage, Oz and
I both put on a brave
face even though we
were suffering physically
and emotionally.

(*Below group*) We love
to be outside and woul
often head over to eith
Carne or Pendow
beach for long walks an
BBQs with Laird and B

(*Above*) Nare Head and the surrounding area was a very special place to us. The Nare Hotel is a lovely family-owned hotel and I am still in touch with the owner, Toby.

(*Below*) Laird's 5th birthday. Oz loved celebrations of all kind and I had got Laird a cake with a Cornish fishing boat on it.

(*Left*) My boys, all over each other like a rash, as always.

(*Right and below*) These were taken at Sam and Hazey's wedding, a truly wonderful and happy day. We had our photo taken aboard HMS *Victory*, but all Laird wanted to do was run about.

rollie and phoned his good friend Stevie Jack, a Scot whom Oz affectionately described as 'a ginger bloke with a dodgy accent'. Stevie had been on the course with Oz, and had passed the first time around. 'What shall I do in this situation?' Oz asked him. 'I've got ten different ways I could go here.'

Stevie said, 'I'm not giving you the answers, Oz. You know what to do, you just have to step up and make the decision.'

Oz said to him, 'You're right, I can do it, I just need time to think.'

He needed that little respite, and the moment of support from Stevie. He went back down, dealt with the situation, defused the bomb and passed the course.

That weekend Mum and Dad travelled to see us. My parents had been eager to come because they knew that Oz would be sent to Afghanistan at any moment from that day on, and was likely to go within days. His outlook was so hopeful and he discussed his plans with them about what he wanted and what he was aiming for. We all knew that passing the course was a biggy for him, a huge personal achievement. He was touched that they came and very proud of himself for passing the course. Despite his concerns about what lay ahead, he felt unique and special that he was one of so few who could do a job that was about preserving life.

I hugged him and said, 'Good effort, Lofty.' It sounds

harsh, but Oz used to love it when I called him that, or knobber. They use such strong language in the Army, and insults become terms of endearment – because his hair was always all over the place I used to call him fathead too.

We'd come home with yet another box full of paperwork Oz had collected on the course. By this time he had collected a stack of files: background material, operating procedures, information about devices and routes for dealing with them. The high-risk guys have to memorise a huge amount of information, and they carry a lot with them wherever they go, so that they can refer to it if need be. They call them bomb doctors, and it's no surprise, because the sheer weight of facts they have to understand and absorb is as complex as anything a medical professional might face.

As well as the stack of files, Oz had a vast stack of kit: summer kit, Arctic kit; stuff for all weathers and all circumstances.

He was always dreadful at organising it all. It would sit in a heap in the corner, but to be honest it needed a room of its own, and until we left Jasmine Cottage we didn't have one. When we moved out to go into the Tidworth quarters, I found all kinds of extraordinary things all over the house: cartridges, handflares and bits of explosives on top of kitchen cupboards, down the sides of furniture and even in his boots. It was all stuff he'd had to use for demonstrations or exercises, where he'd found he had a bit extra and had put it away to use later.

Oz actually enjoyed the demolition work they did. They'd blow things up at Kineton – old cars and other rubbish – as part of their training in understanding the capabilities of the explosives, and for him it was a way of letting off steam.

Not long after he finished the course, Oz wrote me a beautiful card.

HI HONEY,

THANK YOU FOR SUPPORTING ME OVER THE LAST COUPLE OF MONTHS. IT HAS BEEN EXTREMELY IMPORTANT FOR BOTH OF US, AS IS THE NEXT YEAR. I REALLY APPRECIATE IT AND JUST WANTED TO SAY WHAT AN EXCEPTIONAL WIFE AND MOTHER YOU ARE. NEVER FORGET THAT.

THAT IS WHY YOU ARE MINE + LAIRD'S + BO'S. WE HAVE GOT A HOOFIN FUTURE TOGETHER THAT GETS MORE POSITIVE AS TIME GOES ON.

LOVE YOU SO MUCH

OZ xxx

Loving cards like this were written in moments of optimism when he believed and trusted that our life together was on track and we'd put another tick in the box towards moving forward and getting closer to all our plans working out. We had a strong intimacy that only a very few close to him saw. He knew he was likely to be sent to Afghanistan any day that autumn, and he was worried about it, but it was his job, and he was ready to do it. And he stayed focused on a time, beyond that, when he would come home again and we'd get on with making our future.

I was proud of all that Oz was, not least his loyalty to me. Friends of his would tell me, laughing, that when he was away from me and they all went out on the town, he wouldn't go into strip clubs. He'd say, 'I'm not going in there, I'm going to phone my wife instead.' I would get these phone calls all the time wherever he was. If he was out drinking and having a giggle he'd be constantly on the phone, to the point where it annoyed me and I would ask what was the point in him going out?! They'd all tease him over how loved-up he was.

Oz had done all the wild stuff in the past. But he'd long since reached a point in his life where it just didn't interest him any more. He had a family, stability, responsibility, a future.

At Halloween, Oz got Laird all dressed up as a wizard to go out trick-or-treating. Laird was almost five, and wild with excitement about going for the first time. We met up with friends and knocked on a few local doors, and Laird came home with a pile of goodies. Oz and Laird had hollowed out a pumpkin together and gave it a friendly face, and we put a candle inside it and put it in the window.

On Guy Fawkes Night, five days later, Oz organised a big barbecue. He invited friends over and cooked a mountain of food. He let off flares and other bits he had left over from work.

'This is what makes me happy,' he grinned at me, as we watched the firework display. 'You, me, Laird, people we really love and who get us. It's all I want.'

CHAPTER TEN

Oz was expecting to be sent to Afghanistan literally any day. He knew he would go at short notice, and he had prepared himself. He was ready, revved up and on the starting block.

'I'm up for it,' he said, 'bring it on. Send me to war. I need to get this cracked and get on with the bigger plan. It's doing my swede in now, not knowing.'

He thought he'd be back by spring, and that's what he wanted. He had done his up-to-the-minute training, and he preferred the idea of going during the winter for two reasons – firstly the main fighting seasons are spring and summer, so he hoped to avoid the worst conflicts, and secondly he would be able to work in the chill of winter rather than the blazing heat of summer. Oz always preferred the cold. He didn't mind howling gales, ice and snow, and he would choose a holiday sitting in front of a log fire over basking on a beach any day. But, more than anything, he just wanted this next tour of duty to be over. He believed that by then he would have 'done my bit for humanity', as he put it, and would be able to work in Britain until he left the Army a year or two down the line, and could get his pension.

But as day after day passed and Oz wasn't pinged to go, he became increasingly agitated and anxious. He couldn't understand it. 'Why put me on the high-threat course and then hold me back?' he dripped and moaned to his friends. He asked, but he wasn't given much information. He was busy with his day job and duties at Alpha Troop, and he was led to understand that, for the moment, he was needed here, and that was that. But the situation in the Middle East was unveiling and unfolding in front of our eyes daily. He never turned Sky News off. He was on edge, constantly waiting to hear that he had to go, and seldom truly at ease. He fretted over why he hadn't been sent, and when it was going to be. He began to get run-down and ill.

Neither of us was especially religious, but we always went to church on Remembrance Sunday, and then had a roast dinner, and drinks in the afternoon, out of respect for those who had lost their lives for our country. That year, Remembrance Sunday fell on 9 November, and Oz was especially subdued all day. There were more British troops dying than ever before.

A week later, Laird turned five. Oz insisted we have a party. He made a real effort and was on great form, surprising Laird with extra presents, toasting him solemnly with apple juice and helping to entertain a house full of excited children.

Laird had started at the local infant school the previous September, and had made several friends, who would do pretend news reporting and giggle all the time. Touchingly, the thing Laird enjoyed most about school was being a little policeman in the playground, helping to organise games and looking out for other children. For this duty, children were awarded the 'red hat', and Laird was very proud that he'd won it several times. Oz was right behind him. If Laird came home and said he'd got the red hat again, Oz would get out the juice for Laird and wine for us and say, 'I'll drink to that, Laird,' and cook something special for tea. He'd light a candle on the table and insist we all sit down together and raise a glass to remind us of what an achievement it was. 'Laird has got the red hat again,' he would announce seriously. 'What do you think of that, Mummy?' That kind of attention did so much for Laird's confidence and sense of self-worth. They were very important moments for us.

Two weeks after Laird's birthday we had our first wedding anniversary. Oz bought a bottle of champagne and made me champagne cocktails, before taking me out for a curry. He was in great spirits until the end of the meal, when he became quiet.

'I can't stand the thought of losing you and not

161

having this,' he said. 'What if I don't have this again?'

I was shocked. 'Of course you will,' I said. 'We're going to celebrate the next fifty wedding anniversaries! Sadly, I've got to put up with you, and you've got to put up with me!'

He smiled. 'I'm serious. If I go I am probably not coming back, so I need you to promise me certain things. I have thought about what I want.' His mood remained sombre.

'Shut up! What are you talking about?'

He went into detail. I was overwhelmed, as it suddenly felt all very real. I said, 'You need to write this down and speak to the people who matter to you, then.' He had outlined the lot, right down to the very last detail. He couldn't get private life cover as it was so expensive due to his job and the likelihood of him being sent to Afghanistan imminently. He explained that he thought he had left me right in it, as he only had PAX, the military insurance scheme, which is available to HM Armed Forces and their families. But you couldn't even buy a flat with it, he told me. He had no idea how poor it was.

In the build-up to Christmas that year, he continued to be subdued and anxious. He became low, distracted, and ill with the chronic pain of IBS flare-ups. He adored Christmas and normally threw himself into preparing for it. But this time he didn't even want to go food shopping. He'd say, 'Honey, will you go? Can't be around civvies.' He just wanted to stay at home, in front of the fire with Laird.

In the run-up to Christmas, I was working hard and Oz had quite a bit of free time. He and Laird would go round to see Mum most days, for a chat and a cup of tea.

We spent Christmas with Mum and Dad and Jamie. Mum was worried about Oz being so down. 'I think it's since his friend Gaz died,' she said. But Oz said to me, 'It's not Gaz. That hit me hard, I know, but what's getting to me now is waiting to go, and thinking about what I'm going to be dealing with out there.'

I took Laird up to bed and left him to have the talk with my parents that he had had with me earlier that month. They were shocked. Dad said he didn't agree that Oz should be going and that the onus should be on us to bear the issue of death or injury, due to shortages, and a heated debate ensued downstairs as the family had it out. Dad told Oz to make sure he got an executor of his will that he could trust, and to ensure he communicated to those he cared about what his wishes were. He urged him to write down anything that was important to him. He also told him to see those people urgently if he was sure he'd have to go to Afghanistan. My father was visibly upset.

A couple of days later, just before he went back to Didcot, Oz asked me to do his Tarot cards. The Tarot was something I did very rarely, perhaps once every other year. I wasn't sure about doing it this time, but Oz urged me to and I agreed. I had always done them since I was young and I seemed to be gifted at it. However, I didn't really understand why, so I rarely told anyone or did it openly.

The card he chose to show the future was the Burning Tower. I did them again, this time for career, and Oz chose the Burning Tower again. The worst card there is. It signifies death and endings, the worst outcome imaginable and entirely unavoidable; everything you know gone in ruin or catastrophe.

Oz looked stricken. 'I feel this is going to be a really bad year for me,' he said. 'I've got this feeling, as if everything is slipping.'

I tried to lighten it. 'You'll probably just stub your toe when you're at work – you're always a screamer with loads of bad luck! Don't worry, it might just mean that you won't get a promotion or something.'

'No,' he said. 'It's not the card. That just confirmed what I already know and feel.'

It was my turn to choose a card. I hoped I might get something that would lift the mood, but I was startled when I got it in my spread of cards, too. But then I got rebirth after, and the moon. 'See, hun – always light in the dark. Remember that,' he said.

I tried to hide my dismay. 'It's a dark time of year. Perhaps we're both just feeling it,' I said. We went and made supper.

'Let's be positive, forget the cards, we've got lots to look forward to,' I chirped, waiting for him to follow my lead.

He usually did, but this time Oz said, 'No, it's bad. I've got this feeling that if I go out after January or February, I'm not going to be coming back. That's what my gut is telling me.'

There was nothing I could say that would cheer him, and the truth was, it was hard even to try, because I felt worried too.

Laird overheard us talking and asked, 'What you talking about, Dad?'

Oz spoke to just me. 'Mum, you decide, you're the boss, shall I go off sick? It would compromise the job I get when I come out as a civvie, though, and I don't want that.'

'Whoa, whoa, whoa there, honey. Only you can make that call. Don't put it on me, it's not fair,' I said.

He replied, 'But you're the boss. You know I need you to let me off the hook.'

I said I wouldn't ever say or do anything to influence his decision, as it was important to him to get a high-threat tour under his belt. However, I saw how ill he was with colitis; he'd been in and out of hospital. I told him that I didn't think he was fit enough to go and he should tell his regiment – be honest, any commanding officer would listen to our doctor. But Oz said they already knew about his health issues and he didn't want to seem weak. I said I disagreed with not going to them but that we would discuss it later as our son was around.

The next day he went back to camp. In between Christmas and New Year, I had a break from work, and we spent time with Laird, our friends and my parents. For New Year, Oz and I went to Cornwall to celebrate at The New Inn with Jack and Penny. He felt comfortable there, and felt that they let him be him. He could spend time relaxing and chilling out. By this time he was seeing less and less of friends and family back in Cornwall and I had to push him and drive him to see them. He said that no one understood, and that it wound him up being around people who were moaning about trivial things. I could see his point of view: when you've seen the horrific side of war and been through grief and Forces life in quarters, it was so far removed from the lives of others. He was right to stay focused, it was just easier.

On New Year's Eve Oz's mood seemed good. He joined in with the karaoke, and when a little boy aged about eleven said he wanted to sing but was too shy, Oz offered to sing with him and they did a Queen song together. After that Oz became more and more drunk, dancing around to Bon Jovi and Iron Maiden and eventually, by two in the morning, dangling from the door frame, biting the fairy lights. Penny loved Oz, but she was alarmed and told me to get him down. 'You're going to have to stop him, he's going to electrocute himself,' she warned. I did get him down, eventually. But he'd needed a good blow-out.

After the New Year break, we both got back into our working routines, Oz at Didcot and me working from home and from my car, on my rounds of hospitals, pharmacies and doctors. Laird was into his second term at school and seemed OK, and I hoped that, despite the bad omens, the year would be good for us.

Perhaps they won't send him to Afghanistan at all, I thought. After all, he's doing an important job here – it's not as though he's treading water. And he wasn't; with his Para and Commando training, Oz was part of an elite squad kept very busy with antiterrorism work. But living with the only certainty being uncertainty was draining.

I kept a close eye on the news and it was impossible to miss the escalating casualty figures in Afghanistan. Not only were more British troops dying, but the numbers being severely injured and losing limbs were running into hundreds.

The British were still in charge of Helmand province and were formally responsible for security in the centre of Taliban insurgency. Most of the British deaths so far had been at the hands of the Taliban in Helmand. A number of successive military operations had been launched, aimed at pushing the Taliban back and reclaiming land and villages taken by the Taliban, but although there had been successes, the British were still coming under growing attack. In particular, the Taliban were increasing their use of IEDs. Normally in the winter months there is a drop in the level of Taliban activity, but over the winter of 2008/2009 there was no drop; the number of IEDs being deployed continued to increase at an alarming rate, and there were reports that the Taliban were training children as young as five to lay the devices in the roads and fields.

In March 2009, 300 more soldiers were sent out by the British Government, taking the total British presence to 8,300, and a new series of operations was launched. Operation Zafar, in late April, lasted for a week, and was followed by Operation Zafar 2, in mid-May. Both were deemed successful in reclaiming villages from the Taliban and securing an area so that a checkpoint could be built on the road to Lashkar Gah, the capital of Helmand. The way was being prepared for an even bigger operation that would be launched in June – Panther's Claw.

While I looked at the bigger picture of what was in the news, Oz was hearing about how many devices had been found that week or that day. So we had two sides of the picture between us, macro and micro. I was hearing about the desperate shortage of bomb-disposal experts like Oz, the height of that shortage coinciding with this operation and at a time when an unprecedented amount of devices were being used. He was hearing that the metal detectors that the Army was using as a first line of defence were not finding all the IEDs. We didn't discuss it every day, we tried to get on with normal life, but we talked often, and we could see that the picture was becoming increasingly alarming.

Both Oz and I had thought he might be sent out with the additional troops in March. When he wasn't, he became even more edgy.

'I am getting skill fade, and others who passed the course after me are going before me. It's a face-fit culture, it's dogshit,' he'd say. 'And it's getting worse out there all the time. I don't want to go, but I don't have any other choice. Only a few of us can do what we do, they're going to need me.' He got angry, because he said a few men were working really hard while the Fat Ruperts, the career boys, were sitting on their backsides cancelling training to save money, and hiding in training roles, retiring or getting desk jobs instead of stepping up to help the trade. Oz felt it showed a shocking level of selfishness and that the trade ought to be ashamed of itself. 'They should be fighting for us,' he would say. 'Can't they see we're all in this together? We're a team, but they're not doing their bit.'

Perhaps because of the stress of waiting, his IBS was flaring up badly. He was seeing a specialist again, and underwent a second operation to remove the precancerous polyps from his bowel. As with the first, it didn't appear to help. Oz was on steroids and medication as he couldn't sleep. He was losing weight and suffering increasingly severe episodes of pain, which meant more and more he would want to stay at home, saying he didn't want to go out and meet anyone, even close friends like Sam and Hazey. So they would come to us or we'd fix conference calls to keep in touch.

A doctor friend of ours said to Oz over the phone, 'You're not fit to go, you shouldn't be going. You can sign off sick, you're not up to a high-threat tour and you shouldn't feel bad about that because if you go you might compromise yourselves and others.'

Oz tried to get his medical records together to create a case, but unfortunately his admin file was missing. 'In any case,' he would say, 'if I don't go, then who's going to do my job? And who will run Alpha Troop? There isn't anybody, it's on the bones of its arse, it's shocking.' He was in torment over it, desperate to find a way out, but feeling that if he did, he would be letting people die.

There were times when he became almost childlike about it. It was as if he felt overwhelmed by the difficulty of the decision facing him.

We had a family conference about it, the two of us, sitting at the table.

'What can I do?' he said. 'There are only a few other people who do what I do.'

We both knew that he was right. How could he not go, when going would save lives? Oz was so good at what he did and so experienced that he could smell the ground and tell if the tarmac had been taken up and put back down. He used every sense and all his experience to do a job that a young guy of twenty could never do.

I would be in tears, because I felt very strongly that I couldn't be the one to make such a decision for him, but I wanted so desperately to tell him not to go. All I could say was, 'It has to be up to you.' The decision lay so heavily on him, it was a huge burden, an ethical dilemma – to choose himself, and his own life, or to choose to go and try to save as many lives as he could, and accept the huge risk to his own. He'd put his head in his hands and say, 'I can't handle it. This is breaking me.'

Looking back at how desperate he felt during those months before he went, I feel that Oz's courage was immense. To be so afraid, and yet to go anyway, and do what you have to do, is heroism. But he didn't want to be a hero. He wanted to do what was right, but he also wanted to live. Oz did come to a decision that weekend, but sadly the private doctor Oz had been seeing was away in Spain and we couldn't get in touch with him before Oz went to prove he wasn't well enough to go.

So nothing could sort this dilemma for Oz. He was utterly torn – one minute angry and tortured, feeling that he was being hung out to dry and that the government had let the troops down by underequipping them and cutting training programmes; the next minute he'd be saying, 'I've got to go and I'll grizz through it, I'll do what I have to and it will be fine.'

He'd laugh sometimes and say, 'Anyway, what am I going to do on civvie street? Be a driver? Work in a shop? It's scary out there.'

We tried to keep life normal, but it wasn't easy. More than once, Oz simply disappeared, for a night at a time. When he had a few days off he went to visit Andrew and his family in Cornwall. He took his bomb suit. Andrew, who's a strong bloke, told me the helmet, lead-lined and with its own air-conditioning unit, was so heavy that he felt dizzy when he tried it on.

Once when we were in the pub together, Oz picked up a sachet of sugar from the condiments bowl beside it and said, 'This sugar is more use to me than that helmet. At least the sugar gives me the energy I need to think and to do my job.'

At home Oz was happiest in the woods, where he went every weekend when we were back at Jasmine Cottage. We even camped there sometimes. One day he carved Laird's and Bo's names on the tree where he used to sit for a smoke. 'I didn't put our names there, honey,' he said. 'I thought that if anything happened to me it might be too hard for you seeing them there.'

But it was looking ahead to the future that really helped during that time. When Oz was down I'd put my arms round him and say, 'Think of the house in Cornwall that we're going to have, and the carrots we'll grow and the chickens we'll keep and Laird running around chasing them and you sitting by your fire, carving pieces of wood.' He'd smile and say, 'Love that, love you. You talking to me like that is what keeps me sane.'

In May we decided we would put Jasmine Cottage on the market and set the wheels in motion for our next stage. With the profit from the sale we could put a deposit on a house in Cornwall. Oz planned by looking at jobs for after he left the military. We would put Laird into a school down there.

'I want him in a really good school, like the one I went to. With surfing for PE!' Oz would say, and we'd imagine our new life.

It was the thought of this that kept him going as he struggled with his demons.

CHAPTER ELEVEN

In March 2009, Oz had been interviewed by ITN News about his forthcoming deployment to Afghanistan. They were doing a piece on the bomb-disposal team.

In the interview, Oz, with an impressively recent and very rare short-back-and-sides haircut, said, 'Obviously it's a dangerous job . . . however, culmination of all the training we have done, as a team, has prepared me for this deployment in the best possible way. I feel absolutely confident about the job that I'm expected to do and that of my team members as well.'

It was a brave performance, but the truth was that although he knew how to do his job, he didn't feel confident at all about the deployment, and he still didn't know when he was going, if at all. He was still awaiting his medical records that had been lost, and so he couldn't get to a consultant in Didcot to explain how ill he was, what he feared and what our doctor had said.

It was around this time that we started trying for another baby. We'd made progress by putting our house on the market and getting our finances in order. Now it was time to start a new family.

After months of fretting, Oz took his focus off waiting to go to war, because our friends Sam and Hazey were getting married and Oz was to be best man.

Sam and Hazey were an extraordinary combination. She was a Sikh girl from Southampton, he was a lad from Leeds who had become a Royal Marines Commando. They thought long and hard about how to bring together their cultures, families and friends, and in the end they decided to get married three times, with a fun wedding in Vegas for close family and friends, a traditional Sikh one for Sam's family, and a huge reception for everyone.

Before all the weddings kicked off, there was Hazey's stag do, in late March, an event Oz looked forward to for weeks beforehand. Normally the best man would organise the stag events, but Hazey decided to do it himself because it was clear Oz was up to his neck preparing for possible deployment. Hazey had a knack of always seeing the bigger picture, and his love for Oz was evident – he wanted him to relax.

Being the generous man he is, he wanted to treat his closest friends to a really memorable weekend. He invited Oz and his other mates to stay with him in London and he gave them all England rugby shirts, because there was a big Six Nations England–Scotland match on that weekend. They started on Saturday morning by drinking port in the oldest wine bar in London, Gordon's in Villiers Street, close to the Embankment. They carried on in various venues around London, and by the time the match ended, late in the afternoon, with an England victory, they were very happy indeed. The pictures they took that day – ending with one in which Hazey balanced on one leg on the top of an old-fashioned red phone box after getting a leg-up from Oz – tell their own story. They had a fantastic time, and it was good to see Oz looking so happy. Sam's hen party took place on the same night in Bishop's Waltham and we giggled all night at the drunken messages Hazey and Oz left professing their love for us and each other!

The following day, Hazey, who is a qualified pilot, took them all flying, one at a time, in a Cessna light aircraft. Sadly Oz had to miss that part of the weekend because he had to get back to work. He was gutted, as was Hazey.

Two weeks later we also had to miss the Las Vegas wedding, because Oz was on a parachute training exercise, so Hazey asked his close friend, Sergeant Clive Magson – another Royal Marines Commando – to do the honours there.

Oz was getting fed up with the military stopping him being at things that mattered to him. Even though real friends like Hazey and Sam understood, we knew they were deeply disappointed. Friendships in the military are picked up whenever people can physically get together; there is no nine-to-five and life is so different to civvie life. It dictates where you live, what you do, when you have children and where you should school them. But more than that, it dictates what your life chances are also! Oz said he was sure it wasn't for him any more and that he wanted to step back from what he was doing. He often felt fed up when his civvie mates and family moaned, apparently thinking it was a personal choice of ours not to attend things which for them were easy to factor into their lives.

After missing out on Vegas, Oz was determined to make the most of their big wedding reception, which was in Portsmouth on 23 May 2009. The night before, I collected him from Didcot, where he'd just come in from a training exercise, and drove him down to Portsmouth, where he was spending the evening with Hazey and a few of his other close friends. Oz was exhausted after a gruelling week, and hadn't yet written his best man speech, so he wanted to tap Hazey's other mates for a few dits (stories) to include.

I left him there and headed back to Winchester to pick up Laird from his after-school club. We went back to Tidworth to walk the dog and sort our clothes out, and joined everyone for the big celebrations the next day.

The ceremony was held in the historic naval dockyard at HMS *Nelson* barracks and, for the first time in history, Royal Marine drummers played at the reception, alongside a band of Punjabi dhol drummers.

As best man, Oz was Master of Ceremonies for the day, making the brief welcoming speech, introducing the drummers – to much laughter he announced that the Punjabi drummers had made their way 'all the way from India, via Essex' – and making his best man speech, after we'd all eaten a huge feast of Indian delights. He took his duties very seriously, refusing to have a drink until he'd finished his speech, and making sure that everything was going smoothly and Sam and Hazey were having a good time.

It was a wonderful day; one of those truly special days when everything feels right and everyone is happy. One of the happiest days Oz and I ever shared. He was on sparkling form, doing Hazey proud with a speech that managed to be loving and proud and at the same time have everyone in stitches. He'd worked hard on it – he was determined to get it right and he did. Breaking from English tradition, Sam (rather than her father) gave a speech, and it was a bittersweet moment when she turned to Oz, thanked him for being 'our' best man and, having announced to the guests Oz was most certainly soon to deploy to Afghanistan, wished for his safe return.

Oz, Laird and I sat on the top table with the bride and groom, and after dinner we danced until we could barely stand. Laird was with us and he never left Oz's side. When I saw the photos afterwards, there was Laird hugging Oz's knee; Laird feeding Oz a piece of nan bread; Laird grinning up at Oz.

Hazey was still working for the First Sea Lord at the time and, with his permission, they were able to have their wedding photographs taken on HMS *Victory*, the magnificent eighteenth-century warship commanded by Admiral Lord Nelson during the Battle of Trafalgar in 1805, when the British Fleet sailed against the French and Spanish fleets and won. The *Victory*, still a commissioned ship, now has a permanent home in the historic dockyard, where it is a living museum commemorating the Georgian Navy and the flagship of the Commander-in-Chief Naval Home Command.

The pictures we took on the deck of the *Victory* that day, just before sunset, are very precious. Against a backdrop of one of the most magnificent ships ever built, the photographs of us with Sam and Hazey, and of the three of us – Oz, me and Laird – are glowing with laughter, happiness and affection. I felt so good that day, it was wonderful to see Oz back to his old self again, making people laugh as he slid across the dance floor on his knees, dancing with Sam, who was a gorgeous bride, hugging her mum and dad and turning to me every now and then to say, 'This is good, honey, isn't it? This is how it should be.'

I saw him across the room, chatting to the First Sea

Lord, who was among the guests. They knew one another because during Oz's first Afghan tour, two and a half years earlier, the FSL had gone out to Afghanistan for a visit and had announced to the assembled ranks, 'Is there an Oz here?' He'd brought a Christmas card from Hazey. After that, he and Oz sat next to one another at dinner and chatted about the war. 'What do you need?' the FSL had asked him. 'More manpower,' Oz had said. 'Just don't lose your head when you are out there, Oz, too many do.'

It was an emotional day, like all the best weddings, with much laughter and many tears. And as well as celebrating for our friends, Oz and I were celebrating privately, too, because we suspected that I was pregnant again after it dawned on us why I was so exceptionally tired that week and hadn't come on – I was late. Oz was the sort of person who noticed things and remembered dates I didn't. He said, 'Aren't you late? You've been really tired and off your food all week, not drinking coffee either.' We were both stunned because we had been so stressed and busy that we hadn't noticed. I slowed down that night, only having a small tipple and water. It was a couple of years since my miscarriage and we had begun to think that pregnancy might not happen for us again.

Oz was incredibly happy, and so was I. And at that moment everything else – even the threat of him going to Afghanistan for the next few months – seemed somehow less awful. Afghanistan had felt to him, for some time, like the end of the horizon – as far ahead as he could see. Now he once again began to see our life beyond it, with a new baby.

We decided not to tell anyone about the pregnancy for a while – it was still very early. We even kept it from Lairdster. But we hugged it to us, a piece of information we both cherished and would take real joy in sharing a few weeks further on.

'Make sure you look after yourself,' Oz urged me. I promised him I wouldn't overdo it and would put my feet up every night once Laird was in bed. But I wasn't worried. My doctor had reassured me that one miscarriage wasn't unusual. Not that it made it any easier to bear.

Still on a high, Oz said to me, 'Do you know what? I don't think they're going to send me to Afghanistan after all. It's months since I did the high-threat, I reckon it's out of date now, the environment there's changing all the time. They can't ping me out there now.'

Could it be true? Did we dare believe that he wouldn't have to go?

Perhaps it was crazy to think that, with the desperate need for high-threat operators over there, Oz would somehow not be needed. But, crazy or not, that weekend he behaved as though the whole thing had just disappeared and he was off the hook and free. He relaxed, he played with Laird, he made plans for his birthday which was a couple of weeks away, and he began looking at houses in Cornwall on the internet, calling me over to say, 'What do you think of this one, honey?' He even drew a picture of his ideal house, so that if I saw anything similar I should go and see it.

On the Monday after Sam and Hazey's wedding I walked in from work to see Oz on the phone. He was pacing up and down the living room and he looked agitated.

Minutes later he put down the phone and looked at me, his face stricken. 'I'm going,' he said. 'That was Si. Some captain just went out for a week and got sent back with an ulcer and they've pinged me instead. They don't want to send me, he knows what it's like out there. But there's nothing he can do.'

Simon de Gruchy was a good friend of Oz's. A warrant officer in 11 EOD, he had won the Queen's Gallantry Medal in Iraq and now worked in the Operations Room. He was due to come out.

I was trying to take in what Oz was saying. I looked at him. 'When?'

'Next Monday. A week. I've got a week.'

Monday would be 1 June. Ten days before his thirtieth birthday. Thirty was a milestone for a lot of people, but Oz never thought in numbers like that; he thought it was what you'd done with your life that mattered, not the amount of years you'd lived.

I put my arms around him. There was nothing I could say. We had been over it so many times. We both knew what he was facing – blistering heat, too many IEDs, too few high-threat operators.

We had talked and argued and gone over things for months. But now there was very little to say. The decision was made and the next few days would be spent organising his kit and then saying his goodbyes.

For the next couple of days, Oz was silent. When he spoke it was to the point, brief. He'd switched off. I knew he was angry, he felt he'd been wronged, kept waiting too long. Now he was being sent when there were a tiny handful of operators out there who could do his job. There should have been three times as many.

He phoned Hazey to tell him. I could hear him giving instructions. He went off in the car to meet him and talk. He had asked Hazey to be executor of his will, though I didn't know that then. He was away for a night.

For the last few days before he went, Oz was on autopilot. He said to me, 'I'm sorry, I just have to get my head around going now, I can't do anything else. And in case I do die, you need to know what my wishes are. Just write them down, I don't want to go over this again. They are exactly the same, remember, as I told you a few months back . . .'

It was a grim thing to have to do, but in that situation you have to talk about these things. Oz told me that if he came back in a coffin, he wanted me to be there to meet him, on the runway. He wanted me to be at Wootton Bassett. 'I want you to go every time someone comes back,' he said. 'Go and honour them. And if it turns out to be me, I want you there, standing proud.

'If anything happens to me, let everyone know what's going on out there. That would mean a lot to me. Let them know about the shortages and the corner they backed me into, me and the other high-threats. None of us mind doing our job, but we shouldn't be doing five other people's jobs too. Promise me you'll let people know. You've always been gobby. Use it. Promise me! I've never asked you to do anything before and I know if I don't make you promise then you will leave the quarters and do none of it, but it's important to me and the ones on our belt buckle and their families.'

I promised. And I wished, with everything I had, that I would never have to keep my promise.

Then I did my usual thing: the pep talk, Oz used to call it. 'Come on, enough of this morbid nonsense, you're not dying, you dick, man-up, you are a Para-Commando, there is no other man above you. This is us – me, you, Laird – we don't do this.'

When I paused for breath, Oz grinned. 'You done?'

I laughed.

'Save it,' he said. 'I'll probably need it again before I'm out the other side of this.'

Then he said, 'There's another thing. While I'm away,

will you keep me safe? Do your thing every new moon, think of me and send me some good luck. Do it and let me know you're doing it. That will help, knowing that you're looking up at the same moon.'

'Not that you'll need it,' I said. 'You know what you're doing, you're a professional. You will be safe because you know how to do your job.'

Now there wasn't time for anything else. It all happened so fast that there was no possibility of Oz seeing all of his family and friends, no time for visits, or get-togethers or giving presents. Just hasty phone calls, promises to write and reluctant goodbyes.

We celebrated Oz's birthday at home before he went. Cake, presents, balloons, the lot. Oz-style. Laird bouncing all over him in the bed with cuddles, tickles, kisses. Andrew had wanted us to go down to Cornwall to celebrate Oz's birthday and had bought him an engraved bottle of champagne. 'I'll keep the champagne,' Andrew said. 'We'll have it when you get back.'

In the afternoon, he and Laird made pasties together. That was something they loved to do. Oz put Laird's name on his, in pastry, and his own name on the other two. He ate one and put the other in the freezer. 'I'll have it when I get back,' he said.

Laird knew that Oz was going off to the war, and would be gone for a while. He used to say proudly, 'My Daddy keeps people safe, he is a warrior and very brave.' That's what he knew to be true. Oz wasn't allowed to talk specifics about his job in front of Laird.

Oz got all his kit together. Went over it time after time. Medicine for his IBS, plenty of it, because he might not be able to get it there. Loads of specialist extra kit, like gloves, daysacks and special knives he needed. We had to buy everything, as what was issued was rubbish. 'You might need to send me a few more of these, honey.' He gave me a list and websites to get things from. 'I'll probably get through them, so just order them routinely and send to the address I give you when I am there.'

On the Sunday, his last full day, we drove down to Lymington, to where Dad had *Magari*, his boat, moored. Mum and Dad were on board and busy cooking a roast dinner: lamb and lots of fresh vegetables. 'Feed you up, Ozzy,' she said. 'And I'll make you one just the same when you get back.'

'Hoofin Gill, love it, just what I need.' He hugged her, poured a glass of wine for everyone and we sat round the table, all of us enjoying the sunshine. As usual Oz was all over Lairdster like a rash; he wanted to soak up every moment with him.

When it was time to go, Oz hugged Mum and Dad. Promised he'd write. Said, 'Look after the boat, John, and don't forget what I said.' My mum said she wouldn't watch him go and went below deck, teary. I could see my dad was emotional too, but he got us all in the dinghy – Laird at the helm – and dropped us on the quay. Dad said he would play with Laird for a bit in the dinghy. Oz was teary and hugged and play-fought with Laird for ages; he told him he'd be counting the days till we could all be together again. I brought the car round and we said goodbye as Laird was staying with my mum and dad. I drove back up to Tidworth, where Oz packed. Oz was in bits the entire drive home.

I ordered a Chinese takeaway late that night as he packed and went over everything, obsessing. Oz got his favourite wine out of the garage and put it in the fridge, 'For when I get back, wife,' he said. Oz was trying to be positive. We ate slowly and after dinner Oz sat at the table in the kitchen doodling. 'What's that?' I said.

'It's that doodle of the house I want us to have, but I've added some things,' he said. 'Will you look for it while I'm away?'

I looked at what he'd drawn. A small sketch of a house with big windows and a big fireplace, with a list of us as a family below.

'Right,' I smiled. 'I'll circulate it round the Cornish estate agents.' We laughed.

That night neither of us slept much. We held each other tight. Beyond words.

In the morning I decided the only way to get through the next few hours was to tough it out. Be matter-of-fact.

Oz was ready. I was driving him to the base at Didcot, from there he would be taken to RAF Brize Norton for his flight. I had appointments and meetings to get to in

Berkshire, so it made sense to take him myself. It was early, before 7 a.m.; we went in my work car and I drove the first bit before stopping for fuel on the A34. He got out of the car to get a hot drink for us both. We always did it when I drove him up there, just to spend a little time together before going our separate ways.

When he came back I said, 'You drive now instead.' I didn't often let him drive my work car because Oz drove it like a tank, charging over every rut and hole and dip in the road, battering the suspension. I would have to spend hours getting the tracking sorted after he'd finished with it. He was a rubbish driver. He once wrote off a car in the middle of the night because he was rolling a cigarette. The car went out of control, crossed the central verge and rolled twice. I was still paying that off for him, along with some other debts that I was helping him clear. He was always so clumsy – when he messed up, he did it big, my dad always said. Thank God there was no traffic on the opposite side; he'd emerged unscathed and then told everyone he'd hit a deer. This time, though, I didn't care.

He got in, then said, 'Hang on, why am I driving? You always drive me up to camp or on courses or whatever – it's tradition.' He was upset and raised his voice. 'Come on, are you with me on this or not?'

I said, 'Nope, not this time, I will not drive you up.' I didn't want to drive, because I didn't want to be the one to take him to a war he might not come back from.

He copped a look at his watch and said, 'Fine.' On the journey, Oz smoked and we listened to music, silently. As he drove, Oz held my hand, resting it on his leg. It was something he often did, a way of keeping the connection, even when we weren't talking. I looked down at his leg, in his green kit, and his hand, holding mine, rubbing it with his thumb. So familiar and so loved.

The thought was in my mind before I could push it away. That's the last time I'm going to see his hands, his legs even. I felt tired and sick.

His phone rang a lot. Hazey, Sam, Andrew, other friends, ringing to say goodbye, good luck, we'll write. He ignored it. 'This is my time with you, hun. It's precious. I will call them in a bit.'

We got to Didcot and pulled up by the garages, and Oz rolled another ciggie – he'd been chain-smoking the whole way. There were tears in his eyes, and he said, 'I'm just in war mode now, I know I am. I have said all the things I need to say to you and what I expect. You know who to trust and who not to, what to expect from certain people and others; you know who won't help you whilst I am away if you have to move.' We were in surplus quarters off camp and would be moved again soon.

He smoked the rollie and left the stub in the ashtray. He said he felt sick. I did too. I wanted to scream. We were both trying so hard to be upbeat. 'I want out. I don't want this, don't forget that,' he said. But there was no going back, no way out, it was too late.

Time to say goodbye. Oz kissing me and kissing me, passionately, tears rolling down his cheeks. Tears on mine too. Trying to laugh. 'All right bud, I'll see you again in no time. Go on, better get going, I've got to get to work.'

Then I remember driving away, and turning to look back. Oz standing there, his kitbag beside him, watching me go, raising his arm to wave, another rollie in his hand, doing a silly face. His Rizla papers and menthol tips from his rollies left in my car door. Usually I would've tutted and flicked them out, but not this time. Three months, I thought, not long till R&R. I will keep them there.

CHAPTER TWELVE

It is what it is, I thought. He was texting as usual five minutes after we left each other. He knew what he was doing and he would be back with us soon. I said it over and over, like a mantra, but always, lurking just behind it, was the fear that knowing what he was doing wasn't going to be enough. As I was driving, Sam, Hazey and my mum called – all of them were in bits. I didn't have time to text him back.

Within five minutes he was phoning me. 'All right honey? Where are you on the road now? What are you up to? Who you been on the phone to?' I could hear how hard he was trying and I took his cue.

'I'm on the M40, you knob, trying to get to work. Can't wait to see you again.' We talked for ages, throughout his whole drive to Brize Norton.

After I had done my first appointment, he phoned again from Brize Norton and said he'd spoken to Hazey and Andrew and Sam. 'Got to go, hun,' he said. 'Kiss

Laird. Miss you all so much already, this is rrrrubbish! Love you always and forever. I don't know what to give you or say as a Plan B, I'm sorry there isn't one for this.'

'I know. Bye hun. Speak later,' I said. He texted me: 'see you soon.'

Moments before he had to switch off his phone to board the plane, he called Hazey one last time. 'Promise to take care of my family for me, mate,' he said. Hazey promised.

With Oz gone, nothing felt right, or normal. The house felt strange; everything was suddenly flat and silent and empty. No bags thrown in the corner, no empty wine glasses on the table, no towels slung on the bathroom floor. Laird and I both felt it.

I did my best to carry on with life as normal. Took Laird to school, walked Bo, checked on Mum and on Jamie, went to work, did the shopping, cleaned the house, did the laundry – cheerful, practical, functional. But there was a big void in my life and Oz was constantly on my mind. What was he doing? Was he all right? Was he taking his medication, feeling OK? I knew he would be in the transitional phase for the first two or three weeks – acclimatising, training and preparing to go fully operational – and as I watched the news and read the papers, I realised he would be on the front line just in time for Operation Panther's Claw.

Launched at midnight on 19 June, Panther's Claw was the Army's biggest push yet, and was aimed at securing an area the size of the Isle of Wight against the Taliban forces, ahead of the Afghan presidential election which was to be held on 20 August.

Operators like Oz would be vital in clearing the routes and roads of IEDs so that the British Forces could move around more safely and push forward. Suddenly his long wait to go out there made sense to me – he was being held back for this. And if the British push was being stepped up, the Taliban response would escalate too. God only knew what Oz would be dealing with out there.

I watched the casualty figures. By the launch of Panther's Claw, on 19 June, four soldiers had been killed and four had been seriously injured since 1 June, when Oz flew out there – almost all of them as a result of IED explosions while on foot patrol. This number was bound to rise steeply during Panther's Claw.

Then, late in June, when it seemed he had been away and silent for an age, a blue airmail letter – they call them 'blueys' – arrived. I had taken Laird to school and was about to set off to work. I prised it carefully open, anxious not to rip the flimsy paper, and read it over a coffee.

HI HONEY,
    HOPE ALL IS WELL BACK THERE AND YOU ARE HOLDING THE FORT AS YOU ALWAYS DO. FINISHED ALL MY IN THEATRE TRAINING

TODAY SO I AM NOW OFFICIALLY ON LINE.
ONLY ONE PROBLEM, THEY ARE NOT BACK YET.
THEY ARE OUT ON THE GROUND STILL & GET
IN TOMORROW & THEN WE ARE ALL OFF OUT
ON THURSDAY ON A RATHER LARGE
OPERATION – FRONT LINE!! SURE I WILL BE
FINE. LADS ARE BUSY & HAVE BEEN GOBBING
OFF ABOUT ALL THEIR JOBS. SOME EXTREME
LUCK HAS GIFTED THEM & QUITE FRANKLY PUT
THE SHITTERS UP ME, HOWEVER YOU KNOW
ME CANT WAIT TO GET OUT THERE AND GET
STARTED. I HAVE FOUND A LITTLE BLACK HOLE
FOR ALL THE BAD SHIT & A CONCENTRATING
CELL FOR THE TOP TIPS SO I FEEL GOOD &
CONFIDENT. TEAM GOT BLOWN UP THIS
MORNING ABOUT 0100. ONE BLOKE LOST HIS
HEARING, TWO BLOKES GOT FRAGGED FACES +
LOOK LIKE CRAP + ONE LOST BOTH HIS LEGS
ABOVE THE KNEES + ONE ARM + HALF HIS
GENITALS. HE'S STAYING STRONG + HAS MADE
IT THROUGH TO TONIGHT & ON HIS WAY
BACK TO SELLY OAK TONIGHT (NOW). THE
FOUR LADS WERE THAT TEAMS ENGINEER
SEARCHERS FROM OUR GROUP SO MORALE
BETWEEN THE YOUNGSTERS HAS TAKEN A HIT.
HOWEVER WITH NEWS THAT J GOT HIS
HEARING BACK WHEN HE AWOKE & THE
OTHER ARE GOOD, THINGS ARE BETTER

TONIGHT. I LET W DO A DOWNLOAD ON ME SO I SPENT A GOOD HOUR WITH HIM TONIGHT. AFTER HE GOT IT OFF HIS CHEST HE WAS COOL & THEN WE JUST SPUN DITS ABOUT BOMBS. I'M KEEPING A RIGHT OPEN MIND ABOUT ALL OF THIS & JUST WANT TO CRACK ON AND GET MY FIRST FEW JOBS OUT OF THE WAY & GET INTO MY COMFORT ZONE & THEN JUST RULE THE TACTICAL EDGE. I THINK COS IT'S BEEN ON MY MIND FOR SO LONG BEING OUT HERE IT'S NOT PHASING ME. I GOT YOU HONEY AND KNOW YOU ARE UP TO SPOOKY THINGS, CAN FEEL IT!! WILL EXPLAIN WHERE I LIVE WHEN ON BASTION IN ANOTHER LETTER BUT I WON'T BE HERE. DUSTY. ANYWAY, JUST WANTED TO DROP YOU ALL A LINE BEFORE I FUCK OFF INTO THE UNKNOWN FOR DON'T KNOW HOW LONG!! I MISS YOU ALL, ESPECIALLY YOU & JUST HOPE YOU ARE ALL DOING FINE. YOU'RE PROBABLY DOING A LOT BETTER THAN IF I WAS THERE, KNOWING YOU. AT LEAST I'M NOT CLUTTERING UP THE SOFA OR UNDER YOUR FEET ALL THE TIME LOL!! WILL WRITE & PHONE WHEN I GET BACK IN, NOT SURE WHEN THAT WILL BE BUT HOPE-FULLY MY DAYSACK & LAPTOP WILL BE HERE & THEN WE CAN DO SOME OF THAT MSN STUFF. THE INTERNET IS RANDOM & ONLY 250 PEOPLE

CAN GET ON IT AT ONE TIME ON A CAMP WITH 4000 BLOKES OR SO. PLUS I AM NOT GOING TO BE HERE AND ITS ONLY ON IF THERE ARE NO CASUALTIES (OP MINIMISE) AND THERE'S QUITE A LOT OF THEM AT THE MO!!

TAKE CARE HONEY, GIVE LAIRDSTER SOME DAD LOVING

LOVE YOU HONEY & MISS YOUR SEXY BODY ALL OVER MINE, BUMP AND ALL!

HUSBAND XXXXX

The letter made me laugh and cry at the same time. There was so much in it that was typical of Oz. He managed to sound cheerful and upbeat, but he must have felt shocked and deeply upset by what had happened to the young engineers, and especially by Westy's horrific injuries. Yet he hadn't hesitated to be there for his friend Wayne when he needed to offload his anger and grief.

He had written from Camp Bastion, the main British military base in Helmand, and I could hear from his letter that he was preparing himself, mentally, for whatever he would have to face. We had talked often about warriors, about their mental discipline, cool heads, steady hands. We had talked about the picture of a warrior, strong and brave and standing tall. Oz loved that image, it helped him to focus. Reading and re-reading the letter, I thought of him, preparing for the unknown, the dusty tent, the long walk he would take time and time again. And at the same time making light of it all, having a laugh, masking his own doubts and fears, keeping spirits up. To me that was as much a part of being a warrior as courage in battle.

Soon after he wrote that letter, Oz was sent to an area of Helmand known as Babaji. After the initial surge into the area, the British Forces became involved in fierce, close-quarters combat, firefights against Taliban only yards away. The valley floor in that area was littered with IEDs and Oz and his team went through, clearing compound after compound.

In late July another letter arrived.

17-07-09
TO MY GORGEOUS FAMILY XX

HI HONEY – FIRSTLY MISSING YOU ALL VERY MUCH, ESPECIALLY YOU. YOU'VE BEEN ON MY MIND A LOT SINCE I GOT HERE. CAN'T STOP THINKING ABOUT YOU. WE HAVE HAD SOME CRAP TIMES OVER THE PAST FEW MONTHS BUT ALSO SOME REALLY GOOD WHICH STAY FIRMLY IN THE TOP OF MY HEAD YOU'LL BE GLAD TO KNOW. THE CRAP TIMES I PUT DOWN TO THE STRESS WE HAVE BEEN PUT UNDER. WE DON'T EXACTLY HAVE 9–5 JOBS WHERE WE DRIVE 2 MINS TO WORK COME HOME + FULLY

FUNCTION SO I AM CONTENT WE ARE BOTH MOVING FORWARD TOGETHER OUT OF THAT SHIT FOR A HOOFIN FUTURE FOR US AND OUR FAMILY NOT RUNNING AROUND FOR EVERY-ONE ELSE. I LOVE YOU SO MUCH + WANT YOU ALL TO BE HAPPY, NOT STRESSED COS OF ME, BUT HEALTHY AND SETTLED FINALLY ITS MORE THAN YOU, LAIRD + BUMP DESERVE.

I AM GETTING PISSED OFF WITH THIS DAYSACK THING AND WILL LOSE THE PLOT IF I DON'T GET IT BY SUNDAY. WE DEPLOY OUT FOR ANOTHER 2 WEEKS ON THE 2ND PHASE OF THIS OP WHICH HAS ALREADY COST SO MANY LIVES. THIS TIME WE ARE IN WARRIORS (ARMOURED FIGHTING VEHICLES). I WILL BE FINE AS ALWAYS.

HAVE DONE LOADS OF JOBS IN 2 WEEKS (PRESSURE PLATE IEDS, A FIND + EXPLOSIONS). IT'S BEEN INTERESTING AND LEFT SOME INTERESTING IMAGES AND THOUGHTS RUNNING THROUGH MY MIND. MY STONE AND PICTURES OF YOU PROTECT ME + I LEAVE THEM UP WHERE THEY CAN WATCH OVER ME WHEN IN BASTION FOR A COUPLE OF DAYS, OR SAFE WHEN I AM OUT ON THE GROUND. I HAVE ALREADY BEEN LIVING ROUGH FOR WEEKS IN COMPOUNDS WE CLEAR UNDER THE AFGHAN CANOPY THOUSANDS OF MILES

FROM MY WARM GORGEOUS WIFE BUT STARING INTO THE SAME MOON WHICH IS A CONSTANT REMINDER OF HOW LUCKY I AM TO HAVE YOU. I AM PUSHING TO COME BACK AT BANG ON SIX MONTHS. NO ONE IN THIS JOB SHOULD DO MORE AS WE KEEP GETTING REMINDED – STAYING ALIVE IS LIKE A LOTTERY + PATROLLING THE AFGHAN BADLANDS IS PLAYING RUSSIAN ROULETTE WITH YOUR FEET. DEALING WITH BOMBS IS EASY, IT'S THE GETTING SHOT AT WHILST DOING A JOB THAT TENDS TO MAKE ME RUN LIKE FUCK WITH A MAIN CHARGE!! WILL TRY + PHONE BEFORE WE GO OUT ON THIS NEXT OP BUT PHONES ARE A NIGHTMARE.

YOU ARE MY GORGEOUS WIFE, MY SEXY PARTNER AND MY ONE AND ONLY BEST MATE. I MISS YOU ALL SO MUCH AND CAN'T WAIT TO GET BACK + STEER AWAY FROM THE MIND SET I WAS IN BEFORE I LEFT. LOT ON MY MIND. WE HAVE SO MUCH TO DO + NEED TO SORT FOR OUR EMPIRE HONEY –

I AM IN THE GROOVE!! SAY HI TO ALL, TELL THEM THE USUAL: WEATHER'S GOOD, SURF'S UP + BEER IS HOOFIN.

LOVE YOU ALL XXX

HI LAIRDIE MISS YOU, LOTS OF LOVE DADDY OZ X

His humour comforted me. If he could joke, then he was all right. And he had pictures and his special stone I had given him, as a lucky charm and protector.

Three days after Oz wrote that letter, his friend and fellow high-threat operator Captain Dan Shepherd was killed while trying to defuse an IED. Dan was a fellow member of 11 EOD; they had been based at Didcot together and knew one another well.

Dan was twenty-eight and left behind a beautiful, intelligent, strong widow, Kerry. In the thirty-six hours before he died he had cleared thirteen IEDs, while under fire. For this, like Gaz O'Donnell, he was later awarded the George Medal. When I read the citation that spoke of 'thirty-six hours of unbroken activity', I thought about just how exhausted Dan must have been, and how determined, to keep going and keep clearing device after device. The citation also said, 'He was an inspiration to his team; his personal actions directly and demonstrably saved the lives of innumerable Afghans, coalition and British Forces.'

His commanding officer, Lieutenant Colonel Roger Lewis, said, 'Captain Dan Shepherd was an extraordinary officer; composed, compassionate, utterly charming and imbued with a single-minded determination to put others before himself.

'He was incredibly courageous, yet immensely modest about his own stunning achievements. A consummate and technically gifted Ammunition

Technical Officer, Dan understood fully the dangerous nature of his job, yet every day was the first to put his own life on the line.'

Dan had qualified as a high-threat operator in December 2008, just after Oz, and on this tour he dealt with over fifty jobs – each of which would have been made up of many small devices. He was due to come home soon, and to take up a desk job, advising on the management of IEDs.

I learned about Dan's death in a phone call from one of Oz's friends at Didcot. I sat on the sofa, the phone still in my hand, in utter disbelief. Not Dan, I thought. Not Dan, who did the same job as Oz, with the same easy charm. For days I walked around sick. First Gaz, now Dan. They couldn't afford to lose men like that.

I knew that losing Dan would have hit Oz very hard, but this time he couldn't draw the curtains and retreat into grief; he was on active service and had to keep going. He spoke of it very little, but I'm sure he thought of Dan a great deal over the following weeks, as time after time he did what Dan had done, making the 'lonely walk' out to a bomb.

It was only later that I learned that Oz had written to Dan's family, and had said,

I THINK IT'S IMPORTANT TO LET YOU KNOW THIS. HE WILL NEVER BE FORGOTTEN. AS I AM SURE YOU ARE AWARE, IT'S BEEN AN UNFOR-

GIVING SUMMER AND UNFORTUNATELY DAN
HAS PAID THE ULTIMATE PRICE.

I'M CURRENTLY IN OPERATION WHERE DAN
PASSED AND THERE WAS NOT A MAN IN HIS
BATTLE GROUP THAT DIDN'T KNOW HIM AND
HIS WORK. HE WAS EXCEPTIONAL, SAVING
LIVES DAILY IN THE HARSHEST CONDITIONS.

Dan was the 187th soldier to die in Afghanistan. That month, July 2009, was the bloodiest since the war began. In June there were 4 deaths. In July there were 22, and 94 soldiers were injured, 19 of them very seriously – over double the number of casualties there had been in June. Panther's Claw was succeeding in its objectives, but at a desperate cost.

One evening the house phone went.

'Hello gorgeous wife.'

'Alllrrriiight, hun!' I said, smiling. 'Where are you?'

'We're in a compound,' he said. 'I've done my bit, done a few jobs, waiting to get airlifted out now.' It was so nice to have contact and hear his voice. We just talked normally about my day, Laird, admin about his mobile phone contract, news about addresses they gave us in Winchester and what to pack up. We were moving quarters again, closer to Winchester this time, and school.

I could hear war, guns, the crash of bullets, voices shouting. And there was Oz in the middle of it, propped against a mud wall, me sitting on the floor in our hall cross-legged having a chat.

'Honey, I'm aware you think it's cool to ring me now but I can hear all that behind you! Shouldn't you get under cover?'

'I'm fine, just have to wait it out for a bit. Tell me what else is new.'

He talked for the next hour. Catching up on news, telling me a bit about life there, wanting to know about Bo, Mum, and how I was.

'Is it OK for you to use the phone all this time?' I asked.

'Yeah, it's fine. One of the perks of having a sat phone, a gorgeous wife, and no one to tell me not to. I miss you so, so much.'

It turned out that he was calling on the satellite phone the team carried with them. While there was a real shortage of phones in the base camps, out in the field, as team leader, Oz could use the satellite phone whenever he wanted.

He was cool and cheerful. 'Yeah, looks like we're winning this one. That's good, I'm very bored here, waiting to get helloed out, been here a couple of days, be on our way soon. Love you hun.' And he was gone. But after that he called several times, usually when they were stuck somewhere, often with fighting going on in the background, and we often talked for an hour, sometimes two. I tried to keep the landline clear, just in case. Each time he called it was so good to hear his voice. He didn't want to talk about what he was doing, he wanted to know about ordinary things. What we were doing in the school holidays, how the pregnancy was going, had I seen Sam and Hazey, and so on. As if he was on a holiday instead of in the middle of a war.

In the end I'd say, 'I need to work,' and he'd say, 'Oh, sorry, wife, may you have lots of switches [dispense switches]. Have a lovely day, I'll phone you later.'

I kept in contact with Oz's family, left voicemails to say if he'd called. His brother Torben and his mum, Barbara, hadn't seen him in the months before he left, but liked to hear that he was OK.

Oz and his team of twelve often travelled on foot, with their equipment loaded on to quads if the terrain allowed. They had ladders for climbing compound walls and heavy kit to move. They called themselves Team Rainbow, and Oz told a journalist who asked, 'We named ourselves after Zippy, Bungle and George. It was morale. When we're out on a job, people always ask us why we're called Team Rainbow. We could joke about it. Our team mascot is a duck. We call him Corporal Quackers.'

What he didn't say to the journalist was that they also, unofficially, called it Team Toilet Duck, because of Oz's IBS flare-ups.

Stress was a factor that worsened the condition, so I did my best to keep Oz's spirits up, sending him letters and pictures Laird had drawn, food parcels (no chocolate as it melts into a glob before they get it) and a new knife when his old one went blunt.

His friends kept in touch too. Hazey, who had been to Iraq and knew just how much post meant out in the field, sent him a Jiffy bag full of sweets every week. He'd go out and buy packets of dolly mixtures, liquorice allsorts, toffees and bonbons and post them off. 'I'm not much of a one for long letters,' Hazey told me. 'But I want him to know I'm thinking of him. Post is everything when you're out there, and there's always some poor lad who doesn't get any. The others share what they get with him, but it's not the same, you need your own post, and lots of it.'

Sam wrote to Oz, and in early August Oz wrote back.

06/08/09
HI SAM,
     ITS A FEW DAYS TO YOU BOTH MOVING SO HOPE YOU GET THIS AND I APOLOGISE FOR NOT REPLYING SOONER. ITS BEEN MAD HERE. SORRY TO HEAR YOU DIDN'T GET INTO THE MOD POLICE YOU'RE NOT MISSING MUCH AND I'M SURE YOU CAN DO MUCH BETTER SAM. IT ALREADY SOUNDS LIKE YOU HAVE GOOD PLANS UP YOUR SLEEVE & BY THE TIME I GET BACK YOU WOULD I IMAGINE BE WELL INTO BUSINESS WITH SERGE.

Christina Schmid

I CAN'T EVEN BEGIN TO EXPLAIN WHAT IT'S
LIKE OUT HERE, I GOT A GOOD BATTLE
HAPPENING ON MY FIRST DAY HERE, WE ARE
OUT ON THE GROUND PERMANENTLY & NOT
IN BASTION SO IT IS KINETIC 99% OF THE TIME.
I AM IN SANGIN AT THE MOMENT, HAVING
COMPLETED OP PANTHER'S CLAW. WE LOST A
FEW PEOPLE LAST MONTH + A V GOOD MATE.
A LOT OF CASUALTIES TOO. HERE IN SANGIN I
AM NOW REGARDED AS A HIGH-VALUE
TARGET SO EVERY TIME I GO OUT ON A JOB ME
+ MY LADS END UP IN A MASSIVE FIREFIGHT.
GOD KNOWS BUT THEY CAN'T SHOOT
STRAIGHT. ANYWAY IF GETTING BLOWN UP,
SHOT AT ETC ETC IS YOUR THING THEN THIS IS
THE PLACE. FOR ME THOUGH IT'S NOT FUNNY
ANYMORE. IT IS AT THE TIME BUT WHEN YOU
THINK ABOUT IT EVERY TIME YOU ARE OUT WE
ARE AN RPG MAGNET. WE'VE BEEN BLOWN UP,
SHOT AT, DEALT WITH HARROWING
CASUALTIES. I'VE EXPLOITED MORE THAN
ENOUGH EXPLOSION SCENES FINDING ALL
SORTS OF BITS + BOBS. I SUPPOSE WHAT I AM
TRYING TO SAY IS ALL I THINK ABOUT IS
CHRISSY + LAIRD + OUR FUTURE TOGETHER.
OUT HERE IS SURVIVAL + I NEED TO GET HOME
IN 4 MONTHS + FULFIL MINE & CHRISSIE'S
OBJECTIVES. ANYWAY, WILL STOP BORING

YOU NOW. MISS YOU + MARK + REALLY GAGGING TO SEE YOU ALL SOON AND GET BACK TO NORMAL LIFE. I HOPE YOUR MOVE GOES WELL + YOU AND SERGE SORT THE BUSINESS OUT. MISSING YOU BOTH LOADS. WILL WRITE AGAIN.

OZ X

The letter sounded so different to his early letters. The humour had gone, and there was an urgency in his tone that was new. The realisation that he was a high-value target made my blood freeze. It was one of the reasons the high-threat operators didn't wear the heavy bomb-disposal suits. The heat would have made it pretty well impossible anyway, but in addition the suits would have marked them out as easy targets for enemy snipers.

I worried, too, about the 'bits and bobs' Oz found at explosion scenes. He didn't just mean bomb components, or the letters, keepsakes and good-luck charms that operators tucked into their body armour, he meant body parts. Limbs lying in the dust, boots with feet still in them dangling from trees, faces sliced clean off by chinstraps; a bloody catalogue of death that had to be painstakingly collected and then searched for traces of explosive.

It was a scene straight from the depths of hell and I wondered how, if he made it home, Oz would ever find sanity again.

CHAPTER THIRTEEN

With Oz gone I felt very cut off living in the quarters in Tidworth, so I was pleased to move. Oz pinged around so much that we didn't have to stay tied to one particular base, as long as he was within an hour or so of Didcot, London and the South Coast, where he regularly went to top up his training. I started packing to move to Winchester.

I did a box a night, ready for the move. One evening, feeling dog-tired after working all day, walking Bo, doing the school run which was a couple of hours a day in itself and having next-door's kids for tea, I started on the garage. It was kit, so the boxes were extremely heavy, but I wanted to get it done. I stopped for a break and made myself a cup of tea as I felt overcome all of a sudden. As I put the kettle down I felt a surge of pain that left me doubled over. I crawled to the sofa and lay down, but I knew what was happening, I'd been here before. I was so angry with myself.

All I could think, through the long, dark night that followed, as I felt my baby slipping away, was, How am I going to tell Oz? He had already had to deal with so much loss.

I didn't call anyone that night. I couldn't face having to get my parents up, then rousing Laird. They would all have been alarmed and worried and I didn't want the drama of going off in an ambulance and having to deal with hospital staff. So I stayed quietly on my own, and waited. Sorted myself out and did the school run – rescheduled my appointments.

By morning the pain had subsided and I knew it was all over. I called my doctor, who came straight out. He wanted me to go to hospital, and was concerned that I hadn't called earlier, but I told him I'd rather not be admitted unless I absolutely had to.

Physically I recovered fast, but emotionally it was a painful loss. I wrote to tell Oz, then chucked the letter. It wasn't what he needed out there. He phoned. He was sad when I told him, probably much sadder than he admitted to, but he was also practical and calm. 'We'll get over it, honey,' he said. 'We've already got so much, we've got Laird, I just need to come back and be with you and we'll be fine.' He was right, there was nothing more we could do. If we were lucky, there would be other chances. The conversation reminded me that Oz had not yet had a date through for his R&R leave. They are supposed to get two weeks in six months, or one week in four months, otherwise desensitisation sets in.

I really needed him with me, no one else. In fact, when you are in that scenario, you feel even more alone and upset when you have the wrong people around you. The weeks passed and autopilot was the only way I could move forward.

Days later I moved into the new house, which was in Harestock, just outside Winchester.

It was good to be nearer my parents and Laird's school, but I hated the house and the location. We were in army surplus housing again, on a council estate, with empty houses on either side of us and a nice but quiet Gurkha family three doors down. The house was characterless and bleak, I didn't know anyone on the estate, we were miles from any open spaces or woods and I felt pretty rubbish.

I'm sure it all felt much harder because Oz wasn't there with us. Laird and I had moved on our own and I was still grieving for the baby. I didn't have the strength or the will to decorate the house and try to make it more like home as we had in Tidworth. As Oz asked, I left a lot of our things in their packing cases and just unpacked the basics, comforting myself with the thought that when Oz got back we would move again.

I would have moved back into Jasmine Cottage, but it was under offer and the sale was due to complete in early November. I was sad at the thought of saying goodbye to the cottage, but it would give us a good deposit for a new house in Cornwall. I started looking at possible properties online, sending Oz links to anything I liked the look of. When he got a chance he would email back full of excitement, 'Honey, I love that one, don't like that one, bin it, bail on that one . . . can you do a recce on that?'

Twice Laird and I drove down to Cornwall to look at houses in Truro that we liked the look of and we whittled it down to two in Old Kea, an area just outside Truro on the right side for schools that Oz liked. For me and for Oz it helped to think about the future. This was something we could look forward to and get enthusiastic about, when so much else was painful and difficult.

I kept the landline in the new house free, only giving the number to a handful of our closest friends. Oz was phoning whenever he could, and I couldn't bear the thought of him trying to get through on a busy line.

I was still monitoring what was happening in Afghanistan. I didn't watch much TV, just listened to Radio Four in the car, and also read defence news online. IED attacks that year had increased by 120 per cent over 2008, a record for the war so far, and the majority of deaths were as a result of these cruel, hidden, inhuman devices.

In response, the then prime minister, Gordon Brown, announced at the end of August that another 200 extra anti-IED specialists would be deployed in the autumn. There would also be more unmanned surveillance aircraft and better-protected vehicles, all these measures to be paid for out of government reserves, over and above the defence budget.

I laughed to myself; maybe Oz would get some R&R! Or a day when he wasn't on ten minutes' notice to move. The news gave the impression that there would be 200 more people doing Oz's job, but that was a long way from the truth. These 'specialists' were trained to use a Vallon. They were simply men on the ground with metal detectors. It would take a long time to provide extra high-threat operators like Oz, because that involved years of training. I felt the public were being deceived so I pinged the info to Oz in an email. Then sent an email and a letter off internally.

Several people said to me, 'Oh, that's good, isn't it, Oz will be able to ease off a bit,' but of course the opposite was true. Since Dan's death there were even fewer high-threat operators trying to deal with the vast numbers of IEDs.

I was so incensed that I sent an email to the Ministry of Defence to say that as they were sending all these extra people out, did this mean my husband could come home for a rest break sooner than expected? It caused ripples which reached Oz. He phoned me and said, 'What have you been saying?' I told him and he laughed. 'Well done, honey,' he said. 'Love that – you

215

won't change anything though. Harmony guidelines are a joke!' he said.

Harmony guidelines are the rules that are in place to guarantee troops rest between tours of duty.

Oz was operating in what was called the Green Zone, the Helmand River valley, green because it is fertile, though far from safe. It is a landscape of fields and compounds; small settlements surrounded by high mud walls, the mud baked in the sun until it is as tough as concrete. Crisscrossing the valley are the footpaths and alleyways where the Taliban lay their IEDs, directing soldiers towards them by blocking alternative routes with debris, or luring them forward with scouts – men, or sometimes children, who beckon to soldiers, or offer to show them the way. Many of the British deaths had occurred along these paths.

In August Oz was involved in clearing a vital artery known as the Pharmacy Road. This leads east from Sangin district centre to Wishtan, a forward operating base which was so littered with IEDs that it was lethally dangerous and impassable. Oz was attached to the 2 Rifles that were the battlegroup on the ground at the time. Several soldiers had already died or lost limbs there, and Wishtan had become virtually cut off. Three attempts to clear the Pharmacy Road and get supplies through to Wishtan had failed and had led to more death and serious injury.

This was the challenge Oz faced on the day he set out

(*Right*) Oz and Rob Fealey playing with the Scrabble set I had given him for his birthday. You can see all around them the supplies that people had sent to keep spirits up.

(*Below*) This picture is typical of the empty compounds that Oz and others would sleep in when they were out on the ground.

(*Above*) I think this picture really captures the terrain that Oz and his team were operating in. I've always thought it looked like a moonscape. They were working in 50 degree heat, often with less than two litres of water. In the background you can see someone standing in the only patch of shade.

(*Above and left*) Pictures taken during the infamous clearing of Pharmacy Road in Sangin, a clearance that took over twenty-four hours and that Oz would be awarded his GC for.

(*Below*) This photo was taken by David Gill of Oz sat in the place he would smoke and drink coffee.

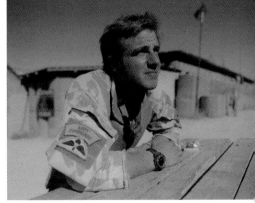

(*Left*) Oz always said that this picture showed him looking grown-up and at his physical peak. This was taken around the time he had made the decision that he wanted out of the Armed Forces. Hazy has the boots that Oz is wearing here after buying them at the kit sale.

(*Above*) Taken in early 2009 of Oz 'digging out' a device.

(*Left*) I love this picture of Oz, but to me he seems to be too thin and not the same man he was at the beginning of the tour.

Oz's teams. (*Above*) Team Rainbow and (*below*) Team Toilet Duck (Corporal Quackers an be seen in the front of the picture!) Rob Nealey (back row, right) made sure that Oz's things were returned to me the way Oz had asked, and explained what had happened.

(*Above*) Wootton Bassett, 5 November 2009, Oz's repatriation.
Clapping wasn't something I had planned, or even thought about,
it was spontaneous. My way of saying publicly, 'I'm so proud of you'.

(*Left*) I felt overwhelmed by enormous pride receiving Oz's George Cross from the Queen, and at the same time by deep sadness that he could not collect it himself.

ght) This was taken
he launch of the
x Fund at the
use of Commons.
e fund has been set
to help support
nb-disposal experts
their families.
low) The Goodwood
tival was my first
cial engagement
Tickets for Troops,
ntastic charity that
n a patron of.

(*Above*) Meeting with David Cameron at International Women's Day in March 2011.
It was coming up to a year since he had promised to make the military covenant
legally binding, and I was questioning him about it. I have been told that I look
very relaxed and that he looks quite defensive in this picture.

to clear the Pharmacy Road, which is lined along both sides by compounds. He and his team set out, early one morning, from Forward Operating Base Jackson, in Sangin. As his men moved along the road searching for IEDs, flanked by riflemen providing cover, they came to a military digger blocking the road, the ground around it peppered by IEDs.

Oz cleared them, painstakingly, one by one, until the digger could be reached and hauled off the road, through a hole blown into the side of a compound wall. He and the team then carried on up the road to Wishtan, searching out the devices planted every few yards, so that Oz could defuse them.

He worked without stopping for eleven hours, with only a couple of litres of water and in fifty-degree heat and made it all the way to Wishtan, clearing the route so that the Pharmacy Road could once again be used to transfer men and supplies back and forth.

It was a superhuman effort. And throughout the time that he worked that stretch, Oz was aware that he was probably being watched from behind the compound walls, and could be targeted by Taliban snipers at any time. This was the extra hazard that meant he had to work on each device as quickly as possible.

Not only that, but many of the devices would be attached to a command wire leading to a detonator which could be triggered by someone watching him. Many times, when working on IEDs, Oz found command wires and cut them, but he knew it was always possible that a wire could be hidden underground and impossible to detect. He once said to me, 'I deal with every device as though you and Laird are on the end of it. That's how I keep my focus.'

In the twenty-four hours following Pharmacy Road, Oz cleared a further thirty-one devices. He was highly regarded as an operator. This was vital for two reasons. Firstly to preserve Afghan homes and communities. Though people could be moved away, a detonation would have destroyed compound walls and homes inside them. Lost homes are not easily rebuilt in a land so desperately poor, and damaged communities would lead to an increase in hostility. But there was another reason – all the parts of disassembled bombs were carefully collected, as forensic evidence, so that those who made and planted the bombs could be identified. It wasn't enough to make them safe – the aim was to identify and capture the people who were manufacturing them and laying them.

It was in late August that Oz met journalist Miles Amoore, who got to know him well and who wrote a long and brilliant article which appeared in the *Sunday Times* on 8 November 2009. It was important to me because Miles really saw what was happening. He talked to Oz about it, he quoted Oz in his story, and reading those quotes I could hear Oz's voice:

'Oz' Schmid was an unusual soldier, not just because
of the lonely and terribly dangerous job he did but
also because of his outlook on soldiering itself. A
former army cook, he volunteered to learn bomb
disposal skills — 'no different from cooking, really' —
and set about protecting people rather than killing
them . . .

I first met him during the Taliban's brutally
successful bombing campaign over the past summer. My
photographer, David Gill, and I were sitting at a
wooden table on the bank of the canal that runs
through the British Army's forward operating base
Jackson in Sangin. An easy-going, fast-talking soldier
with a mop of blond hair and an infectious smile
casually plonked himself down next to us.

He wanted to know what we did. We said we were
freelances. He thought we were bold yet foolish coming
to Helmand without a salary. Then we found out he
defused bombs for a living.

'I once looked into getting life insurance,' he said
with a wry smile. 'It would have cost me £350,000.'
We laughed and told him we couldn't afford any either.
For the next two weeks we'd bump into him in the mess
tent and he'd sit and share a joke over another staple
meal of gravy-covered noodles . . .

'What's it like doing my job? It's like when I used to
cook. You could always get burnt. It's like any other job.
It's the same as stacking shelves in Tesco. You could slip

on milk and break your leg,' he said, his eyes sparkling as he spoke . . .

'I suppose, thinking about it, I've been given a skill or been taught a skill and — well, I don't know, I'm going to sound a bit chav really — at the end of the day it saves lives, it's not killing.

'I go home, and people go, "How many f****** Taliban have you killed?" Well, it's not really about that. It's more about how many lives I've saved, I think . . .

'Every device is different in its own little way . . . you have got to find exactly what it is and come up with the best way of dealing with that, so your mind is constantly focused on that . . .

'My heart's not racing at all when I go in. No, that's not true, there are some points when it does. There's a lot of apprehension, a lot of adrenaline going through you, but it's important to appear calm.

'The guys look at you, they draw strength from you. For the infantry commander on the ground it's a hell of a weight off their shoulders when you come in . . .

'I don't really think about the enemy. There have been a couple of piss-take jobs, though, where they are trying to have a bit of a joke. I found a dollar on top of a pressure plate in Nad-e 'Ali the other week.' . . .

I once asked Oz whether he thought he would get a medal for the work he'd done. 'A friend e-mailed me to *say "you did well" after the Pharmacy Road operation but I just want to come home with my legs.'*

That was something Oz often used to say. That he didn't want a medal, he just wanted to come home with his legs. He wasn't joking. He had witnessed the horror of men who had lost their legs too many times.

September came and with it the new school term. Laird was moving up from Reception to Year One and he felt very grown-up and excited. He knew his dad was due back at the end of half-term, on Sunday 1 November, and he crossed off the days on the chart we had made on his wall. He wanted Oz to be home in time for his birthday. Oz had told me over the phone that he wanted to pay for a party for Laird, a really big one, whatever Laird wanted. I told Laird, who was very excited. 'Will Daddy be there?' he asked. 'I hope so sweetie,' I told him.

In late September another letter arrived.

16/9/09
HI GORGEOUS WIFE,
 WELL WE ARE NOW HALFWAY THROUGH THIS. I AM SO PROUD OF WHAT YOU HAVE DONE + ACHIEVED SINCE I WENT AWAY. IT IS REALLY POSITIVE AND ALREADY IS A MASSIVE STEPPING STONE TO OUR GREAT FUTURE TOGETHER. THANK YOU. ALL YOU DO AND

HAVE DONE + TRULY MEANS WHAT A TOP WIFE YOU ARE. THANK YOU FOR BEING YOU. I HAVE GOT ALL THE SPOOKY THINGS YOU HAVE SENT ME SITTING IN MY BODY ARMOUR + DAY SACK SO YOU ARE ALWAYS WATCHING OVER ME. I FEEL THAT ENERGY AROUND ME. ITS GOOD. I AM GLAD WE HAVE SOLD THE HOUSE (ACCEPTED OFFER) THAT OPENS SO MANY DOORS FOR US. WE DON'T NEED TO RUSH THROUGH BUT NEED TO THROW EVERYTHING INTO IT SO WE NEED TO GET IT RIGHT, IE A PLACE WE CAN BUILD ON, EVERY COUPLE OF YEARS PUT A WEDGE OF CASH INTO IT, EXTEND IT, MAKE IT HOW WE WANT IT WITH GOOD QUALITY FIXTURES, FITTINGS + APPLIANCES AND MY GORGEOUS FAMILY. BEEN THINKING ABOUT IT LOADS.

LAIRD'S FUTURE IS KEY + THAT WILL COME THROUGH WHEN WE GET HIM IN SURROUNDINGS THAT WE BOTH KNOW WILL WORK FOR HIM. IT IS ALL GOING TO HAPPEN AND THE CREDIT LIES WITH YOU. YOU HAVE WORKED SO HARD TO GET IT RIGHT FOR HIM, HE WILL APRECIATE THAT FOREVER. TRELISKE SCHOOL I LIKE IDEA OF TOO BEEN THINKING AND RECOMMEND + THEN TRURO SCHOOL.

TODAY I HAVE 45 DAYS LEFT TILL R+R SO ON

THE BACK IS SOMETHING YOU CAN USE TO WATCH THE DAYS FLY. TAKE IT OUT EVERY FEW DAYS + CROSS THEM. BY THE TIME YOU GET THIS YOU WILL ALREADY HAVE A FEW TO CROSS OFF. I CAN'T WAIT TO SEE YOU HONEY. I REALLY NEED TO BE CUDDLED UP WITH YOU KNOWING YOU ARE HAPPY + CONTENT. I CAN ONLY FEEL THAT WHEN I HAVE BEEN BACK WITH YOU FOR A BIT YOU CAN FEEL MY INTENTIONS FOR REAL. I HOPE YOU GET IT + I KNOW YOU WILL. NOT JUST SAYING THIS STUFF COS I AM OUT HERE. THE MOST IMPORTANT THING IS I TRULY LOVE YOU WITH ALL MY HEART & WANT THE BEST FOR YOU ALL.
LOVE YOU SO MUCH BEAUTIFUL WIFE. XXXX

This is what he wrote on the back of the letter:

46 45 44 43 42 41 40 39 38 37 36 35 34 33 32 31 30 29 28 27 26 25 24 23 22 21 20 19 18 17 16 15 14 13 12 11 10 9 8 7 6 5 4 3 2 1
XXXX HUG + BIG WET KISS XX

His letter was as loving and warm as ever but, as with the letter to Sam, there was none of the humour and enthusiasm of his earlier letters. The cheery 'I'll be fine' was missing. Instead he sounded weary and desperately in need of rest. He was on a constant ten-minute notice period to go out to bombs, and must have been exhausted. No wonder he was counting the days.

CHAPTER FOURTEEN

As September arrived it began to feel as though the end was in sight. Oz was coming home in just over a month – he would be back on Sunday 1 November. By then he would have been gone for five painfully long months.

On 14 September Oz phoned me. He told me that he had fainted, whilst on a parade at a repatriation ceremony, from exhaustion. I was shocked when I heard. He made light of it, but I knew he was seriously compromised. Oz didn't physically break. Ever. For him to show physical signs of fatigue he must have been absolutely mentally and spiritually shattered. I asked him if he'd had enough rest afterwards, and proper food. 'Yeah, well no, it's OK, I'm OK,' he said. But he sounded weary and I was scared.

Between the day Oz left and the end of September there were fifty-three more deaths. All but seven of them, most of whom died in battle, were caused by explosions. At one point, in July, eight men died in twenty-four hours, five of them from the 2nd Battalion the Rifles, in two separate blasts on the same day, as they were on foot patrol close to Sangin.

Foreign Secretary David Milliband said, 'Afghanistan cannot again become an incubator for terrorism.' Opposition leader David Cameron said they were 'fighting to prevent terrorism on the streets of Britain', and Britain's Chief of Defence Staff Sir Jock Stirrup warned of more casualties to come.

As Oz had asked me to, I went to as many repatriations as I could manage, several of them for two or more of those who had died. Each of them heartbreaking. And every time, as I stood in Wootton Bassett and paid my respects, I sent Oz a silent message.

'Please don't make me stand on the other side of the street, honey. Keep going. Grizz through it. Get home.'

I took some comfort from thinking that without Oz defusing device after device, there would have been many more deaths, both military and civilian.

It had been a busy weekend, but no more than usual. I walked miles with Laird and Bo, visited my parents, shopped, cleaned and sorted out our stuff for the coming week. On Sunday Oz rang. He sounded tired, but cheerful. 'Full moon tonight, hun, do your thing, say something positive for me?' he asked me. 'It's kept me going – I will be looking at it thinking of you all too.'

'Course I will,' I told him.

That evening, as usual, I tucked Laird into bed and read him a story. Normally I would then go downstairs to read, call friends or watch TV. I'm a night person, I often stay up very late and have buckets of energy, I'm a powerhouse and can keep going past most people. But that night, without even consciously thinking that I was tired, I fell asleep on Laird's bed.

I woke at around 4 a.m., disoriented to find I was fully clothed and Laird was asleep on me, in his pyjamas. As the realisation dawned that I had missed doing the wish for Oz, I ran to the window. The moon had disappeared, and I felt distraught.

'Oh my God, what have I done?' I whispered. 'I've done it every month. Why now?' I told myself it didn't matter, that it was just a bit of a silly tradition, that I should forget it. But I couldn't.

Every phone call with Oz those last few times was painful. He sounded uneasy, and I felt miserable.

Days later, in mid-October, Afghan soldiers spotted a massive bomb in the Sangin bazaar close to seven large cans of diesel. About forty civilians were in the area at the time, all of them within range of the bomb. The terrified soldiers did not alert the civilians or evacuate the area, afraid the Taliban were watching and were only holding fire against them because the civilians were there.

It was Oz who got the call. He went in, defused the device and saved all of them. Just another day's work.

Soon after this, Andrew received a letter from Oz that was chilling. He said that he knew he was a marked man, one of the Taliban's prime targets, and that he feared it was just a matter of time till they got him. He spoke of his respect for them, said they were clever, and that it was essentially a game of wits. But they only needed to be lucky once, whereas he needed to be lucky every time. He wrote that he was missing me and Laird more than anything.

Everyone Oz wrote to noticed that his letters were less jokey and upbeat, more dispirited and weary. To some extent this wasn't surprising: what man at war for several months wouldn't feel more dispirited than when he began? But everyone who loved Oz felt worried about him, his exhaustion, the pressure on him, and the daily confrontation with huge risks.

There was a desperate shortage of high-threat operators in Afghanistan at that time. Gaz and Dan Shepherd had died, and in October Oz's close friend Dan Read, another high-threat ATO, was injured in a blast and sent home. Oz and Dan were the same age, and had trained together, and they were both with 11 EOD. Dan had grown up in Kent, but he lived in Cornwall, where his wife Lorraine was a serving police officer, so he and Oz shared a love of Cornwall too. Dan was a lovely guy and Oz was hugely relieved that Dan's injuries weren't life-threatening, and that he would recover, but it was another man down. Of their small group of high-threat ATO friends, that left Oz and another friend, Ken Bellringer, still working out there, and Oz knew they were both key targets and both under enormous pressure.

In one phone call he told me that a lot of the men were being sick before going out to fight, knowing how high the chances were of being shot or injured. Oz did his best to keep morale up, chivvying them along with, 'Come on fellas, we can do this, let's go.'

Soon after the letter to Andrew, another letter arrived. This one was addressed to Master Laird + Bo Schmid and under 'sender' he had written 'SSgt "Dad" Schmid'.

HELLO LAIRDY

HOW ARE YOU?? I HAVE HEARD FROM MUMMY YOU HAVE BEEN SUCH A GOOD BOY AT SCHOOL AND AT HOME. I AM SO PROUD OF YOU SON AND WILL TREAT YOU TO SOMETHING REALLY GOOD ON R+R (WHEN I COME HOME) SO YOU HAVE A THINK WHAT YOU WOULD REALLY LIKE TO DO AND WE WILL DO IT. ALSO IT IS YOUR BIG '6' BIRTHDAY, PLEASE WRITE TO ME TO TELL ME WHAT YOU WOULD LIKE. I AM SO PROUD OF YOU LEARNING REALLY HARD AT SCHOOL. YOU ARE SUCH A GOOD BOY LAIRD.

LIFE OUT HERE IS GOOD LAIRD. THE PEOPLE OVER HERE WILL HOPEFULLY HAVE A BETTER

LIFE BECAUSE WE ARE HERE, SO THE PLACE GETS BETTER ALL THE TIME.

RIGHT, GOT TO GO TO WORK. I REALLY MISS YOU LAIRD AND CAN ONLY SAY THANK YOU FOR LOOKING AFTER MUM. I LOVE YOU LOTS.

BO,

SIT. LISTEN IN. HEARD YOU HAVE BEEN A GOOD BOY. DON'T BELIEVE IT, HOWEVER, YOUR TREAT WILL BE ME WALKING YOU EARLY IN THE MORNINGS WHEN I GET BACK + THEY WILL BE LONG ONES. IF YOU ARE GOOD I HAVE SOME LEFT OVER JERKY YOU MIGHT LIKE!!

MISS YOU BO. XX

Oz had put all his fears and worries aside to write a beautiful letter to Laird, who was thrilled to have a letter of his own, and insisted on reading Bo his message. 'What would you like for your birthday?' I asked Laird. 'I want to see Daddy,' he said. 'I want to have my birthday with him.'

I began to believe that his wish would come true. I knew Oz was weary and that it must all be taking a terrible toll on him. But he had made it this far; despite all his fears and doubts he had been unbelievably brave and had endured everything that came at him. All he had to do was keep going, and he would be home.

I began to feel more confident. I even planned a

party, ringing our closest friends and inviting them for the weekend after Oz got back. I knew he'd need a few days to rest and get used to being home, but then he'd want to see his friends.

Two days before he was due to leave Afghanistan for home, Oz called again. As usual, I had kept the landline clear, and when it rang I ran to pick up the receiver.

I could hear immediately that he was low. He had been out of contact for several days, and he sounded shattered.

'I feel like shit,' he said. 'Honey, I just feel really bad, I've got this odd feeling, like dread, I don't feel safe, it's bad. Have you got it too?'

I had. In the pit of my stomach I felt a lurch as he spoke. I had been uneasy, anxious, and had a feeling of dread, but I didn't want to say that.

'You're tired,' I said. 'It's OK, you'll be back soon. Do what you did the last few months in the next couple of days, hun. You got forty-eight hours left, that's all.'

'Honey, I'm mentally and spiritually hammered, I'm hanging out. I've been away too long, worked too much, and if it's too much for me it's too much for anyone. But I can't let it show. I've got to keep positive and strong, they've got to trust me. If anything happens to me, I don't want them to blame themselves, I've seen that too often.'

Oz used the expression 'hanging out a bootneck' to tell me how tired and desperate he felt. It means he's had it, finished, can't go on and needs help. It's an admission soldiers wouldn't make until they feel desperate, one they try never to make, and I was truly alarmed.

Oz was still talking. 'If anything happens, those lads will always think, what have I done? They'll think they could have done something differently. But it's nothing to do with them. If I fuck up now it's not their fault. If something happens you've got to let them know that it wasn't their fault. We're getting dicked here.' That meant being targeted and patterned.

His team were the men – some little more than boys – whose job it was to support him. They spent almost all of their time together and I knew how strong the bond was, and how responsible Oz felt for them. But the way he was talking now frightened me. And he hadn't finished.

'There's another thing. If I don't make it, I want you to stand there at the side of the road and be proud of me. Hold your head up, show them all you're proud of what we did. If those lads see you looking sad they'll feel worse. Don't let me down or let insurgents get the satisfaction of seeing you in bits too.'

I promised him, and then told him I wouldn't need to stand at the side of the road because it would all be fine.

'I don't think it will,' he said. 'And I don't believe you, don't lie to me, you feel it too, don't you?'

We never could hide anything from one another.

'Maybe it's because it's your last forty-eight hours, you know. You just have to get through this last bit, then you're free.'

'I wish you could come and get me,' he said. 'I need you. Just come and get me now, honey.'

'I wish I could,' I said, tears running down my face. 'But I can't. You've got to stop talking like this, you're just tired. You can push for forty-eight hours.'

'I need to speak to Laird,' he said.

The mum in me kicked in. 'Don't speak to him now, honey, you're too down, he'll pick it up. Take ten minutes, have a little chat with yourself first.'

He agreed and, as he rang back, Laird came down from his room and said, 'Mummy, that's Daddy, I know he wants to talk to me.'

'I'm OK, I'm calm now,' Oz said when I picked up.

I handed Laird the phone and he went upstairs and they talked for about ten minutes.

When Laird gave the phone back, Oz said, 'I'm calm, honey, but I can't help how I feel. I don't think I'm coming back, cos I'm cuffing it now. I'm drained – it's hard to explain.'

I tried to lift his spirits. 'You know you'll probably just bang your arm getting on that helicopter to go back to base.'

He was quiet for a moment. 'Honey, give me the pep talk.'

I took a deep breath. 'OK, you've done it before, you

233

can do it again, you've done it every day now for five months, you can do it; you have so you can. You can get through this and do what you need to do and when you do I'll be waiting for you, loving you and we're going to be in a happy new place. I am so proud of you. I look at the men I see day in day out and there isn't anyone above you. Your strength and loyalty are something you rarely see any more in men or people. You are unique and I will never leave you or let you down. You can be a house husband when you come home – you have done your bit for humanity ten times over.'

'Thanks honey. I've got to go. I love you.'

'Love you so much too, hun.'

That night I barely slept, and the next day I felt dreadful. I had never heard Oz sound so low and it had shocked me. I kept the phone beside me all evening, hoping he'd ring. I wanted to ring him, but I couldn't, so that night I emailed – 'please email me. Don't go out on the ground tomorrow, cut the last day, don't do it.'

He never got it.

That night I slept fitfully, and then I dreamed that Gaz O'Donnell was standing in front of me. 'Don't worry, Chris, I'm here to get him when he comes over,' he said, 'I'll hold him. I won't let go.'

'What are you on about?' I said. 'You've got no arms.'

Gaz just looked at me and smiled.

The next morning, Saturday 31 October, I woke at

6.30 a.m. with a feeling I'd never had before. It was as powerful as thunder. I felt a heaviness, an exhaustion, and as I stood up all the life just seemed to drain out of me.

It's today. He's going or has he gone yet?

I felt it so surely that it was in the floor beneath my feet as I got out of bed, and in the air around me as I went downstairs to let Bo out and make Laird's breakfast.

I felt numb, suspended in time, as I went through the motions of life. I knew that all I could do was wait.

At nine I phoned my mum and told her I wasn't going to take Laird to his swimming lesson that morning, because I didn't feel well.

'What's going on, Swiss?' she said. 'You sound so quiet. Oz is home tomorrow, you should be happy.'

I paused. 'He's not coming home, Mum, I know it.'

'Now that's daft, course he's coming home,' Mum said, but she sounded uneasy.

'I just need you to come over because I can't stay in.'

'I'll come and take Laird for a bit, but you stop all this. You never worry. You're just worrying when there's no need. The move, work, Laird, it's a lot to deal with and you are nearly at the end now. It's probably just all a bit too much now the end is in sight.'

Mum arrived at ten to eleven. 'I won't be more than an hour,' I promised.

I went to get fresh air and walk. I picked things up as I walked, feathers, berries, leaves. I loved the woods and the wind on my face, I just sat and listened. Felt drained. I just knew something was wrong.

I took a photo of the woods using my mobile phone. It was 11.30. I wept, as my heart broke, until I felt completely empty. Then I went home, shut the curtains and wrapped myself in a duvet on the sofa.

Mum was worried. She knew that I never normally stop – always busy with things that need doing. Normally running around on Halloween too, shopping for bits, taking the dog out, getting Laird to his Saturday swimming lesson. She settled Laird with a colouring book in the kitchen and came in.

'What's going on, Swissy?' she said.

'I can't speak, Mum.'

'Don't be ridiculous, what exactly has happened?

'Just get the feeling he's gone.'

'You don't know that, you're being irrational. It's the last day of nearly six months, when you spoke to him he was tired. You need to face it, you don't know.'

'He's dead, Mum.'

She looked at me, exasperated.

'I don't know what to tell you,' she said, 'but I know I've got to apply rationality. We don't know anything. Now you need to get up and take that child out.'

'I can't today.'

She stayed for another hour and we all ate together. She was annoyed with me for being down.

I stayed on the sofa, Laird playing beside me.

At five Mum rang. 'Are you all right? Have you eaten?'

She knew me so well. I had fed Laird but couldn't face food myself.

'Yes, Mum, don't worry,' I fibbed.

An hour later some of the other mums from the estate came round knocking to ask if we wanted to go trick-or-treating. Laird looked at me, pleading. 'Please Mummy, can we go?'

I pulled myself together. You have to, with a child. Washed my face, found a little bag for Laird to collect goodies in and we set off. The other mums and children were chatting and laughing and it helped. Although I still felt detached from reality, I went through the motions and felt a little better.

After a couple of hours of knocking on doors and filling Laird's bag, we came home.

I thought about the last Halloween, a year ago, when we'd had a barbecue. Oz adored Halloween. He would have been sitting outside, by a fire, if he'd been home. We both loved Halloween.

I told myself I was being silly. If anything had happened, I'd have heard by now, surely? It was eight, so 11.30 in Afghanistan. Oz should be getting back to Bastion, ready to hand over and come home.

I ran Laird's bath, ordered the Chinese food, got out the bottle of wine I'd saved and left it on the side in the kitchen, towelled Laird dry, got his pyjamas on, put him to bed and read him a story.

He was so excited. Talking about Oz coming home, about his birthday, about showing Oz his wall chart, where he'd ticked off all the days.

As he chattered I looked at his small, sweet face and thought, I'm being a fool, I've imagined the whole thing, of course Oz is fine, of course he's coming home, how stupid of me to doubt and dread things without knowing the facts. If anything had happened, I'd have heard by now!

I kissed Laird, went downstairs, opened the bottle of wine and got out a glass. I would drink a toast to home-coming, reunion, togetherness. I had kept the wine for five months, it even moved house with us.

Laird called down – he knew he wasn't allowed downstairs once he'd gone to bed. 'I can't sleep, Mummy.' Of course he couldn't, no surprise there. Tanked up with sweets he didn't usually have and waiting for Oz.

I went back up the stairs and sent him into my bed, picking up his favourite Richard Scarry book and settling down beside him to read it.

And then the knock came that signalled the end of our world.

CHAPTER FIFTEEN

'I think we should let them in, Mummy.'

I looked at Laird, his little chin set, determined to be brave, and I knew I had to be strong.

I wanted to throw our things into a bag, slip out of the back door while they waited at the front, pack us into the car and run away, miles from here, away from all that I knew was coming. Oz had known that's what I would want to do. He'd teased me about it, just before he left. Said, 'I know you, Swissy, you'll take off if you get the chance, avoid all the fuss. But you can't do that, you've got to do me proud.'

'Daddy's dead, isn't he?'

'Yes,' I told Laird.

'Where is he? Will they bring him in? I'm going to help get him in.'

He thought they'd got him outside, in a coffin with a flag on it. He'd seen the repatriations on TV; we always said they were coming home.

'No hun, they're just telling us the news.'

Laird ran downstairs and I followed. He opened the door and said, 'Do you know my Daddy? You're not allowed in if you don't know him.'

Oz had said to him that when he was away, no man was coming into the house apart from Granddad, JJ (Jamie) or the men we knew that he worked with. 'Never let them in the house unless I know them,' he'd told Laird.

They said no, they didn't know him.

Laird said, 'What happened to him?'

They couldn't tell us anything. Only what we knew already. That Oz was dead. They said they weren't allowed to leave us, so I let them in and they stood in the hallway.

Laird ran to the living room and put on Sky News. He'd seen Oz do it many times when anything happened. I used to tell Oz to switch the rolling news off, but he always watched it.

I explained to Laird that it wouldn't be on the news yet, it was too soon. He went out into the hallway. I followed, and we sat on the stairs together. He shouted, 'If you don't know anything, go.'

They went out the back door and waited.

I put my arm around him. 'It won't be OK now,' I told him. 'It won't be OK for a long time. But it will be OK one day.'

He said, 'I'm going to be brave, I'm going to look after

you, Mummy.'

I said, 'No Lairdy, you won't. I will look after both of us. Daddy is gone but we are still here and I will look after you. I need you to help me, and I will ask you when I need help, but you are my baby. Daddy would want you to know that he's very proud of you for saying that, but I am your mum and I will look after you.'

I told Laird I needed to phone Granddad to come and get Bobo. The dog was going mad. I'd shut him in the kitchen and he was kicking up a terrible racket because Oz had taught him to keep barking if he was ever shut in anywhere or if there were strangers in the house.

I phoned my parents and Mum answered. 'Mum . . .'

She heard the grief in my voice.

'Swiss, what is it?'

'Mum . . .'

'Oh no, no, not Oz, oh my God, you knew. John . . .' She wailed and then we both sobbed for several seconds, then Dad took the phone.

'Can you come and get the dog, Dad.'

'Why's he barking, what's going on? Your mother's in bits here.'

There was a moment of realisation, a pause, and then, 'He's dead, isn't he?'

'Yes Dad.'

'OK, I'm coming to get the dog, if you want us to have Laird we'll take him too, whatever you want darling, just let us know. I'm on my way now,' his voice breaking and my mum crying in the background.'

I put the phone down and turned to Laird. 'Granddad's coming, he's going to take you and Bo to be with him and Nana tonight. I've got some people I need to telephone, and things I must do.'

We went upstairs together to the loo, and I looked in the mirror. My face was blotchy, streaked with tears, and my hair was all over the place. I splashed some cold water over my face and ran my fingers through my hair. 'You do your make-up, Mummy,' Laird said solemnly. 'Daddy would want you to look pretty.'

Laird was trying to be a little Oz.

'I will. In a bit. First we need to put some things in a bag for you to take to Granddad's.'

While we waited for Dad I phoned Shelley, a good friend of mine – our children went to school together.

'I'm coming over,' she said as soon as I told her. 'Don't move, I'll be there in half an hour.'

She was warm and practical and just the kind of person I needed around me that night.

Dad arrived and put his arms around me. 'I'm sorry, Swissy, so sorry, we loved him too. Just tell us whatever you need. If you can't phone, text, we'll be on the other end.'

He loaded Bo into the car before coming back for Laird. 'Come on, Lairdy, having you come and stay with us. Got your bag? Great, let's go, see you in a bit, Mum.'

By the time they left, the house was beginning to fill with people and the phone wouldn't stop ringing. There were two command cars outside, two men were posted at the front door, two at the back.

I called Torben, Oz's brother. He was quiet, in shock. He asked me if we could wait before releasing the name, have a period in which to grieve privately. I told him we couldn't; we had to release his name immediately. Not just for the families of soldiers out there, but for the men in Oz's unit, who knew and loved him – otherwise people would be wondering who it was, rumours start, people worry and it is dangerous. I asked Torben to go and see their mother, let her know, and then let me know when he'd done it and when they had told the family there. He did.

I had some photos from a photographer called David Gill, who'd been in Afghanistan. He'd thoughtfully sent them to me a couple of weeks earlier. I went and got one of them, an image that has become so familiar now, because it's been in the papers hundreds of times. Oz, rumpled hair, sweet grin, on the dusty ground on one knee, his helmet in front of him, looking up at the camera.

'You need to make a statement to go with the announcement on the Ministry of Defence website,' they said to me.

I did the statement as I knew how important that was. As soon as it became known that a soldier had died in

Afghanistan, every family of a serving soldier would be terrified that it was their husband, son, sister, brother, daughter who had died. Oz had always said to me to get his name out there fast if it happened.

I told them that I needed to check that his family had all been told. Then we could release it. My statement read:

'Oz was a phenomenal husband and loving father who was cruelly killed – no, correction – MURDERED on his last day of a relentless five-month tour. He was my best friend and soulmate. The pain of losing him is overwhelming. I take comfort knowing he saved countless lives with his hard work. I am so proud of him.'

I said it without even thinking.

I rang Hazey. I kept phoning and phoning but there was no answer. Eventually Hazey must have seen the missed calls and he sent me a text, 'In a club with Sam and Tamara. What's up? Are you and Laird OK?' I sent him one back. 'He's dead.'

Hazey and Sam were in a nightclub in Gunwharf Keys, in Portsmouth, with their good friend, Tamara, who was visiting from London. Oz knew Tamara, as they had all socialised together in London and had attended the Massed Bands of HM's Royal Marines at the Royal Albert Hall, where Oz had gallantly rescued Tamara's stiletto shoe! They'd been wining, dining, dancing and generally being silly, having a great time. The text must have been shocking, but at the time I couldn't think what else to do. Hazey had showed it to Sam, who said, 'Is she messing about?' Sam froze, Hazey froze and Tamara sensed blackness. Hazey said, 'Get our coats, I'll be outside.'

Once outside, Hazey called. 'What do you mean, he's dead? He isn't dead, tell me he's not dead.'

I started wailing. I couldn't help it, Hazey was so close to Oz, me and Laird. Telling him made it so real. And I could feel his grief down the phone line, he was crying and kicking something. I could hear the merrymaking in the background, people laughing, dancing, shouting. And Hazey, saying, 'It can't be true, my God, it can't be true, not Oz.' He asked me if they should come, and I said tomorrow.

'You know you have to carry him, Hazey.'

'Yeah,' he said.

As soon as Sam came on the phone she managed the word 'Chrissy' before we sobbed in devastation. We both knew our lives had changed forever.

I phoned Sharon, the mother of Rob Nealey, Oz's number two. The guy who was never more than a few yards from him during any operation, his right-hand man. Sharon and I had become good friends over the past few months, swapping any news we had. Oz got in touch more than Rob, because he could use the phone, so I'd let her know what they were up to, and that Rob was fine. She would hear soon that someone had died, and I needed to let her and Rob's girlfriend Charlotte know it wasn't Rob.

'Chrissy I'm so sorry. What happened?' It was something I would hear over and over again, and all I could say was that I didn't know. No details had come through yet.

I called Andrew, Oz's oldest friend from Cornwall. He and Amanda were in his flat above The Old Ship, watching a film. When he saw it was me on the phone he said to her, 'That's a call I don't want to take, I don't want to pick it up.' He knew. By the time he picked up, I could hear Amanda crying.

I couldn't settle. I just wanted to do what he'd asked.

'How about getting some rest?' Shelley said.

I told her I couldn't. I had too much to do. I needed to contact the friends Oz had nominated to carry his coffin at the repatriation. He'd given me the list and I'd promised I'd make sure they did it. I knew the Army would provide bearers, but Oz didn't want that. He wanted it done his way, with his friends, not six guys who didn't know him. Oz had been very prescriptive about what he wanted. I knew I had to insist on that. He'd said, 'Don't you dare let just anyone carry me.' He wanted the men he'd served with, the men he loved and respected.

I knew them all, and I knew how hard this was going to hit them. I felt drained, it was difficult to get my words out, but I had to keep going. I think it was then that I made a decision, born out of love for my husband. I knew I could and I would grieve for him for the rest of my life, but at that moment I needed to do what he had asked me to do. I've got a moment in time to stand up and let everybody know who he is and celebrate his life and my grief is secondary to who he is and was.

I was strong, I knew that. I would show Oz how much I loved him, by doing all the things that would make him proud – standing tall, speaking out, making sure things went the way he wanted, and letting people know what he and the others out there had been through.

Next to call was Deano, Dean Taylor, the guy Oz had been to Afghanistan with the first time, his former boss. Oz respected Deano; he was always one step ahead of Oz on the career ladder and he was another quirky guy. Oz used to call him Badger: he'd take photos of badgers whenever he saw them, usually as road kill, and send them to Deano.

'I knew it was him,' he said. 'I'm coming tomorrow but I can't now cos I've started drinking.'

I said, 'You're carrying him.' He said, 'Yeah, Roger that, I am.' Charlotte, his wife, was my rock and came the following day.

One by one I rang the others. Pete Royston, another Marine, Si de Gruchy, the guy who'd phoned Oz to say he was pinged to go. Woody, another colleague, and

Moxy. And one by one I heard them break down, shocked, grief-stricken, unable to take it in. Pete was in Wales and one of the others was in Germany, but they said they'd be back the next day, and every one of them promised they'd be there to carry him and would do him proud.

I was exhausted, sick of the phone ringing. I launched it across the room and smashed the base. I kept throwing up. Screaming 'No', and shaking uncontrollably.

The rest of that night passed in a blur. People came and went, my mobile rang nonstop as word spread, until I couldn't answer it any more, couldn't go over the same words again and again. Shelley took over and I went to bed, where I lay, exhausted but unable to sleep.

The next morning a colonel and a visiting officer arrived. The colonel told me how sorry he was and left. The visiting officer introduced himself as Staff Sergeant Adie Lambert, and said he would be with me for the next few days, sorting out all the paperwork and the official side. He explained that Oz was high profile, the media were going to be around a lot, and the Army wanted to keep things under control and give me support.

I realised then there would be no time to grieve. An Army death is very different to a civilian one, especially in these circumstances. My house was going to be full for days, there was a lot to do, and I just had to cope. I went upstairs and washed my face again. 'You can do this,' I told myself. 'You have to do this. And you have to do it well, for Oz.'

I liked Adie from the start, he was sweet and honest. I told him, 'I haven't done this before, but I will do my best, I promise. Whatever you need I will try to give you. I will try and ensure I do everything that I have to.'

Adie produced a purple folder of paperwork about a foot thick that had to be completed, clearing a space on the dining table for it; forms for this and that, permission for the repatriation, autopsy, inquest. A huge amount of paperwork. 'We'll get through it, bit by bit,' Adie promised.

People began to arrive early. Deano and his girlfriend Charlie came with a bottle of Bombay Sapphire. Then Hazey and Sam came. They had lain awake all night, Sam said, just stunned, unable to speak, watching the dark and then listening to the birds begin their dawn chorus.

Hazey put his arms round me and I collapsed into them. I felt broken and could only sob, 'Hazey, go and get my Oz and bring him back to me.'

I said the same to Dean. I was inconsolable. Charlie just held me.

Late that afternoon, Dad rang. 'Do you want Laird to come home, love, or should we keep him for a bit?'

I knew what I needed to do.

'Bring him back, Dad. He needs to get ready for school tomorrow.'

It was tempting to find a way to block everything out, at least for a few days. But in that moment I understood that life has to go on, people have to eat, sleep, wash, dress, go to work and to school, no matter how enormous their pain. And while it felt as though the loss of Oz had ripped my heart out of my body, I knew that what I could still do, and must do, was look after my little boy, and give him as much of a sense of security and normality as possible, despite the nightmare that had descended on us.

CHAPTER SIXTEEN

The next morning I got up early, let Bo out and then got Laird up and ready for school. I was on autopilot, so tired that I could barely think. Everything seemed surreal; it was as though someone else was going through the motions of making porridge, brushing hair, cleaning teeth. All those routine, everyday things that have to happen, even when your life has been irrevocably altered.

Laird was quiet but composed as the two of us sat at the table, trying to eat.

For so long we had hoped that by that Monday morning, Oz would be home. We would have gone to collect him after he flew in on the Sunday, hugged him, kissed him, told him excited, disjointed bits of news, taken him home to find Bo leaping about, cooked him a huge, fresh meal, told him how much we loved him and had missed him.

We would have put Laird to bed, and then sat and

talked over a bottle of wine. I would have held him
close, felt the warmth of his body, looked at his
beautiful hands, his sweet smile.

I couldn't think about it, dared not let myself go
there, or I knew I would not be able to go on. Instead I
did what Oz did, put it all in a little box in my head,
marked 'visit later'. Except that the box leaked, the
memories and the ache of loss slipped out through the
cracks, just as the tears leaked from my eyes, even as I
wiped them away and forced myself to put on a coping
face.

In those circumstances many families keep their
children off school, sometimes for weeks, but I felt that
if I didn't take Laird to school then I might never do it.
I understand why others don't, but I felt that for Laird
routine was important, and at school he would have
respite from the atmosphere of grief at home, the house
full of people, uniforms, paperwork, the phone
constantly going, people in tears. Better for a five-year-
old to have time away from that, to play with his friends
and feel that life goes on.

He was in Year One then, and had a lovely teacher.
We arrived a little early and I went to talk to her, bracing
myself to tell her. She was warm and kind, and practical.
Laird said to her, 'My Daddy was very brave and my
Mummy and I are going to get through,' and she smiled
and said, 'Yes, your Daddy was very, very brave, and you
are right, you will get through.' She had tears in her eyes.

I said I would pick him up, and turned to go.

She came after me. 'Oh Chrissy . . .' She gave me the biggest hug and I just fell down sobbing.

'I will collect him. Go and look after him, don't fuss him,' I said.

I felt I wanted to be with Laird, but I needed him to be with his friends as I needed to be with mine.

Back at home, Adie was waiting for me. For the next few days he would spend every day at our house, from 8.30 to 5.30, and longer if necessary, dealing with all the paperwork, admin, forms and official necessities. He was the perfect mix of formal and friendly, and I found him a great support.

Adie told me that I would be allocated a driver, to take me wherever I needed to go, in the coming weeks. There was a rota of drivers, but the one who came most often was George, a big man with a mad Glaswegian accent. George proved to be a real friend during those weeks. He had an Arnold Schwarzenegger satnav that made me laugh and his advice and support was always spot-on. He drove me to the many official appointments I had over that period, and as I began to find myself on an escalator, having to make statements and appearances, he would say to me when I climbed back into the car, 'You nailed that,' 'Well done, that told them' or, 'That's my girl, Oz would be proud,' or, 'Too right, hun.'

During those first weeks, George was privy to our

grief-stricken lives. He did so much more than drive me around. I can remember him running around a play centre in his green kit for Laird's birthday party, which Oz had booked. Ordering me to get a bite to eat and telling me to take a break or I'd collapse.

That first Monday morning, Adie showed me the announcement of Oz's death that had appeared on the Ministry of Defence website.

It is with great regret that the Ministry of Defence must confirm the death of Staff Sergeant Olaf Sean George Schmid, of the Royal Logistic Corps, in Afghanistan on the afternoon of Saturday 31 October 2009.

It was followed by a piece about Oz, his life and his death, which I was only able to read properly later on. It included a short biography and an account of his rise through the ranks as a top ATO. My quote came next:

Christina Schmid, wife of Staff Sergeant Olaf Schmid said:

'Oz was a phenomenal husband and loving father who was cruelly murdered on his last day of a relentless five-month tour.

'He was my best friend and soulmate. The pain of losing him is overwhelming. I take comfort knowing he saved countless lives with his hard work. I am so proud of him.'

After that came a quote from Rob Thomson, the commanding officer of 2 Rifles, the group Oz was working with in Afghanistan,

> *Lieutenant Col Robert Thomson, Commanding Officer*
> *2 RIFLES Battle Group said:*
> *'SSgt Oz Schmid was simply the bravest and most courageous man I have ever met. Under relentless IED and small arms attacks he stood taller than the tallest. He opened the Pharmacy Road and 24 hrs later, found 31 IEDs in one go on route SPARTA. Every single Company in 2 RIFLES adored working with him.*
> *'I adored working with him. No matter how difficult or lethal the task which lay in front of us, he was the man who only saw solutions.*
> *'He saved lives in 2 RIFLES time after time and for that he will retain a very special place in every heart of every Rifleman in our extraordinary Battle Group. Superlatives do not do the man justice. Better than the best. Better than the best of the best. Our thoughts and prayers are with his beloved family.'*

Those words meant a great deal to me and I read them many times. Rob Thomson could not have bestowed higher praise, greater acknowledgment or deeper warmth. To call Oz better than the best was a true accolade, and Rob's words seemed to come from the heart.

255

There were many other accolades.

Lieutenant Colonel Gareth Bex RLC, Commanding Officer Counter IED Task Force, said:

'SSgt Oz Schmid was a brilliant IEDD operator and a superb soldier. We loved him like a brother; he was a much adored member of our close knit family.

'His example will urge us on with greater determination as we continue the C-IED fight he fought so valiantly. He had such a bright future ahead of him in a career that he so blatantly loved; the Army has been robbed of a superb talent.

'With his tousled hair and boyish grin his effervescent presence was always good for morale and he had an infectious enthusiasm.

'Once met, never forgotten his wicked sense of humour was legendary; he received so many accolades from the Battle Groups for his professionalism, courage and vibrant personality.

'It was an honour to serve with him and a privilege to have been his Commanding Officer. He will be revered forever in 11 EOD Regiment RLC as a hero and an inspiration to all who follow him; he takes his rightful place alongside recent fallen comrades WO2 Gaz O'Donnell GM+Bar and Captain Dan Shepherd.

'SSgt Schmid stood proud amongst some formidable men serving here in Afghanistan; the tag "legend" is frequently bestowed nowadays but in his case it is

rightly justified – SSgt Schmid was a legend.

'His courage was not displayed in a fleeting moment of time; he stared death in the face on a daily basis. Many soldiers and ordinary Afghans owe their lives to SSgt Schmid's gallant actions and his sacrifice will never be forgotten.'

These tributes, and the many others that appeared on the website and began to appear in the press, didn't bring me comfort. In his time on this earth, Oz had done extraordinary things. People were walking around, living their lives, because he had saved them. I couldn't – and still can't – think of any more noble purpose or achievement in a life.

Bit by bit I learned the details of what happened to Oz on his last day. The account on the MoD website said:

SSgt Schmid died instantly following an Improvised Explosive Device (IED) explosion in the Sangin region of Helmand Province.

At the time he was commanding an Improvised Explosive Device Disposal (IEDD) team who were dealing with a confirmed IED.

Working in concert with an Advanced Search team he was conducting a manual route search to clear devices in the vicinity of the Forward Operating Base and was defusing the device when it initiated.

He was doing what he did every single day out there, defusing bombs. I knew that however tired he might have been, he would have been doing it for his team, so that they could come home, with the job completed in time for their R&R – otherwise they might have missed their slot entirely.

Later, I met Colonel Seddon, who led the technical investigation, a few weeks after the funeral. He showed me photographs of Oz kneeling over the devices which killed him. They were taken a few moments before death. I could see a compound wall in the background, and the wires poking out of the ground a few yards in front of it, Oz, deep in concentration, looking at them, thinking about how he would deal with this particular scenario.

The next photographs were of a crater in the ground, where the bomb, and Oz, had been. There are scraps of burned paper lying about, parts of the letters and photographs Oz carried tucked into his body armour.

Rob Nealey phoned me, after Oz died. He told me they had managed to get everything – and I knew he meant every part of Oz, as well as all the letters, photos and other things he carried on him. Rob was proud of that, it was a point of honour, not to leave anything at all that might become a Taliban 'trophy', and I told him how grateful I was. I knew that he and the rest of the team had put themselves in danger to do what they did and how gruelling it must have been for them.

They hadn't had a body bag with them, so they put Oz

into a black grip – a holdall – they had, and lashed it, with him in it, to the back of the quad bike and trailer they used to carry their stuff around in. That way his men – and I can only imagine the shock and grief they felt – got him back to base. From there they had to wait hours (as there were none available) for a helicopter to take him back to Camp Bastion so that he could be formally pronounced dead by a doctor. There was a hold-up because no doctors were available; they were busy tending to the injured, as those who were still alive took priority over those who had died. That was one reason why it had taken them ten hours to let me know he had died.

He had died at three in the afternoon, 11.30 in the UK. I had been in the woods, feeling that something was wrong.

Grim as the details were, I preferred knowing the full story. I knew how horrific it must have been for his men, straight after the blast, but they didn't let him down, they did what they had to do and got him to the base so that he could be brought home. I was grateful to them, especially Rob Nealey, who was so close to Oz, both as a friend and literally in his job, and who is a modest, loyal and big-hearted man.

Many of Oz's colleagues phoned me or wrote.

His loss is singularly one of the most significant during this campaign, as his skills and expertise are hard fought and won; the British Army is a lesser organisation without him. He was a man very much at the top of his game. His enthusiasm and energy knew no bounds – he lit up a room with his personality and oozed professionalism, which was absolutely infectious to all who were fortunate enough to work with him, myself included . . .

Despite the considerable risk of operating within the Sangin area, young men like Oz continue to go out and it is as a result of their determination and dedication that we are beginning to make tangible progress . . .

I hope that you, Laird, family and friends under-stand that your ultimate sacrifice will not have been in vain – we will see to that. Oz saved countless British and Afghan lives this summer; of which you should be justifiably proud – we are. We all remain absolutely committed to ensuring success is achieved and losses such as this only serve to strengthen our resolve.

Meeting the people who have proved to be such good friends has been one of the positive things to come from the tragedy of Oz's death. I knew some of his friends before he died, but others, whom he served with in Afghanistan or elsewhere, I have got to know since and they have been unfailingly supportive.

Oz was to be flown back to Britain, to RAF Lyneham, on Thursday 5 November – in three days' time. The repatriation ceremony would take place at Lyneham, and he would, like so many before him, be driven through Wootton Bassett on his way to the John Radcliffe Infirmary.

This was the first of many ceremonial and public events I would need to get through and I knew I needed to do it with pride and dignity, for Oz. For the hundredth time I wished I could pile our things into the car, take Laird and Bo, and run away. I would have liked to go to my nan's cottage, up on a Welsh hillside, far from everything, and just walk for miles, curl up in front of the fire, be with Laird and think about Oz, in my own way and my own time. Away from the phone calls and the questions, the paperwork and the plans. Just be allowed to grieve. But I couldn't do that. Oz had been so specific about wanting me there to meet him, he had mentioned it again in a phone conversation only days before he died. I faced it head-on.

I kept going with Laird's routine, taking him to school and picking him up each day. On the way out of the school, a couple of days after the news broke, I bumped into Pearl, a learning support assistant who had been with Laird's class in Reception. She knew Oz, because he used to drop Laird off. She held my hand and said, 'Darling, you're doing fantastic. If I'm feeling this grief, Christ knows what you're feeling. I just want you to know I'm right behind you. I'd love to give you a hug, but I'm not going to stop you, I just wanted to say that to you, I saw how he was with you and Laird.'

I said, 'Pearl, can I have that hug?' So there, in the corridor, she put her motherly arms around me and gave me a beautiful hug.

Later I met the head teacher, who talked about the need for counselling, but actually what Pearl gave me was exactly what I needed at that point. Sometimes, in those early, raw days, talking about it isn't what you need. There is a wealth of evidence now showing that sometimes pushing you to talk isn't right for everyone, and those after the 9/11 attacks who suffer from the worst PTSD and issues are those that had counselling early on or for long periods.

Before the repatriation, the lads who were to carry Oz arrived and went to Lyneham for rehearsals. It was important to all of them that they conduct the ceremony with perfect precision, in a manner that would honour Oz. So they drowned their sorrows at night, but during the day they squared up and prepared themselves for what was to come.

I spent those days at home, going through the endless paperwork with Adie, finding black clothes I could wear for the ceremony – looking after Laird and fielding calls. I got so tired that my parents stepped in and told me not to answer the phone. They spent a lot of time with me, taking calls, making cups of tea and helping me with Laird and Bo. Most of the time my mobile and the landline were going at the same time – it was relentless. And people wanted to know the same details. I just couldn't keep going over them – what happened, when, how, what, why, which? And each time I explained, it hit me harder. My Oz was gone, my baby, my family. I was a widow. All the plans, the hopes, the dreams we'd had, blown apart.

The sale of Jasmine Cottage was due to be completed on the Friday after Oz came back, 6 November. I felt bad, but I wouldn't go ahead with any big decision at that time. I didn't know where our lives would turn next. I could stay in married quarters, but I loved that cottage, it was where we had first lived together and it was part of our lives. I wasn't ready to let it go.

In all the chaos and turbulence of repatriation day, there was yet another huge change coming – I was made redundant. My boss was apologetic, it wasn't personal; there was a recession on.

I would find another job, but it was a miserable blow.

CHAPTER SEVENTEEN

Before Oz left Camp Bastion he was given the very moving send-off accorded to every serving soldier who dies in Helmand.

In a generous letter which paid warm tribute to Oz, one of his former bosses, Major Wayne Davidson, of 11 EOD at Didcot, said:

Events conducted in preparation for Oz's repatriation to the UK will be done in an extremely honouring and dignified manner. This is the least that can be done in theatre for a soldier who has paid the ultimate sacrifice. A ceremony will be held for him on Camp Bastion which all the soldiers of varying nations will attend, where duty permits, and pay their respects to him. Thereafter he will be given a ceremonial ramp parade when he is placed onto the aircraft.

Camp Bastion houses 30,000 soldiers, not just British

but many other nationalities as well, and has grown to the size of a town. There is a memorial there which lists the names, on gold plaques, of every soldier who has been killed in the line of duty in Helmand province. When a soldier dies, those who can will gather for a ceremony, held by the padre, after which a single bugler will play the Last Post before the casket is carried on to the waiting plane. I have been told that this simple farewell is intensely moving and, on the night before Oz came home, I sat and thought about what was happening three and a half thousand miles away and about Oz's friends and colleagues there, honouring him as they said goodbye.

Oz was coming home, and I would be there, as I had said I would be. It was never easy having life-and-death conversations with Oz, but we had had to do it, more than once, and he had always said that repatriation was hugely important to him. He had said, 'You will be there, promise me, as my wife, that you'll be there, honey. Just you on that runway. When I get off that plane, dead or alive, you are the only one I want to see on that tarmac,' and even though I was sickened by the thought of watching Oz return home in a coffin, I had promised.

He had said to me, 'If I die, don't run around for everyone else, the military, family, friends. You do things on your schedule; Laird and you are the priority, do what's right for him and for you.' So far I felt I'd been run ragged, trying to cope. But, for the repatriation, I knew I needed to get through the day in my way. So rather than have one of the Army drivers take me to RAF Lyneham, I drove myself after the school run. If I'd gone with a driver I would have been expected to get there a couple of hours early, or even to stay in a hotel nearby the night before. I didn't want that, I wanted to walk Bo, take Laird to school and then go home, put on a simple black dress and jacket, with Oz's medals pinned to the front, and do the drive in my car, our route, with my music. I drove through Marlborough, which is a lovely route, and I thought about that last journey I had made with Oz, in the same car. His Rizlas and menthol tips down the side of the door. Still there where he'd left them.

I had thought about taking a friend, but I was afraid that, if I did, they would be in bits and I wouldn't be able to focus, I would go to bits too. I wanted to be able to control myself, handle the situation with dignity and do Oz proud, as his friends would, carrying him, and I knew that I would manage that better on my own. If I had someone else there, I would worry about them instead of doing what I needed to do.

As I drove, all I could think was, My husband's dead. I want to be with my son and my dog and get away, leave all the red tape and ceremony behind and be in the woods. But I wouldn't do that.

The first stop was a briefing in a hotel close to the

airport. I was used to briefings, so I treated it like going to work. There were about twenty military people waiting there. They told me what would happen, the order of the day, the purpose of the repatriation and so on. I had to sign more paperwork, it was a military handover for the body to the coroner in Oxford, and then I was driven to the air base in a command car.

I pictured Oz laughing at all the official stuff going on for him. He'd have said, 'All this for me?' Especially as his plane was late and everyone had to stand around waiting – he used to say to me, 'The RAF are never on time,' and they certainly weren't this time. I was offered coffee and sandwiches. I took the coffee, but I couldn't eat. The lady serving it was lovely, and at one point I saw her looking at me with real tenderness. I wondered whether the pain I felt was showing more than I knew.

As the plane approached I was taken out on to the tarmac. The six bearers, Oz's close friends, marched out to line up, at attention, as the plane dipped low and flew past – a tradition when a body is on board. It circled again and landed some distance from us, for security clearance. During the half-hour this took, we went back inside.

Finally we went out again to see the plane taxi into place in front of us, and the hearse draw up behind it. As the engines whirred to a standstill, the bearers marched out to the back of the plane, where the ramp was lowered, and they disappeared inside, behind the black curtain hanging over the entrance.

The next part I didn't see, Hazey told me about it afterwards, and it made me smile to picture it. The flag-draped coffin had been placed on a stand at the top of the ramp. Oz's pals, in immaculate uniform, but every one of them commando underneath, me included, in Oz's honour, stood around it, and one of them, strictly against regulations, brought out a hip flask and proceeded to pour them each a tot, including one for Oz.

Then, as the startled RAF team looked on, they toasted him. 'Welcome home, Oz.' Each of them said their goodbyes, then they said, 'OK Oz, let's go,' shouldered the coffin and reappeared down the ramp, to place it gently in the hearse. From there Oz was taken to the chapel, where I was able to spend a few quiet minutes alone with him, to say goodbye, privately. 'Finally. You are home. Not as we planned though, is it?' I just sat there for an age in a room, draped over the coffin.

Moxy gave me a poem that he thought was very me, and he was right. It was Maya Angelou, 'Still I Rise'.

A little later the coffin was returned to the hearse for the drive to the John Radcliffe Infirmary, via Wootton Bassett. I waited there in advance, along with Oz's mother Barbara and brothers Torben and Greg, and friends, including Sam, and Malc, who wanted to pay his respects to Oz.

It was easy to stand in the place I had always dreaded – on the other side of the street, the side reserved for the families and close friends. It wasn't a bomb. I was alive, that's the way I looked at it. At least I had some of him back, at least Laird and I were still here.

I wasn't going to let anyone get the satisfaction of seeing that it was breaking me. Nothing would stand in the way of my love and honour for him. I got the strength from him. Listening to the words he said in my head. I thought about the fact that usually when an operator is hit his team members are too. I was so relieved that they were all OK. That was rare, and I knew Oz would have been pleased.

Opposite us were the regimental standard-bearers, and as the church bell tolled and the car carrying Oz approached, at walking pace and with a police escort both before and after him, the standards were lowered to the ground as a mark of respect.

The car stopped in front of us, and with Barbara – who, unlike some other mothers, chose to attend and must have been feeling the most terrible grief, but who showed immense calm and dignity throughout – after Sam had done so, I stepped forward with two flowers, one for me and one for Laird. Barbara is a private person who has never wanted to say a lot in public, but she did say, with great generosity and compassion, 'I hope his work will be a contribution to making Afghanistan a safer place for British troops and the Afghan people.' Her words appeared in a *Times* obituary for Oz, published just after the repatriation.

Many others surrounded the car with us to put flowers on it, and then we stepped back to the pavement. I blew Oz a quiet kiss, and as the car moved slowly forward, I began to clap, and I whispered, 'Well done.' Clapping wasn't something I had planned, or even thought about; it was spontaneous, the only way I could think of to say publicly, 'I'm so proud of you.'

Oz had said to me many times that he wanted his team to see pride from me. He said, 'If they've seen me blown up, Swissy, the last thing they need is to see even more pain and devastation. I want you to be absolutely proud of me and stand there and be appreciative and show your love for me and be as positive as you can about what I've achieved and what I've done.'

After the cortège had passed, I was approached by a television crew and asked to comment. I had to think on my feet. I told them that I was pleased to have Oz home, that he was an absolute hero, that his friends had done him proud carrying him and how proud I was of him. I told them that he was one of a select few high-threat operators who put themselves in danger every day, and that there weren't enough of them. And I said that Oz was a protector, not a destroyer; he loved his family, life, his team and wanted everybody to be safe. I finished by saying, 'He was my best friend and I really, really will miss him, he was the best part of my day.'

As soon as I could, I escaped the crowds and went home. I collected his engraved goblets from the sergeants' mess on the way home. I picked Laird up from my parents, who had collected him from school, and went back to the house, feeling wrung out and hoping to shut the door on the world for a few hours. But what we couldn't escape was the sound of fireworks. They were going off all around us, and we pulled back the curtains and watched. I felt as though every one of them was for Oz. It seemed a fitting tribute.

Laird seemed to be coping well. During the day he was tired and sometimes angry, but at night he didn't want to be alone, especially in the new quarter that was dire in comparision to the other one or Stone Terrace, and not homely at all. So I put him in with me for a few days. It helped us both.

Once Laird was asleep, that Guy Fawkes evening, I went downstairs, sat at the kitchen table and wept. I had promised myself, and Oz, that I wouldn't cry in public, but I needed to be able to cry in private. For Oz, for Laird, for his family and mine, all of us who loved him and had lost him, and for the uncertain future I was now facing, without even the security and familiarity of the job I had been doing for over ten years.

Exhausted and emotionally blitzed, I wanted some

sense of normality before facing Oz's funeral, so I unplugged the landline and stuffed my mobile in a drawer and then spent a quiet couple of days, trying to get back into a routine with Laird, and seeing only my parents and a couple of close friends. It wasn't until Saturday afternoon that I checked my calls and realised what had been going on. There were messages from newspaper journalists and TV stations and I realised that not only had Oz's repatriation been shown on the Thursday evening news along with me clapping – but so had the interview I had given. Since then, my clapping Oz had become a major talking point. That brief gesture, unplanned and lasting only a few moments, had caused a huge reaction.

Some people thought I was being showy and insensitive, others congratulated me for making a proud statement on behalf of all those who had been killed in Afghanistan. The response amazed me, but I realised that it had got people talking about Afghanistan, the role of the Army there and the men who were dying, and that was a good thing, and certainly something that Oz also wanted – awareness of the Afghanistan conflict.

Not only were the press trying to get hold of me, but the Sherriff of Cornwall's office had left a message asking me to a special Remembrance Sunday service the following day at Truro Cathedral, in memory of Oz.

I had expected to spend Remembrance Sunday

quietly at home, or perhaps to visit the local church, as we used to, but I had to be in Cornwall if the service was for Oz. I phoned Mum, who agreed to come over that evening in order to be around for Laird when he woke up. 'I'd love a day with my grandson,' she said, and I explained to Laird that I would put him to bed but Nan would get him up and stay with him till I got back.

I went to bed for a few hours before getting up at four in the morning to make the long drive down to Cornwall in time for the service. I arrived at 10.30, just in time. It was a beautiful service, Oz's home town honouring him in the cathedral where he was once a chorister, and his whole family were there.

After saying my goodbyes I walked out of the cathedral, planning to head back to my car and get home to Laird, when I was stopped by a Sky News reporter. He was nice, offered me a coffee, which I was grateful for, to warm me up, and asked me to give him an interview. I was surprised, but I thought, why not?

He asked me what Remembrance Sunday meant to me. I told him about the Remembrance Sundays Oz and I spent together, going to church and having a roast, and how important it was to Oz.

Harry Patch, the last surviving soldier to have fought in the trenches in the First World War, had just died in July, aged 111, so I said, 'Harry Patch and the other veterans of the Great War were marvellous men, but they've gone and it is time for Olaf and the others who have died to become the new faces of war. Our appreciation needs to move forward.'

Oz and I felt this very strongly. There is, as there should be, such deep respect and appreciation for the fallen of the two world wars. But less attention has been given to the fallen of recent years, in smaller wars. The men and women dying in Afghanistan are every bit as brave and as deserving as those who fought in the world wars. They too are fighting for their country, and for freedom, but because most people aren't feeling the effects of war first-hand, it doesn't seem as real, or as important.

That night the interview was shown on TV and I was stunned by the speed with which the reaction I was getting snowballed. I hadn't sought or expected it, but when I was asked to give interviews I decided to use the opportunity to speak out, about the things Oz and I had talked about, the need for our troops, especially in Afghanistan, to be given more support, to be better equipped and less overworked, to have more recognition from the government and the public, and to be appreciated and rewarded for what they do.

There are those, and I have complete respect for them, who have campaigned against the war in Afghanistan. But rather than debate the rights and wrongs of the war, since it is happening and our men and women are there, I wanted to voice my support for them, to encourage others to do the same, and to ask the government for more highly trained bomb-disposal operators to get the job done. I didn't want to make political points, simply to appreciate the troops whose job it is to protect our homeland, the ones caught in the middle, aside from politics, who are simply getting on with doing their jobs and struggling to have a family life at the same time.

It was to be the beginning of a roller-coaster ride that didn't stop, and wouldn't let me get off. I hadn't ever imagined being a public figure, but because I was not afraid to make a gesture, and to speak out, I became a figurehead, speaking on behalf of many who could not speak out for themselves.

So much for packing Laird and Bo into the car and taking off. Suddenly I was inundated by calls from the press, requests to give TV interviews and calls and letters from military personnel past and present, and from the public, the vast majority of them supportive and appreciative.

This letter, written a few days after the repatriation, was typical.

Dear Christina,

Firstly may I convey my sincere sympathy for your terrible loss. I can't start to imagine how you feel.

I was moved to write to you after I saw your picture in the paper. Your attitude to your loss is amazing and inspiring. Your husband was a true 110% hero and I have no doubt he would have been so very proud of your approach. Your strength, I am sure, will give strength to countless others.

I wish you all the best in the coming weeks and years, as you say, you must continue on with your plans for you and Laird. You will remain in the thoughts of myself and my family.

Letters like this touched me deeply, I was overwhelmed by people's kindness and generosity.

This was another typical comment, on an internet forum,

I've been listening to this articulate, brightly intelligent and determined woman on the news all week, and can't help but be moved by the heartfelt and immensely self-controlled tributes she's been paying to her husband; it's almost like she's become his personal battle-standard-bearer, such is her respect and devotion to his memory and deeds. It makes you feel proud to be British; we don't just know how to make great men and soldiers, we know how to make great girls too.

It seems to me to be utterly cruel and incredibly inhumane, that on top of the grief of losing her husband Christina is now without a job and has a young son to support. I'd imagine that at the moment she's still caught up in the shock and daze of having to deal with Olaf's death, and working will be the last thing on her mind until at least the New Year. But my God, how cruel and wrong can it be, that she now hasn't got a job to go back to when she most needs all the help that she can get?

I was so touched by caring comments like this. I was indeed proud to be Oz's standard-bearer, and if that was the impression coming across, I felt very happy. That was what he wanted, and it was something I could do for him. As for the comment about my job, I appreciated the thoughtfulness of this person, and many others. They were right, I had no idea what I would do, but I felt as if I was in a black hole, simply functioning, and I couldn't even begin to think about how to climb out.

CHAPTER EIGHTEEN

A week later Laird turned six. How, in the midst of the turmoil and grief and interviews and funeral planning, to manage a birthday party for a small boy?

Despite my insistence that I would look after him and not the other way around, I knew that Laird worried about me and was trying so hard to be brave and good and helpful.

He knew I was hurting, and I knew he was, and neither of us could take each other's pain away. But what I could do was give him one day away from the quarter, a day in which all the unhappiness was suspended and he could run around, eat too much cake and play with his friends.

Besides, the party was already booked, at Oz's insistence. He'd hired a play centre, with slides and bouncy castles and a ball-pool. Laird had asked me, a few days after Oz died, 'Am I still having my party,

Mummy?' and I had said, 'Yes, of course you are, it's going to be great.' It was the first time I'd seen him smile since we'd heard the news.

It wasn't easy – children's parties are exhausting at the best of times – but at least twelve screaming six and seven-year-olds were distracting, and I got through it with help from my parents and George, the driver, who insisted on coming along and giving excited little boys piggybacks all afternoon.

That night, tired but happy, Laird snuggled into bed. 'Thank you for my party, Mummy, it was lovely. Daddy was there as a little ghosty watching!'

'Me too, gorgeous,' I said, kissing him. 'Daddy would have loved it, wouldn't he?'

Laird's birthday was Monday 16 November. The next day, while Laird was at school, Hazey phoned me.

'Chrissy, Oz's things have come back. As his executor I've got to go and collect them, then I'll bring them over to you first thing after the school run. Meet you at the quarter, OK?'

It was good of him to let me know and to do it so quickly. I had asked them to send Oz's things back exactly as they were, scruffy, worn and thrown in a heap. I didn't want a nice, tidy pile of neatly folded laundry. Oz was a scruffbag, and I wanted his stuff just as he'd left it.

Hazey spared me the details of what it was like for him collecting Oz's things. It was only later that he told me how tough it had been to walk into the vast hangar at RAF Brize Norton and see four large cardboard boxes sitting in the middle. He'd been told to open them and go through the contents and divide the things up into piles – anything electrical, clothes, personal effects like letters and anything to do with his work.

Doing that was extremely hard for him. The last time he'd seen Oz had been at his wedding. Now, he picked up Oz's boots, the ones he wore everywhere, and sat with them in his hands. Oz had even turned up to his stag do in them and got a lot of ribbing as a result. Hazey smiled, but he was never far from tears.

Oz's laptop was dead and there were no photos on our family camera.

When everything had been sorted and security–checked, Hazey was allowed to pack it all back up to bring to me. He arrived that evening, brought the boxes in and put them in the sitting room. I wanted to go through them when Laird was in bed. Hazey and I shared a beer and I thanked him – being executor wasn't an easy job.

I opened the boxes immediately. It was an immensely difficult thing to do.

There were his T-shirts. The green gilet that he practically lived in – the one he'd been wearing the day we met in Winchester. And his favourite black, down-filled Rab jacket. There were little holes in it, where sparks from his roll-ups had burned into it and he'd patched them with green tape. It smelt of him. It was so warm, that jacket, he used to wear it on Arctic nights in Norway. He'd be on the phone to me in flip-flops, a towel, and the Rab, and everyone used to take the piss out of him. He probably wore it every night in Afghanistan too; it was battered and honking, but I loved it all the more for that as it smelt of him.

There were grubby socks, his battered boots and his shemagh, the square cotton Arab scarf often used in Eastern countries, wrapped around the face and mouth to keep out dust and sand. Oz loved it, he wore it all the time; he used to wrap it around his face and ears when it got cold at night. I buried my face in each one of them, drinking in his smell.

My letters were there, battered and grubby and full of sand, as were all the letters from his family and friends. Laird's drawings, several with glitter sprinkled all over them. Oz had told me he kissed them when they arrived in the post, and got glitter all over his face. The lads thought it was hilarious when he sat in a briefing without realising he had glitter on his cheeks.

There were his washing and shaving things, a small tin full of empty shells, the lighter I had given him for our wedding, his ring and a couple of manuals. Each item I took out of the box held memories, they made me smile, they were all so distinctly Oz, his style, his mould, his touch.

That night I took the Rab to bed with me and cuddled

it, as I would continue to do for many, many nights. And Laird had the shemagh, and from then on he slept with it wrapped around him.

I put the remainder of Oz's things back in the boxes and stored them in a spare room. I knew I had to decide what would go in the kit sale. The dog moped and sat around outside the door.

Apart from the things that came back from Afghanistan, which I wasn't ready to part with, Oz had a huge amount of kit – not only the stuff he'd left at home but stuff he'd left at his base. He was a bit like a tomcat: he had left his imprint everywhere; all over the house and everywhere else that he'd ever been.

Tradition dictates that, after death, a kit sale is held at the wake. The idea is to create a quick pot of money to help the bereaved family, who might have to wait some time for any official payout. The kit is laid out and friends and colleagues bid for it; it provides mementos of a lost friend, and helps the family at the same time.

Contrary to what most people might expect, the kit sale is always an occasion for much hilarity and fooling about, perhaps as an antidote to the heartbreaking loss that it represents. Oz's sale was held in a hangar at Stonehouse, in Plymouth, where Oz had been for his happiest years, and I went down there for it.

The kit was all laid out and Oz's mates went to the bar first, had a few drinks, and headed down to the sale. Some of them had dressed up, and proceeded to strip naked as items were sold, and there was a lot of wild hilarity.

It was a mark of how much Oz was loved that his things sold for extraordinary prices. One sock went into three figures. I was offered huge amounts of cash for his Rab, but I wasn't going to sell it. I needed to have it near me.

In the end they raised a magnificent amount, and soon afterwards I was handed a cheque. I was deeply touched. I wasn't sure what to do with it; it didn't feel right to spend money they had given with such love. In the end I put it into a savings account in Laird's name so that one day he could have it, as a legacy from Oz.

Just after Laird's birthday I heard more devastating news from Afghanistan. Ken Bellringer, another high-threat ATO who had trained and worked with Oz, had been desperately injured in a bomb blast on 15 November. Ken, a warrant officer and a warm, easy-going, big-hearted man, had gone to the aid of another soldier who'd got stuck in mud in a ploughed field. He'd been pulling the chap out, when the bomb functioned, killing the soldier he was helping and injuring Ken. He had lost both legs, the fingers of one hand and the thumb of the other, and his pelvis was also shattered.

Ken, who was thirty-seven, had been flown back to the UK and was in Intensive Care, with his wife Chris and children, seven-year-old Harry and eleven-year-old

Neeve, at his side. Doctors had given him a ten per cent chance of surviving – all any of us could do was to pray for him.

The news left me reeling. First Gaz O'Donnell, then Dan Shepherd, then Oz and now Ken. All capable men and husbands with families, at the top of their game, all high-threat ATOs absolutely vital to the Army. All comrades, close friends who worked and saved lives together.

How many more would there be?

I couldn't let myself think about that, or who might be next. I needed to focus on Oz's funeral first. It was to be held at Truro Cathedral, on Tuesday 24 November. It would be a full military funeral, a huge occasion, and I hoped that I could get through it with dignity and deliver a eulogy that would do him justice.

He had told me to bury him in Winchester. However, I decided on Truro, where his mother and brothers and his oldest friends were, and where almost every single person looked on him, fondly and proudly, as a local boy. The wake afterwards would be held in Plymouth.

I travelled down to Cornwall by car. George was driving, as I sat in the back, writing the eulogy. That five-hour journey gave me the peace and quiet I needed to think about what I wanted to say, to convey just how special Oz was, and how much he had done for others.

At the cathedral it was freezing, dry but windy. Not only had a thousand people gathered inside but, despite the cold and grey day, hundreds had gathered outside to pay their respects.

As I walked in I looked around and saw so many of his friends, so many people who loved him. There was Belinda from The Artillery, sobbing her eyes out, there was Andrew with his family, Jack and Penny from The New Inn, and Dan Read, another high-threat ATO and good friend to Oz who had been in Afghanistan with him. He had come back in September after being injured and was now, thankfully, recovering well.

There were friends and colleagues from all the battle groups that Oz had served with: the Paras, the Marines, the Commandos, 11 EOD.

Oz was carried, once more, by his friends. As Hazey put it, 'No one was going to carry him but us, we wanted to be there from the start to the finish.' And they were; they carried him into the cathedral and out again, and then into the crematorium for the private family service afterwards.

As he was carried in, the pipers who had just come back from Afghanistan and who Oz would have listened to over there, played 'Amazing Grace'. It was a deeply poignant start to a service that honoured Oz, celebrated his life and brought together all the different parts of his life, and so many people who had truly loved him.

It opened with William Blake's 'Jerusalem', one of the most poignant and lovely of hymns, after which tributes were given by Major Kier Head, Commanding Officer of the Royal Logistics Regiment, and Lieutenant Colonel Rob Thomson, Commanding Officer of 2 Rifles.

Major Head said that Oz had the intelligence, intuition and bravery to 'take that long walk' to the location of an IED and was a 'consummate professional . . . an emperor amongst men.'

Rob Thomson spoke of how Oz had cleared the notorious Pharmacy Road in Sangin. He had previously said that Oz was better than the best of the best. That he was the most courageous man he had ever met and saved lives time after time. Today he said, 'At the end of the eleven-hour clearance, for which he was permanently point man and in which he had cleared five IEDs, he had enabled us to bring my C Company back into the fight. The resounding success of that operation was entirely due to the heroic, selfless acts of Staff Sergeant Schmid. I still marvel at his indomitable spirit that day and his ability to find fun, even in the face of the most terrible threats. Oh, and twenty-four hours later he cleared another route in Sangin, this time dealing with thirty-one devices in a single twenty-four-hour period.'

The Cathedral Choir, of which Oz was once a member, sang Fauré's *Requiem Cantique de Jean Racine* and then Deano stood up to pay his tribute.

He reminded the congregation of Oz's wilder side. The six speeding tickets he picked up in France, his habit of parading around stark naked except for his green Royal Marines beret. It was lovely to have laughter in the midst of all the sadness. At the end Deano simply said, 'Sleep well, mate.'

Then it was my turn. Oz had said he wanted me to speak, and as I stood up and walked to the lectern, with so many eyes on me, I felt that I had to see it through in the way that Oz would expect. No tears – save those for when you're in private. Deano stood beside me, for a bit of moral support. I was prone to fainting.

My eulogy lasted only for a few minutes, but it came from the heart.

I've chosen to speak because Oz said to call us husband and wife was an understatement, and even best friends didn't do us service to describe our relationship; he said we were a unit.

In my eyes my husband, my son's father, was a warrior. Warriors are unique. Our protectors, not destroyers. Oz and troops like him join to serve traditional warrior values: to passionately protect the country they love, its ideals, and especially their families, communities and each other. In past conflicts, where there was an immediate threat to our shores and our existence, soldiers were never plagued with self-doubt about the value of their role in society, and a people and their soldiers were once close in unity. We might disagree with a war. However, I hope through Olaf's death, my public storytelling and appreciation, our community display of respect here today can serve to bridge that gap and unite us once more with our troops. I would personally like to thank you all for coming and showing your support.

I hope the work Olaf and others like him undertake on our behalf is not taken for granted any more or goes unnoticed by our leaders. For Olaf has certainly raised the bar. All the families of lost and injured servicemen should be able to expect our peacemakers to show us they are working just as hard as he did. For at present too many die, too many veterans exist in silence, too many are left with horrific disabilities while the rest of our community proceed with business as usual. Oz's death can never mean business as usual again for our son or me. There's just too much that time cannot erase.

Most of you will have known Oz the joker, always up for a giggle. However, I lived with a very different man. Particularly in the last eighteen months I've stood by him through, as he described, his toughest, darkest challenges ever. When he felt compromised, overwhelmed, threatened, I've wiped his tears, carried him and fought his fears for him. Becoming his widow has been the hardest thing I have ever done for him. He has made me so proud, and I hope he would be of me too.

I am fiercely loyal to serve him in death as I did

289

when he was alive, however much it's breaking me. Oz lived and stood for something he believed in and in the end he paid the ultimate sacrifice for those beliefs. We now have a duty not just to honour what he stood for but to live lives which honour the sacrifice he made. Please do not allow him to die in vain.

As I made my way back to my seat, I touched the top of his coffin. I was relieved that I had managed it all without stumbling, I was aware that there was applause, and I was hugely grateful for the support.

In the planning of the funeral we had tried to include something that would have meaning for everyone closest to Oz, and the next hymn was one that I had specially chosen, a modern hymn, a bit of a hippy little song really, that said so much about my relationship with Oz. It's called 'Your Love Echoes Around the World'.

Your gentle love has sweet embraced
The memories I had to hold
When I close my eyes
I see your face
Your love echoes around the world

In my dreams I hold you close to me
In the stars you shine like gold

It's the beat of your heart
That sets me free
Your love echoes around the world.

As the shadows fall the sun will rise
I surrender you my soul
And I know you will guide
Me there to you
Your love echoes around the world

Your precious love and sweet embrace
Is all I have to hold
But I know one day
I'll see your face
Your love echoes around the world.

After a reading from Revelation and the address, the choir sang 'For the Fallen', that moving poem with words written by Laurence Binyon, that contains the lines:

They shall not grow old, as we that are left grow
old:
Age shall not weary them, nor the years condemn.
At the going down of the sun and in the morning
We will remember them.

This was followed by prayers, and the hymn 'Thine Be

291

the Glory', chosen by Oz's brother Torben, the com-
mendation, the Last Post, silence, Reveille and the
blessing.

The mourners were asked to stay seated as the final
salute, three rounds, was fired outside by men from the
RLC, and then Oz was carried from the cathedral on the
shoulders of his friends as I followed.

After the cremation I travelled to Stonehouse, where
many of Oz's closest friends had gathered for a wake in
the sergeants' mess. When I walked in arms were thrown
around me and a drink was thrust into my hand; there
were tears and laughter and everyone had something to
say. After the formality of a very public funeral, this
warm, intimate affection was just what I needed and Oz
would've liked and wanted.

CHAPTER NINETEEN

Our second wedding anniversary fell eight days after Oz's funeral. It was the day Oz had said he feared he would never see. 'What if we don't have this again?' he had said to me on our first anniversary. It had been his worst fear, and mine, and the reality of it was hard to bear.

I decided to go back to the hotel where we had married, and Rob Thomson said he would come with me.

Rob was the lieutenant colonel who commanded 2 Rifles, who had been with Oz at Pharmacy Road and who had called him the best of the best. He had become a good friend. We met there at Lainston House for a bite to eat and a coffee. A generous and eloquent man, whose initial MoD statement about Oz has been repeated many times in the media, he wrote to me just after Oz died, saying:

You will know only too well that Oz was one in a million, but I can honestly say that he was the most courageous man I have ever had the privilege to fight, laugh and drink brews with. He worked for each one of my five Companies and every single one loved his infectious 'solution offering' way. I was deeply in his debt and I told him so as I said farewell to him in Sangin on 21 October. He gave me a big 'Oz hug' and I had to walk away before he saw my tears.

The Army has lost a rising and uniquely talented star – rarely have I seen such a coincidence of professional brilliance, attractiveness of character and physical ebullience. He would have gone all the way and I am so sorry that you have lost him . . .

Rob had said in his letter that he wanted to come and meet me, and soon after that he got in touch. It meant a lot to me to meet and talk to someone who had been with Oz in Afghanistan, who had known him well and seen him work. Rob was able to tell me what things had been like there and he told me several funny anecdotes and stories so typical of Oz. I had asked him to speak at Oz's funeral and he did, warmly and eloquently, and I was glad of his offer of lunch on my wedding anniversary.

It was a hard day to get through, one of the worst yet. But going back to Lainston House helped. It was good to remember how happy we had been, and to spend a couple of hours there, talking to Rob about Oz. Afterwards I headed off to get Laird from school and we went home for a quiet evening.

I tried hard to keep Laird's life as normal as possible, to be the one to take him to school and pick him up. He had told me that he didn't want to go to after-school club any more, because Oz used to pick him up from there. So if I couldn't be there at 3.15 I would ask a friend to take him home, or my parents would help out, then I would have him for supper.

Laird understood what had happened to Oz. He asked me questions, and I made sure the world stopped so I could answer them for him, but it was painful. Children amplify your grief. More than once I found him in the room where I had put the boxes of Oz's things, just looking at them. It breaks my heart to see him, simply missing him. He used to say, 'Let's get all the best scientists and get a time machine and get him back!'

My parents and my brother were grieving too. Mum and Dad had both adored Oz, and his death had left them feeling bereft, and of course deeply worried about me and Laird. Dad, who seldom showed his feelings, would go out to the woods with his dog, to the tree where Oz had carved Laird's and Bo's initials, LS and BS, and cry for Oz there. His sense of loss was so deep that he decided to sell his beloved boat, *Magari*. He couldn't face sailing it again without Oz, and he couldn't set foot on deck without remembering the last meal we had all eaten there, the day before Oz left. Mum was also deeply upset. She sold the cottage in Snowdonia.

My uncle and his children travel and some have left the country, so we had no need to keep the cottage. It held so many memories of Oz. Oz's friends, many of whom are now out of the military, plan on leaving the country and say enough is enough.

As for me, in the month since Oz had died I had existed in a frenetic whirlwind. Between the repatriation and funeral, Remembrance Sunday, Laird's birthday and my wedding anniversary, the phone had not stopped ringing. More than one of Oz's friends rang me at three or four in the morning, tearful and drunk, in bits over losing him. The trouble was, I was grieving too.

I thought things would quieten down after the funeral, and that I would have time to get back into a proper routine with Laird and to think about what to do with my future. But far from quietening down, things became even more hectic.

The eulogy I gave for Oz seemed to strike a note with a lot of people. I got messages and calls; people came up to me in the street and letters poured in to thank me for speaking out for those who had suffered in the Afghan war. Overnight I found myself regarded as an ambassador for the dead and injured and their families, and a campaigner for the military men and women who were unable to speak out in their own interests.

I even got a letter from royalty – one letter said: *'What an incredible lady you are, you showed the whole nation courage, bravery and strength . . . I am in awe of you.'*

Gordon Brown, then Prime Minister, wrote a long and very warm letter in which he said:

It is with the greatest sadness that I write, on behalf of Sarah and myself, to offer our personal condolences to you and your son Laird on the death of your very brave husband Olaf. Sarah and I have both read and been profoundly moved by your eulogy at Truro Cathedral. Your husband's courage was legendary and he was, and always will be, an inspiration to our country . . .

I also had a very kind letter from Defence Secretary Bob Ainsworth. All the letters were warm and I was grateful to those who had taken the time to let me know how they felt. But one letter in particular touched me deeply. It was from a retired major, Philip Malins. He wrote to Brigadier C. J. Murray of the Royal Logistics Corps, who forwarded the letter to me. It said:

You will have seen the text, published in today's Telegraph, *of the wonderful, courageous, inspiring and so deeply moving tribute paid by his widow yesterday at the funeral of Olaf Schmid.*

I am a 90-year-old RASC Territorial from 1938, the only one so far as is known commanding Gurkhas and

Japanese Infantry fighting on the same side to be awarded an MC.

From Olaf Schmid's medals worn by his wife at his funeral I cannot see one for gallantry. He is reported in the press as having cleared some 60 unexploded devices, an immense achievement of calm courage.

If it has not already been done can you, as head of the Corps, initiate action for the posthumous gallantry award to be received and cherished by his equally gallant widow, Christina. I am sure this would be the wish of all those serving and who have served in our armed forces, and of the general public.

This former territorial soldier's generous words meant a lot to me. Not everyone approved of my outspokenness, but the majority of people who contacted me, including many military, and former military men and women, did.

Brigadier Murray's accompanying note said,

People keep telling me what a star you are! Of course I know that already. Despite all the huge pressure on you, you've found the time to be supportive of everything the Corps is doing in the most ferocious of circumstances. Thank you.

This was the point for me. I wanted to be supportive. I felt so strongly that the men and women in the Armed

Forces are doing a difficult job, brilliantly. What I wanted was to do what Oz asked and raise awareness for the dead and broken, to bring respect and appreciation for all those serving, not all of whom necessarily believed in the war in Afghanistan. And to add my voice to those campaigning for better conditions, Harmony guidelines, equipment and awareness for high-threat bomb-disposal operators and their families.

I knew from Oz that there weren't enough high-threat ATOs, and that there wasn't enough equipment, and that some of the equipment that was provided wasn't suitable for the job – like the heavy protective suits that were too hot and attracted attention to ATOs. And I knew that he and the rest of the men and women out there felt underappreciated by the public back home.

Most people in Britain felt very removed from what was happening in Afghanistan. And while some were disinterested, others opposed British involvement there. This was hardly surprising, given the complex and con-troversial political background to what was happening, but the result was that the troops, risking their lives daily, felt sidelined. I knew that Oz had felt people didn't really care, and that was sad, because whatever the political rights or wrongs of our troops being there, the fact was that they were there because they had no choice, facing death and injury every day, doing a difficult and dangerous job, and they needed to know that people back home cared.

I felt that if I was being approached, I had to seize the moment and get that message across. So when I was invited to do newspaper and magazine interviews and to appear on *Newsnight,* talking to Kirsty Wark, and on Radio Five Live talking to Victoria Derbyshire, I accepted. Television appearances, in particular, weren't daunting; I wasn't facing a bomb, was I?

I didn't want others to go through what I, Oz and Laird had. I was doing it for Oz. Flying his flag, telling people what his message had been. I talked about his measured, calm strength and what an awesome man he had been. I talked about how we could all show more support and appreciation for our troops. And I talked about the deaths and the injuries, in particular the increase in amputees. Inevitably the deaths got more attention, but the number of men coming back without one, two or three limbs was increasing daily.

Some of the messages posted on the internet or sent to me in response were so heartening. It meant a great deal to me to know what Oz did was recognised. One message said:

VCs have been rightly awarded to men who, on the spur of the moment, throw themselves onto live grenades to save their comrades. Men like Staff Sergeant Schmid did this every day of their battle front experience in the

full knowledge that they could die in an instant. What
more can a man do for his fellow Man?

Another said:

No one can ever know just how many lives Olaf saved,
we just know he did, many, many times over. If that
doesn't deserve recognition then what does? He
certainly has my recognition and I'm sure countless
other people's too. It's not just me who owes Olaf a
massive thank-you, or the soldiers he saved, but the
whole country.

How I wished Oz could have known of the warmth and
appreciation generated towards him. He would have
been amazed at the attention, and he would have felt so
heartened. But while I was grateful for the recognition of
what he did, any talk of medals – and there was plenty
– made me feel a little uncomfortable. Of course I
believed that Oz deserved one, but that wasn't what
mattered to him. If anyone ever mentioned medals to
him he'd laugh. He didn't need or expect a medal.

As December wore on and Christmas approached, I
began to dread it. Christmas had been so special to Oz.
I wished I could just go to sleep and wake up the other
side of it, but I had Laird to think of, and for a small boy
Christmas is special, even if Daddy can't be there.

In mid-December I received a letter that made

Christmas a little easier to bear. It was from Major Tim Gould, Commander of the Joint Force EOD Group in Afghanistan.

It comforted me a great deal as it said that the troops in Afghanistan knew what I was saying, and thought it was a good thing. And of course Tim Gould said things about Oz that warmed my heart.

There was another thing that cheered me, too. Ken Bellringer, the horrifically injured ATO who had been given only a ten per cent chance of survival, had pulled through, and though he would have to undergo many months in hospital and many operations, he would live, and go home to his family. He was one of the most severely injured men to survive Afghanistan, and would need great courage to face the future. But then Ken, like all the men who dealt daily with bombs, had great courage. Around the same time I heard about Ken, I learned that Dan Read had asked to go back to Afghanistan to finish the tour of duty that had been interrupted when he was injured. He wanted to be back with his team, doing what he knew was vital work, when there were so few others to do it. He could have waited until after Christmas, but he didn't, and the respect I felt for him was huge.

Just before Christmas, Gordon Brown announced that an extra £150 million would be spent on counter-IED efforts over the next three years. Once again I was asked to comment. I said it was a start, a small start, but not far enough. They weren't getting it.

The trouble was, no amount of money would conjure up more fully trained high-threat operatives. That would involve finding men and women with the right ability and temperament, and then training them for years. But I hoped that at some future point there would finally be enough people doing the job to prevent anyone having to become as exhausted and drained as Oz was by the end of his tour.

Lots of Oz's friends got in touch, calling and sending cards and messages to say how much they missed him and that they were thinking of me and Laird.

In the end I went to Cornwall for Christmas, to Veryan, where I rented a cottage and invited a few friends to come. I went to see Oz's mum, went for long walks with Laird and was grateful for Jack and Penny's warm hospitality at The New Inn. But it was a tough time, and I felt I was mostly coasting along while other people celebrated, smiling in the right places, going through the motions, doing my best to give Laird a happy time.

I survived Christmas and the New Year, but it was tough. I was managing to keep going, but only just. I knew it wouldn't take much to topple me.

CHAPTER TWENTY

As the bleak, cold days of early January arrived, I felt desperately low. There seemed to be no respite from grief, no easing of the constant ache that was missing Oz, no replacement for the future we had lost, only reminders.

I felt so exhausted. We had plans and hopes and dreams and now they were gone. I didn't even know where to live. I was living in the married quarters to save cash until my redundancy money came through. Laird and I were in a house where Oz had never lived and we had never settled. Half our stuff was still packed into boxes waiting for Oz to unpack it – most of it was his, after all.

I could have gone back to Jasmine Cottage, but it was so full of memories that I was afraid it would be too hard. Yet I couldn't face looking for somewhere new either. I thought about moving to Cornwall, as we had planned, but that didn't feel right – at least not yet. We needed to be near my parents and Jamie. So for the moment we stayed where we were, and I began, half-heartedly, to look for a house for us near Laird's school.

Then came another piece of heart-rending news. Dan Read had been killed, blown up as he was defusing an IED, on 11 January. He had only been back in Afghanistan for a month. Dan had been gutted when Oz died, and I knew Oz would be gutted now. He and Dan had trained together and were the same age. They had joined the Army in the same year, and they were close friends with a deep bond. Dan had written in one of the books of remembrance for Oz.

Like Oz, Dan had those special qualities that a high-threat ATO needs. He had already made safe thirty-two improvised explosive devices, saving many lives, before the blast which killed him.

Dan, a joker with a huge grin, had been brought up in Kent, but he lived in Newquay, Cornwall, with his wife Lou, who was a police officer.

Major Kier Head, second-in-command of 11 EOD Regiment, said Dan was a man the Army could not afford to lose. 'There are only a few specialist operators in the Forces and it takes time to grow them,' he said. 'The operator needs to be intelligent enough to understand the technical intricacies of these devices, intuitive enough to understand the enemy's likely plan to deploy them, brave enough to conduct that long walk to the suspected location of the device and clever enough to add all these factors together to develop the best render safe procedure.'

He said for Dan to return to his team after his injuries from an IED took an unbelievable amount of courage – 'a very, very special type of man. Dan was that officer, was that soldier.'

Dan's funeral was held in Truro Cathedral on 5 February, just two months and a few days after he had attended Oz's funeral there.

Dan's death accentuated both my sorrow and my anger. The toll of high-threat operators had now reached four dead and one desperately injured, all of them friends, part of the same small group. How many more would have to die? My resolve deepened to do anything I could to help. And requests were still arriving daily, for interviews, to attend functions and to make television appearances.

I tried to be selective, choosing those that would be most responsible and do most good. When the *Panorama* team approached me to help them make a programme about Oz and the others like him, highlighting the work they did and the shortages and difficulties they faced, I knew I had to say yes. It would mean a lot of work, but it would also mean finding out more than I already knew about what really happened and it was a big opportunity. And I had to do that, because if we knew what went wrong, we could try to get it put right. So I accepted.

My involvement with *Panorama*, and with other media projects, gave me a much-needed focus. Since I had no job to go to any longer, I needed a purpose to my day or I would be in danger of crawling under a duvet and staying there. Financially I was all right for the moment, since thankfully I'd always been careful with money and saved, but I needed something to do, in addition to being a mother, that would give meaning to my life now that Oz had gone. And fighting for justice for Oz, and for those who went before and who followed him, seemed more important than anything else I could possibly do. I needed answers to questions like why was there such a shortage of trained ATs, which had led to a cluster of deaths? Why had Oz not had his R&R and why were they forced to work with only two litres of water per day in fifty-degree heat?

While I was grateful to be offered the opportunity to get involved in such valuable projects, and I did get fired up and excited about what they might achieve, I still felt, most of the time, as though I had been run over by a truck and every part of me, inside and out, had been broken. Just because I got out of bed, put on a face for the world, went out there and did what he'd asked, it didn't change the fact that I was grieving.

One morning in mid-January, as I walked back to my car after dropping Laird at school, the mother of Laird's friend in his class stopped me. 'I don't want to freak you

out,' she said, 'but my mum wants you to get in touch
with her.'

I knew Laird's friend's mum well, and had seen her
mother sometimes – she always said hello to me if we
bumped into one another. But why would she want me
to get in touch?

'She says she's got a message for you, Oz wants to say
something,' she said, looking embarrassed. 'You know
Mum does all that spiritualist stuff, and she keeps
asking me about you. I haven't upset you, have I? Ball's
in your court.'

'Don't worry, I couldn't be any more upset than I
already am,' I told her. 'Tell your mum I'm not sure, I'll
have a think about it.'

'Fine, no pressure.' She smiled and I got into my car,
and I drove home feeling very unsure about what to do.
I had heard that her mother was a member of a
spiritualist church, but was that something I wanted to
get involved with?

Spiritualists believe that we all die physically and that
some aspect of the personality or mind survives this and
continues to exist on a spirit plane. And some
spiritualists believe they are able to contact those who
have died and to pass on messages.

Did she have a message for me from Oz?

I thought about it for several days. The thought of
hearing from Oz meant so much, but was that really
possible?

In the end something brought us together. The lad's jumper was in Laird's bag, so I took it round to his mum's. When she opened the door she said, 'Mum said you were coming, he's come through again. She has no idea what it means.'

Neither did I, except that in the bathroom that morning I had been thinking about whether to call her mum.

A couple of days later I phoned her and she said, 'Hello Chrissy, I'm glad you've called, he's just been here in my bathroom this morning. How soon can you come and see me? I never normally tell people to come, especially not this early after a bereavement, but he's come straight through and he keeps saying, "Will you speak to her, where is she? I'm here, I want to talk to her." He's been to see two other people in the same church as me. He's very persistent – annoying also, isn't he?' She was lovely. I cried, but she was positive. 'Don't be scared, anytime is fine. Just let me know when you are ready.'

I had to laugh – it was so Oz. Refusing to go away or give up.

I went to see her the next day, just after lunch.

She beamed at me as she opened the door. 'I'm so glad you've come, he's chattering away to me.' We went inside and she offered me a coffee.

'He's saying coffee, white, one. Man-up. Oh, and what an awful taste, it's something like liquorice. What is that?'

I smiled. 'His liquorice rollies, with menthol tips, he always smoked them. And that's how he talked, he always said "coffee, white, one," and "man-up" – they were his phrases.' She had got his intonation exactly right.

'He's telling me so that you'll know it's him,' she said. 'He says always forever, you two. You're round a table, he's saying always forever, my love, even through death. You'll always be married to me. Why's he saying that?'

It was a big thing with Oz. He used to say, 'There's only one, always forever, you and me. If anything happens to me I want you to be happy, live with someone, have kids, share all your money, but don't marry them. You're my wife, you'll always be married to me.' Lucy went on. 'He says, he is sorry.'

For several minutes I couldn't speak.

And there was more. 'He says why have you shut everything out? Why are you shutting the curtains? And what's this "have a little chat with yourself" thing? He says you should do that.' I had been shutting the curtains during the day all the time.

I laughed, thinking of all the times I'd told him to have a little chat with himself when there was something he needed to sort out or work through. Was he telling me to do that now? I'd always left the bedroom curtains open when the moon and stars were out; I loved the moonlight flooding into the room. But since

Oz died, I'd closed them, shutting out the moonbeams the way I wanted to shut out the world.

She went on passing messages – things that only Oz and I knew, beautiful things he'd said to me. At one point she and I were both in tears and she said, 'Why am I crying, I don't normally cry, but the things he's saying are very special, he was a soppy sod when it came to you.'

By the time I left, I felt better. It was so wonderful to hear his words, just as he had spoken them to me. I was grateful to her, I felt she had thrown me a lifeline, something I could hold on to when things got really dark.

After that I opened the curtains again on moonlit nights. And I talked to Oz, all the time. I'd walk around the house saying, 'OK knob-head, what are you up to? I'm just off to get Laird then I'm going to see Mum and Dad, I'll give them your best.'

I've been back to see her a handful of times, on those days when everything feels truly bleak and without hope. She always passes on an Oz message, in his distinctive style. And it helps me to keep going and keeps me grounded. I wasn't really a believer before, but I am open to things like that now.

Some friends were wonderful, but a lot of people didn't know what to say to me. Anyone who's been bereaved will say this – people get awkward and uncomfortable; they don't know whether to mention what's happened or pretend it didn't, so they avoid you, or keep it brief. You find yourself helping them, instead of the other way around. You smooth things over, act as though you're fine. And that can get exhausting.

Some people would say to me, 'Well at least you've got Laird.' I found that really odd. As if Laird was some kind of consolation prize. I'd lost my husband, and whether or not I had a son didn't change the fact that I grieved deeply. Another widow I got to know later, Kirianne Curley, whose husband Steve, a Marine, died in Afghanistan, said the same thing. She was left with a son, William, who was just eighteen weeks old, and while, like me, she was glad and grateful to have a child, it didn't lessen the grief she felt for Steve. 'If anything,' she told me, 'having a child worsens my grief, because I'm grieving for him too, losing the dad he will never remember.' Try as they might, people often don't get it. So you have to just try and feel the intention and not listen to the assumptions they make and some of the thoughtless things they say.

When I felt really down there was one friend who always managed to make me laugh. Bec was mum to Lizzie, who was Laird's age and was in the same class, and Thomas, who was younger. After Oz died, Bec came forward and chivvied me out of self-pity, time and time again. She looked a bit like Dawn French in polka dots and pearls and talked with a very upper-crust accent, and she was absolutely punishingly honest. She was my daily text-pest, 'Morning', she'd text. I'd text back trying to sound cheerful and say, 'Yup, I'm fine', but she could see right through it and she'd call me and say, 'Bugger that, darling, come on, we're going shopping and for coffee and you can tell me how shit today is.' 'Stay vertical, please, don't show me up in public.' She was hilarious.

She was a perfectionist. She'd ring me and say, 'I'm very cross with myself, I left the tortoise out and it wasn't warm enough and then I made a walnut cake and it didn't rise properly, so rubbish day, but then I thought of you and bought you a flowerpot for your front door. It said welcome on it, then when I turned it around I could write "Push off" on the back. Love it! I thought.

She once caught me with a Harvey Nichols carrier bag and said, 'Ooh, what have you got?' I told her it was just spare tights, as I'd laddered mine in London. She looked disgusted. 'For goodness' sake, Chrissy, live a little, will you? You can't go into Harvey Nicks and come out with just tights! Jesus, lady.'

She was always trying to get me to 'brighten up a bit'. 'Why not try a red mac with that?' she'd say, as I appeared in yet another black dress, 'Or some red pumps?' Because of her I started to dress more like the old me and eat a little more healthily instead of just one meal with Laird.

When Bec decided I was running around too much and needed to slow down, she would make a big bowl of rice pudding, put cling film on the top and stick it in the boot of my car. 'That'll slow you down a bit,' she'd say. 'Try speeding home with that in your boot.' She wouldn't let me take it out and I'd have to set off home with Laird at about ten miles an hour because I wasn't about to risk rice pudding all over my car.

The thing about Bec was that not only did she make me laugh at a time when very little did, but she was also deeply sensitive. She had been an Oncology nurse and she knew all about suffering and bereavement. I never felt she was ignoring my grief – she would talk about Oz, but at the same time she encouraged me to have fun and to see that life hadn't ended, even if it felt that way some days. On those days when I thought about Oz, I could still see him skipping in and out with Laird, gorgeous ass Oz and beautiful happy Laird. Bec used to say to me, 'I just don't get it, I just don't get life, it's bollocks! But it always feels worse if you try and ask yourself why,' and she was right.

Despite the concern of my parents and the kindness of friends like Bec, and Hazey's wife Sam, who was also a good and loving friend, life at that point still felt very much like a vortex of despair. I haven't felt angry, but I don't feel that I have moved on much. Receiving accolades such as the 'Bravest Woman of the Year' and 'Communicator of the Year' awards aren't things that I enjoy, they are just acknowledgments of the fact that Oz isn't here any more. Perhaps inevitably, I get regular bouts of shingles, a tingling, burning, viral rash in the nerves in my back, caused by the chickenpox virus, which flares up with stress. It gives me headaches and temperatures, as well as discomfort, and leaves me feeling run-down and exhausted for weeks on end. For a while I had several lots of antiviral drugs, but unless I take them all the time it keeps recurring. More recently I have found that acupuncture has really helped me.

Once again I felt tempted to drop everything and run away to the Welsh hills for some healing. But with Laird at school and the projects I was involved in beginning to rev up, it wasn't an option. Instead I took Laird to Cowley Manor for a weekend, so that we could have a peaceful couple of days together. It was somewhere that we'd had fun with Oz in the past; we could go for a moonlit walk, squelching through the mud in our wellies, wrapped in our warmest coats and enjoying fresh food.

CHAPTER TWENTY-ONE

Working on the programme for *Panorama* was both fascinating and disturbing. In the making of it I was able to talk to all kinds of people I might not otherwise have had access to, and it was an education that left me reeling.

I spoke to many of the guys Oz had worked with on the ground, and I learned just how tough it had been for them, carrying their kit in fifty-degree heat, walking to jobs because there weren't enough helicopters or armoured vehicles, or there was no oil for the quad bikes, lasting on a litre of water a day because they couldn't carry more, falling asleep on jobs because they were so shattered.

They were living in compounds with no running water, and dealing with up to forty-five IEDs in a hundred-metre stretch of ground. When they cleared an area, there weren't enough lads available to guard it, so the Taliban would just slip back in and replant devices

317

all over it. They felt that for every two steps forward, there was a step back, so that although progress was made, it was slow and painstaking.

It was said in all the reports that Oz defused sixty-four devices, and was defusing the sixty-fifth when he died. But this is inaccurate. He may have gone on sixty-four jobs – other reports said seventy – but each job involved countless devices. There is ample evidence of this. For example, I was sent a series of photographs of Oz at work, by a photographer called Michael Yon, who had posted them in an online report. Michael said that on the single mission during which the photos were taken, Oz and his crew destroyed several dozen bombs.

Just after the Pharmacy Road clearance, Oz defused thirty-one devices in twenty-four hours. Even on the day he died, he was on his third job, tens of devices clustered together, by three in the afternoon, having been working since early morning. I have no doubt whatsoever that he defused hundreds over nearly five months.

Most high-threat operators, pre-Afghanistan, had worked on perhaps five bombs in the course of several years. In Afghanistan, what they were being asked to do was off the scale. In 2008 the threats from IEDs grew by 400 per cent, and by the time Oz got there in 2009, it had risen a further 400 per cent. In Helmand alone, an average fourteen devices were being made safe every day. It meant a level of pressure for high-threat operators and their teams that was previously un-heard of.

One of the guys who helped with the programme was Staff Sergeant Kim Hughes, another high-threat ATO who had been in Afghanistan at the same time as Oz. Kim was the same age as Oz; they had trained and worked together and they both belonged to 11 EOD.

Kim said, 'When it comes to physical fighting, the firefights, we will win every time; we've got better weapons and we do it better. The only way they can attack us is the IED threat, and at the minute it's just off the scale. It's ridiculous how many there are out there. It's like fighting an enemy you can't see. Everywhere you go you have to be a hundred per cent, you can't switch off for two minutes.'

Yet the Army had not been prepared for this. When they first deployed to Afghanistan only 'limited consideration' was given to dealing with the threat of IEDs. It was only later that they realised how lethal and pervasive the Taliban's weapon of choice was, leaving the Army to fight an unseen, silent enemy that could strike every time they took a step forwards.

To make matters worse, in 2002 senior military advisers suspended the recruitment of high-threat IED operators for eighteen months. The MoD's own figures show that this decision meant that by 2008, ammu-nition technicians were forty per cent under strength. And that shortage affected Oz, Gaz O'Donnell, Dan

Shepherd, Ken Bellringer and Dan Read directly. They were left trying to cover work that should have been done by double the number of men – and given the rise in IEDs, by many more. The Army was caught on the hop, and they paid the price.

When Gaz O'Donnell died, several high-threat operators left the Army, further reducing numbers. One of them, Rick Hartley, spoke to me for the programme. He said, 'It was an accumulation of things really, why I left, the main one was carrying a friend with Oz off a plane in a coffin, which is just a massive reality check.'

It was the same dilemma Oz had faced, and agonised about. I absolutely understood why Rick and others like him chose to leave. That Oz chose to stay and face what came is a source both of enormous pride and frustrated sadness to me. He could be here with me today, but if he was, he would not have been the man I married.

Exhaustion was another aspect of what happened to Oz that I wanted to investigate. Most soldiers were sent back to Camp Bastion for regular rest breaks every four weeks or so, but in the five months he was there, Oz never did. He never had regular breaks; there was no one saying to him, 'OK, you need to stop now, take an official rest.' There was no one thinking 'bigger picture'; thinking that perhaps if he rested it would help him.

In fact the opposite was true, Oz was permanently on ten-minute standby, day and night, to be called out to another device. If they got time between jobs, they were writing reports, prepping, but still not officially resting. We know that they are in a high-risk group for PTSD and combat stress issues years down the line. So, even doing the most unsafe, dangerous of jobs, they still weren't as safe as they needed to be in order to make decisions about themselves and their troop.

One of the men who spoke to us for the programme was Colonel Stuart Tootal, who had commanded 3 Para Regiment during some of the fiercest fighting in Helmand. He resigned from the Army in 2007 over his concern about the welfare of his soldiers.

He told us, 'Soldiers like Oz will push themselves and will keep stepping up to the plate. What's the danger if they don't get those breaks? Reverse shot. They will get increasingly tired, their performance could degrade, they will be less alert and they might miss things, so risk increases. Two or three days in Camp Bastion makes the world of difference to someone who has been in the line doing these high-risk tasks for several weeks.'

Of course the Army has guidelines about rest breaks and lengths of tours, but they were drawn up before Afghanistan, and with so many IEDs and so few operators, it was impossible to stick to the rules. The Ministry of Defence's own research shows that fewer breaks leave soldiers more susceptible to combat stress and post traumatic stress disorder.

I was able to put all of this to Colonel Bob Seddon of the Royal Logistics Regiment, the Army's senior bomb-disposal officer, or principal ammunition technical officer, who had shown me the last photographs of Oz ever taken, just minutes before he died, as he crouched over the bomb.

He said he was concerned about the pressures, physical and psychological, that the operators were facing, and he told me, 'We could certainly use more high-threat teams in Afghanistan. We are seeking now to bring people back into high-threat IEDD operations who have been out for some time, we are looking for more senior officers to become more involved, but it will take some time before these measures can come into play and what it does mean is that the existing cohorts are going to be under pressure. I'm very concerned about that.'

The £40,000 operational tour allowance that was publicised for high-threat ATOs was a start. However, it was not enough – it was an acknowledgement that they ought to be viewed differently and paid for getting on their belt buckle.

Making the programme took several weeks, and during that time I thought of little else. It was due to air in late May, and I wondered what the response of the Army, and politicians, would be. Yes, there were more high-threat ATOs being trained and recruited, as Bob Seddon had confirmed, but was that it, or would there be any further response? I hoped that the programme would at least provide a talking point and perhaps even result in increased funding for better equipment for the Army. Seddon resigned the day it aired. That the resignation was linked to the *Panorama* episode was, in my mind, beyond doubt. *Panorama* was about to expose just how serious the situation was, and the Army had to respond in some way. But his departure brought me no comfort. In fact, I was concerned that if Bob Seddon had been the one taking responsibility for the failures, who would do so once he had gone?

When the programme aired I felt very proud of it. I was grateful to *Panorama* for highlighting the problems and for allowing me to be part of that. And the response was enormous – once again I was asked to give interviews and talks and many people, military and non-military, got in touch to say thank you for highlighting what was really going on in Afghanistan. The programme was ground-breaking; there hadn't been a documentary about Afghanistan as honest or as detailed.

It opened people's eyes and paved the way; since then there have been a number of other documentaries, not topic-specific to bomb disposal, but dealing with the situation in Afghanistan. Many of them have been excellent, all of them looking in greater depth at what the Army is actually up against in this war, and high-lighting the shortages of manpower and equipment.

I didn't watch it. I knew it was factually correct and I had the information to take to the new coalition government, who said they were pro-Forces and committed to trying to fix the problems of the previous government.

I went to see them, backed by News International, and asked for cash for training and equipment so they could up the numbers of operators, train them with enough resources, give them equipment to make their job efficient and safer . . . as Oz had said in his interview.

Overall responsibility for bomb disposal was taken off the RLC and given to the Royal Engineers. Now, hopefully, training would never be suspended again, and high-threat and bomb-disposal teams, searchers and ATOs would be well respected and supported going forward.

In spring 2010 I was invited to receive the Elizabeth Cross, a commemorative award for the families of Army personnel killed in action or as the result of a terrorist attack, and a recognition of the support the families give and what they go through.

Families have long been recognised – in the First World War they received a scroll and a bronze plaque and in the Second World War a scroll, but this is the first time there has been a medal and it was instituted by the Queen.

The first medal was only given out in August of 2009, so it felt very new and special to receive it, in a simple ceremony, from Princess Anne. It is a silver cross against a laurel wreath, with floral emblems of England, Scotland, Ireland and Wales in each leg of the cross. It is very beautiful and was accompanied by a scroll which said: 'This scroll commemorates Olaf Schmid, who gave his life for Queen and Country on 31 October 2009.' I was also given a miniature pin-on version of the cross.

I had heard rumours that Oz had been put forward for a bravery award. Of course I felt he deserved recognition, but I had no idea what, if anything, he might be given. Then a friend called to say, 'Oz has got something with first-class honours.'

When I was informed, officially, that Oz had won the George Cross, I felt overwhelmed by enormous pride and at the same time by deep sadness that he would not be able to collect it himself. I could hear him saying, I want to walk away with my legs from this tour, or alive, not with a medal.

The George Cross is a medal won by only 161 people – including Oz – since its inception in 1941. It is on a par with the Victoria Cross, but while the VC can only be awarded to military personnel 'in the face of the enemy', that is, in battle, the GC is an equivalent award, instituted in 1941 by the Queen's father, King George, for civilians and military personnel who have shown the highest degree of bravery in situations other than direct battle. He felt, rightly, that acts of outstanding bravery were taking place for which the terms of existing military and civilian decorations were not deemed appropriate.

In the same honours, Dan Shepherd was awarded the George Medal, and Kim Hughes, who had helped to make the *Panorama* programme, also won the George Cross.

I was so delighted for Kim. Like all the other high-threat operators I had known, he was a modest, easy-going and down-to-earth man who did what he did with no fuss and no expectation of recognition. Yet he had performed what became known as the single most outstanding act of explosive ordnance disposal ever recorded in Afghanistan.

In August 2009 he was called to disarm a minefield at a helicopter landing site, surrounded by the bodies of two troops and four others, including stretcher bearers, who had been seriously wounded and stranded by exploding devices. The area was effectively a minefield, watched over by the enemy, and the men were stranded within it.

Kim and his team were called into this harrowing and chaotic situation to get the casualties out and recover the bodies. Speed was absolutely essential, and Kim worked tirelessly to clear a path to evacuate the injured. One of the devices he disabled was within a metre of one of the injured men and he knew that any error would be fatal to him and the others, yet he kept a cool head and disabled device after device. It was an extraordinary act and Kim's medal was richly deserved.

On 18 March 2010, Kim and I both went to the panelled ballroom of the Honourable Artillery Company in the City of London to receive the framed citations from Air Chief Marshal Sir Jock Stirrup, Chief of the Defence Staff.

It was another very emotional day. I wore a black cocktail dress that Oz had loved, it was off-the-shoulder and had been his favourite, but unfortunately I didn't realise we would be going outside to take the pictures and it was freezing cold.

At the ceremony I met a lovely woman, Didy Grahame, who was Secretary of the VC and GC association. I hadn't realised there was an association, but Didy, whose father was a VC, chatted merrily away, explaining that not only was there an association, but there was always a lot of work to do, contacting recipients of medals and their families in connection with various functions, keeping an eye on the locations of all the medals and of course welcoming new members. 'We're a small organisation,' she said, 'there are just twelve VC holders and twenty-one GC holders living, but the families represent all those who have gone, and it's a very friendly connection that binds us all together.' I liked her enormously, and when she said, 'You should come along dear, get involved,' I promised I would.

Oz won his medal for three incidents in particular.

The first was the clearing of Pharmacy Road in August 2009, the second was defusing the bomb in the bazaar in October and the third was the incident in which he died.

His citation said:

Staff Sergeant Schmid was a High Threat Improvised Explosive Device Disposal (IEDD) Operator in Helmand from June 2009 until his death in action on 31 October 2009.

He deployed at the height of Operation Panchai Palang (Panther's Claw) and went immediately into the fray, into one of the most physically draining, mentally intense and hazardous jobs in Helmand.

Typically having to deploy on foot, thereby precluding the option of specialist protective equipment and severely limiting the use of remote-controlled vehicles, he spent long periods of time in close proximity to Victim Operated IEDs (VOIED) and in the gravest personal danger. Before his death in action he responded to 42 IED tasks, personally dealing with 70 confirmed IEDs. A number of examples illustrate his bravery.

An infantry company based in Wishtan province was isolated by a substantial minefield and the infamous 'Pharmacy Road', the only resupply route, was blocked by a medium-wheeled tractor and another vehicle, both blown up by very large IEDs.

Intelligence, unenviable first-hand experience and numerous unexplained explosions from the area indicated that the area of the stricken vehicles was laced with IEDs.

At 0800 hours on 9 August 2009, as temperatures soared past 45 degrees Celsius, Schmid started work.

Within only a hundred metres he found and cleared an IED, and once within 100 metres of the vehicles, intent on using a remote controlled vehicle (RCV) and remote explosive clearance devices, he deployed an RCV that struck an IED and was destroyed.

Schmid moved forward without hesitation and, well inside the most lethal arc of any device, manually placed explosive charges, clearing a route to within five metres of the vehicles.

His team then moved to clear a compound adjacent to the stricken vehicles to drag them off the road. When a second IED was found, Schmid made another manual approach and rapidly got rid of it.

A new approach to the vehicles from the compound was explosively created for the hulks to be dragged clear. Schmid painstakingly cleared up to both vehicles and his first trip took an hour. He was relying on his eyesight and understanding of enemy tactics alone.

Despite the threat, Schmid again decided against explosive clearance; time was critical so he placed heavy and cumbersome chains onto the stricken vehicles, the riskiest of enterprises given the very high likelihood of booby traps, and the vehicles were finally dragged clear. As the light started to fade, Schmid then personally led a high risk clearance of the road where the vehicles had been, manually disposing of two further IEDs.

The clearance had lasted 11 hours. It was physically, mentally and emotionally draining, but the road was open and the company resupplied. The resounding success of this battle group operation was entirely due to the heroic, selfless acts of Schmid.

On 8 October 2009, Schmid was tasked in Sangin district centre to deal with an artillery shell reported by Afghan National Army (ANA) soldiers.

On arrival the ANA led him, unsuspecting, directly to the device.

He was now not only at grave personal risk but immediately realised that the many unsuspecting civilians around him in the bustling bazaar were also in peril.

Time was not on his side.

He quickly assessed that the shell was in fact part

of a live radio-controlled IED intended to cause maximum casualties in a well populated area. The nature of the device also meant it was almost certainly overwatched by the bomber controlling it.

Without any consideration for his own safety, Schmid immediately decided to neutralise the IED manually. To do this he knew he was employing a render safe procedure that should only ever be employed in the gravest of circumstances and which is conducted at the highest personal risk to the operator.

In an instant, Schmid made the most courageous decision possible, consciously placing his own life on the line in order to save the lives of countless Afghan civilians and demonstrating bravery of the highest order and well beyond the call of duty.

At the end of October 2009 Schmid was involved in an operation near Forward Operating Base Jackson in Battle Group North's area. Having dealt with three IEDs already that day, Schmid and his team were transiting to another compound when a searcher discovered a command wire running down the alleyway they were using.

Schmid and his team were trapped in the alleyway with no safe route forward or back as they did not know in which direction the IED was situated.

...

Knowing that his team were in potential danger, he immediately took action to reduce the hazard. Schmid eventually traced the wire to a complex command wire IED in that it incorporated three linked, buried main charges.

He was killed whilst dealing with the device.

Schmid's actions on that fateful day, when trapped in an alleyway with no safe means of escape, probably saved the lives of his team. These occasions are representative of the complexity and danger that Schmid had faced daily throughout his four-month tour.

His selfless gallantry, his devotion to duty, and his indefatigable courage, displayed time and time again, saved countless military and civilian lives and is worthy of the highest recognition.

Reading this, and recalling his letters and phone calls, it was hard not to feel that Oz was actually 'in the face of the enemy' most of the time when he was in Afghanistan. But the technicalities were not what mattered. His bravery had been recognised, and in the following weeks I received an avalanche of mail, not least from Oz's delighted colleagues and bosses.

Ash Cooper wrote to say, 'It was with huge pride and satisfaction that I saw Oz had received the appropriate level of national recognition for his genuinely incredible efforts. The term hero is bandied around perhaps too liberally, but Oz absolutely deserves to be called a hero.'

General Sir Kevin O'Donoghue, the Master General of Logistics, wrote, 'The George Cross sits at the top, no less important or revered than the Victoria Cross . . . Bravery is perhaps that virtue which soldiers most hope to have attributed to them, when spoken about by those with whom they have served.'

There were letters from many senior Army personnel, and even from the Duke of Gloucester, who is Deputy Colonel in Chief of the Royal Logistics Corps. But the reactions I enjoyed most were those of his friends, like Hazey, who simply said, 'Good effort.'

CHAPTER TWENTY-TWO

The anniversary of Sam and Hazey's wedding, on 23 May, is another date that's a very poignant one for me. That had been the last time that Oz and Laird and I were truly happy together. It was such a wonderful day, I found it almost impossible to look at the photos of us, laughing, dancing, full of hope, without getting that familiar black, heavy feeling.

Within a couple of days a black cloud had descended on us, and a week later Oz was gone and I would never see him again.

There was nothing I could do to help the day pass more easily. I had hoped that now, almost seven months on, the grief might get a little easier, but if anything the opposite was true. The initial wave of adrenalin that had carried me through the aftermath was gone, and in its place was the raw daily pain of missing him, day in and day out.

*

On Wednesday 2 June I got up early and travelled to Buckingham Palace with Laird and my parents. Having received the George Cross citation, now was the time to collect Oz's medal. It was half-term, which meant Laird didn't have to miss school, but it also meant that there was a lot of extra traffic about, as families headed to London to see the sights.

I had very mixed feelings about this day, and about the medal. Everyone was so pleased for me when he won it, but it seemed to bring his loss into even sharper contrast. I found it so hard to be doing something for him that he should have been there to do. In the end I decided to make it as good a day as possible, even though I didn't feel that way inside.

Oz's achievements were part of history, and this day would always be part of our history as a family.

The sun shone and I wore a yellow dress, for peace. Laird wore a suit and looked so grown-up. We drove, but halfway there we had a puncture. Thankfully we had left lots of time, and we managed to change the wheel and set off again.

We had our palace parking sticker on the car, so when we arrived we were directed to the parking area. Then we were escorted inside and up to a beautiful room, with doors flung wide to a balcony overlooking the gardens. It was a warm day.

The Queen was conducting a number of other medal

ceremonies first, and though we had been invited to watch, we decided we would rather not. I felt that seeing other lads getting their medals when Oz couldn't accept his would be a bit like someone holding a megaphone in my face shouting, 'Your husband's dead.'

The staff were gracious and friendly; they brought tea, sandwiches and fresh apple juice for Laird, and chatted to us as we waited for an hour or so. Laird, like any seven-year-old, was bored and ran around the room and out on to the balcony.

'Where's your helipad?' he asked one of the staff.

'It's over there,' the chap replied, indicating the furthest reaches of the gardens.

'Can I go down there now please?' Laird asked.

The man smiled, 'Yes, I'm sure we can arrange that.'

They talked us through what the Queen would do, and as the time for her arrival approached, Mum grew very emotional.

'Would you like to come this way now?' the chap asked. 'Her Majesty will be with you shortly.'

We followed him through to another glorious room we were told is the Music Room. On the way they showed us the room where President Obama was received. It was lovely to think of all these beautiful rooms being used, rather than sitting empty; it felt almost like a family home, albeit a spectacularly grand one.

When the Queen came in she came straight over to us

and smiled. She wore a dress with yellow flecks in it and I felt she was a lovely, strong, calm presence, and found her very beautiful. She didn't rush at all; she made us feel that she had all the time in the world.

After the introductions, she asked how our journey had been.

Laird told her about the puncture and she said, 'Oh, I do understand, we had one a couple of days ago. I was with my husband and we couldn't get the wheel nuts off, we had to wait ages.'

Laird, who was not overawed in the least, said, 'What you need to do is what my Mummy does. Whenever you have a new car, go into the tyre place and chat to the men and they'll undo those nuts from the factory just a little bit and then you can undo them yourself by hand and you won't have to struggle.'

'Oh really?' Her Majesty replied, smiling. 'Right I'll do that.'

She was playful, chatty, warm with Laird. I hadn't been expecting her to be so natural. She said to him, 'How do you feel about coming here today for your father?' and he said, 'I'm happy to be here, but it's very hot, I like your balcony it's beautiful.'

She turned to me and said, 'I know what your husband did and there are no words to express my admiration.' Her directness and warmth floored me, but I was determined not to cry.

'My family and I have listened to you on Radio Four

and read the press,' she continued. 'We're very impressed with the way that you have conducted yourself. I try to listen and follow what is happening.' Her voice was soft and I could feel she was genuine.

I thanked her, and an assistant brought the medal over, on a red cushion. The Queen took it and held it between her hands as she talked to us for several minutes, about the George Cross, how it had been started by her father and its history. She spoke about how significant an award this was and said, 'I'm very humbled by the work that they all do and particularly what your husband did.' She referred to him as 'your husband', never as Staff Sergeant Schmid. There was a sense of intimacy and connection, and she held the medal as though she were infusing it with her warmth and good wishes.

As she handed it to me, tears filled my eyes. I looked at Mum, who was crying, and I knew we were thinking the same thing. He should be here.

The medal was white gold, a simple and very contemporary design, and was attached to a bright, sky-blue ribbon. It reminded me of the colour of Oz's eyes – everyone used to notice his eyes. I was very tearful and remarked upon the colour. She listened.

After spending time with us, the Queen said goodbye. I had managed to maintain my composure in public so many times, but in the face of the kindness and warmth of the Queen, I could not. When faced with anything quiet or a one-to-one meeting, I would often break. I was the opposite to others in their grief.

The staff member arrived to escort us back down through the palace and as we started down the sweeping staircase, Laird giggled. 'If Daddy was here he'd slide down the banisters, wouldn't he?'

He was so right. Oz was always making us laugh, fidgeting, jumping and sliding down banisters, and these were perfect, wide ones. He'd have loved them. And he'd have loved the medal. I pictured him pinning it on, with a cheeky grin, and saying, 'What do you think?'

The member of staff, true to his word, took us out into the gardens, where Laird did aeroplane arms all round the helipad and they let us take photographs. There was a small lake, and Laird ran down to it and back – he had a long car journey ahead so a bit of exercise was a blessing. The gardens were beautiful, old and established, with fresh, green grass. I was so impressed they utilised the palace so thoroughly and enjoyed the lovely, chilled atmosphere.

That night, at home, Laird said to me, 'I don't need a medal to tell me how good my Daddy is, I just want him back so he can help me with my Lego. I'm going to design a time machine so I can go back in time and see him.'

CHAPTER TWENTY-THREE

Our palace visit was a wonderful experience, one that will stay in our memories always. But while I loved Oz's medal and was enormously proud of it, I didn't know what I was going to do with it. To keep it in a safe would be a terrible waste, but it was worth a great deal of money, perhaps half a million pounds, and I couldn't exactly pop it in my jewellery box.

The answer arrived via Didy Grahame, whom I went to see in London, in the VC and GC Association offices in Horse Guards Parade. 'Why not put it in the Imperial War Museum?' she said. 'It will still belong to you, but will be beautifully displayed, beside the other VCs and GCs – there are quite a number of them there. It's so important that people can see them, for inspiration.'

I made contact with the museum and made a number of visits. It seemed like the perfect place to display Oz's medal. I wanted to include something personal with it, as many others had, so I put his iPod there too. He listened to it all the time in Afghanistan, as a way of escaping what was going on around him. He loved music, a whole range of classical and pop. It was an item that was pure Oz.

Di Lees, Director General of the museum, asked me to work with them a couple of days a week as a volunteer, to help promote the museum and its collections. It was sadly having its funding cut, but they very much want to keep it free entry and needed to develop a higher profile and encourage more people to come.

I was introduced to Lord Ashcroft, the businessman, philanthropist and politician, who owns the world's largest collection of VCs and who donated the money for the Ashcroft Gallery to be built at the very top of the Imperial War Museum, in the heavens, under the dome. The museum is housed in what used to be Bedlam, the Hospital for the Criminally Insane, a stunning building, but protected. They can't add on wings, they can only go up, so that's what they did, and the new gallery houses the VC and GC collection.

Michael Ashcroft told me he was writing a book, *George Cross Heroes* (he had already written *Victoria Cross Heroes*), and he asked me to contribute to the book, which was published in 2011. The proceeds from which were donated to the VC and GC Association. He told the stories of every George Cross hero – all but four of whom were men. In the entry for Oz he outlined what

Oz had done in Afghanistan and then added, 'There are many outstanding tributes in this book to many worthy GC recipients. But the tributes to Staff Sergeant Olaf 'Oz' Schmid from his commanding officers and comrades are not only hard for anyone to match, but they also come from the heart.'

In the foreword, to which I gave a great deal of thought, I said:

> Oz was a unique maverick and I feel the award captured the essence of him and everything he represented. I had always known that Oz had been consistently brave in all areas of life, particularly his bomb-disposal work in Afghanistan. However, after I learnt about the exact circumstances in which Oz had died, I decorated him in my own mind with a gallantry medal because I was convinced he deserved one. When it was announced much later that he had been awarded the George Cross, I felt an overwhelming sense of pride . . . I also felt a sense of justice that Oz's relentless bravery had, finally, been publicly recognised. I know that if Oz was still alive, he would have been 'wowed' by what has been said about him.

In July I was asked to Number Ten Downing Street to become a patron of 'Tickets for Troops', a charity set up to do exactly what it says – obtain tickets to events across a broad spectrum, from concerts to theatre to sporting events, to give to serving members of the Forces, or to those discharged on medical grounds. I had no hesitation in saying yes, and my fellow patrons included, among others, Samantha Cameron, Gary Lineker, James Blunt, Jeremy Clarkson, Freddie Flintoff, Sir Michael Parkinson and Lawrence Dallaglio.

Since I became a patron I have worked hard for TFT, often two or three days a week, attending corporate events and persuading organisers to donate tickets, not just a few cut-price ones, but regular donations of full-price tickets over several years, as a way of showing appreciation for the Armed Forces and all they do.

I also offered support to the Child Bereavement Trust – speaking for them about forces children and bereavement in particular – and became involved with the VC and GC Association, getting to know Didy Grahame, whom I liked and admired enormously. One day, helping out in the office, as a volunteer on a regular basis, would be great, as long as Laird is settled – it is still very much early days for us.

Keeping busy has always been my style and, after losing Oz, it helped me to immerse myself as much as possible in good causes and in publicising, as much as I could, the cause of the troops in Afghanistan. I felt, in some way, that by helping them in any way possible, I was doing something to make Oz proud of me.

I was also asked to become a regular contributor for

News International and its publications. They are pro-Forces and very supportive and professional, offering me a platform for the causes I wanted to promote, so I accepted. The first assignment I had was an interview with David Cameron, the new prime minister, who at that point had been in office for just seven weeks. It was published on 4 July and I was extremely proud of it. I didn't hold back when talking to David Cameron, I asked him about funding and equipment, about harmony guidelines, military covenant, pay and pensions and support for dependants and families. I also asked him how long we'd be in Afghanistan for and what he felt was important.

The week after, the government pledged a further £67 million for counter-IED teams. He knew that the only way to ease the workload on men like Oz was to put more men on the ground, and he stressed that the war was working in the sense that there were fewer terror plots coming out of Afghanistan and Pakistan. He said, 'A few years ago, seventy-five to eighty per cent of the plots we faced in this country came from that area. It's now more like fifty per cent. Why is that? Because we cleared al-Qaeda out of Afghanistan and the Pakistanis are making some progress at clearing some of them out of Pakistan'.

He told me that Afghanistan was the biggest responsibility, and the biggest challenge, he faced, and he promised to look at the length of military tours and to protect the £9 million funding the government had allocated to help military personnel suffering from stress. He also promised to look at military widows' pensions. After Oz died, I was given a pension of just £6,000 a year – £4,000 for me and £2,000 for Laird, all of it taxable. A pitiful amount.

It was a challenging meeting and I hoped very much that it would play a part in raising awareness of the issues and helping to bring about a better deal for troops.

In late November I was given the Communicator of the Year Award by the Institute of Internal Communication, for championing better equipment for soldiers in Afghanistan and for my patronage of the Tickets for Troops charity. The announcement said:

Christina has spoken powerfully about a number of issues affecting the Armed Forces and has presented her own BBC1 *Panorama* investigation into the work of high-threat bomb-disposal officers.

Earlier this year, Christina became a patron of the charity, Tickets for Troops, which offers free tickets for big events to soldiers, sailors and airmen.

Her fellow patron, Samantha Cameron, wife of the prime minister, has praised her 'remarkable strength' and her campaigning work on behalf of troops serving abroad.

I was delighted by this generous recognition and went up to the Landmark Hotel in London to receive the award. In my heart, I collected it for Oz, because in the end, everything I did was for him.

I kept busy, I did what I could, I accepted invitations that I thought might further the cause of supporting the Armed Forces, and, as time went by, many people thought I had 'got over' losing Oz. I was good at putting on a public face; smiling, dressing smartly, saying and doing the right things. But I still missed Oz as much as ever.

The people who saw me in public didn't see me in those dark moments – and there were still so many – when I felt I couldn't bear the sense of loss, and knowing I would never see him again felt like a tidal wave of pain that I couldn't fight.

The anniversary of his death was a grim day, and what helped to get me through it were the letters and calls from Oz's friends and colleagues. Rob Thomson wrote, 'Please be aware that you are still very much front and centre in my prayers and thoughts. One year on your pain and grief will not be diminished and I still treasure the memory of the one and only Oz . . . I will find time on 31st October to pause and remember your husband and acknowledge the sacrifice he has made for his fellow soldiers, his country, and for the betterment of the people of Afghanistan.'

I appreciated letters like that so much. It would have been easy for people to disappear after the initial wave of grief, but many did not, and their kindness helped me to get through.

In February 2011 came another major hurdle: the inquest. It had been delayed for sixteen months, a ridiculously long time, during which I was acutely aware that it was something I had yet to face. It was held in Truro, and from the start I felt it was a sham.

When I arrived I was seated facing the window, looking out on the cathedral where Oz's funeral was held, and facing the men who were going to be witnesses. It felt desperately uncomfortable.

I felt that I was treated curtly and without proper consideration and there was no concession whatsoever made for the sensitivity of the occasion.

In her opening speech the coroner made it clear that she would not be looking further than what happened in the minutes before Oz died: to my mind a complete failure of the purpose of the inquest.

In my opinion it was to be another whitewash inquest, avoiding controversy, without recommendations or any glimpse at the bigger picture, no deeper interest in saving lives or looking at the real issues. Just another box-ticking exercise.

Before witnesses were called we had to sit and listen to a long, detailed and gruesome autopsy report. It was appalling to have to listen to how Oz's pliers, which I had bought, were found inside his thorax, and other gruesome details. But I could have withstood that if I had felt that the underlying purpose of a coroner's court were being upheld.

Long before the inquest, the day Oz had died, I had asked for bloods to be taken. I had kept asking where the toxicology report was. It would have shown whether he had eaten and drunk enough in the hours before he died, and what level his blood sugar was at, what his cortisol levels were, so you could see if he was functioning and fit. But no toxicology report was ever done, despite me being told that one might have been carried out. I was unsure as to why I had been told potentially conflicting stories.

As far as I knew, he hadn't eaten since early morning – nine hours before he died. That would have affected his ability to make clear decisions – a vital part of his job.

He was desensitised and therefore compromised. It is a fact that he hadn't had R&R – as Harmony guidelines state he should have had – of a week every four months, at the very least. This would have been a vital respite, so that he could have been away from his 'ten-minutes' notice to move', and had a break from being a troop commander for a short space of time. It would have given him a chance to rest and come back with a fresh attitude to risk.

But none of those factors which clearly affected him the day he died were raised, only the actions in the moment.

It is fact that he was not a safe operator prior to that job. No matter what, he was compromised and unsafe that day, and I believe that the military and his seniors failed to ensure he was as safe as he needed to be. That is not Oz's fault. Why should Laird and I suffer if the Army failed him? No matter what his job was, you will not be able to say the cause of death until you have ruled out those factors and you can say he was fed, watered, rested as per guidelines – only then can you say he was mentally, spiritually and physically fit that day. I felt that again the UK chose not to raise the bar, but instead to slope its shoulders and pull its Teflon coat around itself, allowing these conditions to continue. It is, in my mind, despicable.

After a couple of hours I made the decision to leave. I felt that this inquest could have been a real opportunity to expose some truths and make recommendations, and nothing of the sort was going to happen. Nothing would be addressed. Instead it was being implied that the blame for what happened lay with Oz, because he was a little rushed that day, and because he had spoken to Laird two days earlier, and Laird had said, 'You need to come home now, Daddy.' Perhaps he wasn't himself that day but, even if that was true, that was not why he died.

I was not about to have my son or my husband blamed for Oz's death. He was a professional at the top of his game, he knew what he was doing, he had done it so many times before. This was his third job that day. Yes, he was desperately tired, he hadn't been given breaks and that should have been addressed, but he would not have made a mistake in a situation like that. I believe the device may have been detonated by remote control. But no witness could say for sure.

I was represented by the British Legion, who asked questions on my behalf, and my friend Sam stayed on for the whole two days, to report to me about the proceedings. But it was clear to me that the whole thing was an attempt to brush everything under the carpet. No one was going to be allowed to bring out any truths about how the Army let Oz down by failing to give him proper rest breaks.

Colonel Bob Seddon, the Army's senior bomb-disposal officer who resigned at the time of the *Panorama* programme, told the inquest that in the month after Oz's death the Army had fifty per cent of its desired level of IED specialists, and that it was a constant battle to keep up with new IEDs developed by the Taliban. But this information, which might have led to questions about how tired and overworked Oz was, went nowhere. Instead emphasis was put on the fact that Oz seemed more impatient than normal during the fatal patrol, and that Laird had told him it was time for him to come home.

The coroner said, 'It was his last day before rest and

recreation and he was apparently keen to get the task done and anxious to clear the area.' Recording a verdict that Oz was unlawfully killed while on active service, she added, 'There was nothing in the operation which fell below what might have been expected and that could have contributed to his death.'

I felt let down, I had not got justice for Oz. The evidence and conclusions had tarnished him, and the whole truth had not come out. I was furious. I felt they had subtly discredited Oz by saying that he was rushed or impatient or distracted. Whereas the conclusion should have said that he hadn't been looked after properly, or been given proper rest breaks. He was over-worked. The inquest didn't look into anything other than what happened to his body, whereas I wanted a fuller picture of the build-up.

It was frustrating and sad – such a good opportunity lost. The brief, as with so many other military inquests, was clearly to avoid all controversy.

I put the inquest behind me, as much as I could, and got on with the work in hand.

Over the following months, I gave as much support as I could to the Royal British Legion's 'Honour the Covenant' campaign, with News International, which aimed to have the Military Covenant made law. I attended International Women's Day and asked Cameron directly why he hadn't honoured his promise to make it legally binding. He said that Libya and Japan had kept him extremely busy. I said, Didn't he have the guts to do what he said he would? Can't he handle the job? Didn't he promise almost a year before to make it legally binding? I said, If Oz said he would do something, then he would honour that promise. Cheeky, I know!

The Military Covenant was an agreement, an informal understanding, referring to the government and the nation's duty of care to the Armed Forces. It was used to refer to adequate safeguards, civil rights, rewards and compensations for military personnel and their dependants, who agree to risk their lives for the country and forgo certain civil rights in return for being looked after by the state, housed, clothed, fed, paid, and receiving access to health and education for their children, wherever they are asked to live.

Under the legal terms of the covenant, soldiers who were injured would be compensated and cared for and so would the families of those who'd died. Although these commitments were honoured, they were not laid down in law, and they were not good enough. I was shocked to discover, for instance, that the paltry widow's pension would be removed altogether if a widow remarried.

To our great delight, in May 2011, David Cameron announced that the Military Covenant would become law, under the new Armed Forces Bill. This was a complete U-turn, because in February the Defence Secretary, Liam Fox, had ruled out codifying the covenant in the bill.

The prime minister put the Armed Forces bill back a week and used an article in the *News of the World* to explain the decision: 'The high esteem we all have for our Armed Forces will soon be given the recognition it deserves – as part of the law of the land. I'm keeping my word. We owe them. If we are asking our Armed Forces to do dangerous jobs in places like Afghanistan and Iraq, we have to ensure that we are doing everything we can for them in return.'

The covenant would apply to all three services, setting out rights to healthcare, housing and education for Forces children, including a doubling of council tax relief to fifty per cent for those serving overseas and a £3m fund for schools with high numbers of children from Forces families. The government also committed to caring for injured veterans who need prosthetic limbs and to giving personnel better access to cut-price public transport.

In addition, action was promised to improve military inquests. Veterans who have suffered genital injuries were also promised access to IVF treatment, either privately or through the NHS. It was estimated that the entire package would cost £45m a year.

It was a great victory for all those who had campaigned, and for the *News of the World*, which, despite all the awful phone-hacking scandal of the past, had raised its game.

That night I sat at the kitchen table with a glass of wine and raised a toast.

'To you Oz. Well done, honey.'

EPILOGUE

October 2011

Two years on, there are times when I feel I am only just beginning to grieve, and other times when, just for a moment, I can laugh at something and not feel a surge of pain because Oz isn't there to share the joke.

The hurdles are always there – the anniversaries, birthdays; all events, markers in life that arrive so relentlessly, every one of them accompanied by that awful lurch of awareness on waking: he's not here.

I still miss him so much. Every single day.

It can be silly things that set me off. Civvies. Small things people moan about that I know he used to despise as trivial. I hear someone click a cigarette lighter and the distinctive sound reminds me of how Oz used to light his rollies with his Zippo. I open the freezer to get out some fish fingers and see that pasty, the one he made with his initials on it, and it physically hurts. I guess I ought to throw it away. But I can't. Just like I can't clear the last Rizlas and menthol tips out of the car.

Sometimes I sit in the dark for hours and think about him. I don't ask why, I know that's futile. Only people who really knew him and were intimate with him, slept, ate, lived and fought with him, knew him. As he said, anyone else is a cling-on, hun, or history. Only trust these people, he'd say when he was alive. Thank God I listened and remembered that.

Laird and Bo and I moved out of quarters into a new house out of the centre of Winchester a few months ago. I picked it because it was surrounded by hawthorn and had a stream running past and a great big rock beside the gate. I know Oz would have approved. We've got the little fire pit we all used to sit beside out in the garden.

After the inquest my dad, who is a very practical man, said to me, 'That's enough now, it's time to move on. I will not stay in this country we've worked so hard in and for and pay taxes and see such wrongdoing. I know one thing, you broke the rules when they said you wouldn't change things, Swissy – you have, you know. Oz did and you did. We're so proud of you both.'

None of us who loved Oz are, or ever can be, the same.

In fact, the lives of so many of our friends and family have changed since Oz was killed. I sometimes wonder what Oz would make of all that has happened. Biscuits from Alpha Troop, whom he loved (Biscuits, like many, had a tattoo for Oz), and his wife Charlie had a baby, maybe committing earlier than they would have done, but it brought them closer. Others can't talk about it properly and it tears relationships apart. Hazey found peace by saying farewell to his best friend in the back of the C17 during the repat ceremony. He didn't talk about it after Truro – I suppose it was his way of coping. Unfortunately Sam found that approach difficult to come to terms with, and she and I will talk for hours, sometimes sitting in silence, knowing what each other was thinking. In the end her strong Warrior Sikh faith helped channel her grief into positive actions.

Mum and Dad are now living abroad, to find a bit of sun and get away from memories and what they hate most about modern British society.

As for me, I don't think it matters where I am. I am linked to him in a thousand ways, small and big. Even in my work. I did try going back to pharmaceuticals, briefly, on a freelance contract, but it reminded me of my old life. The pressure to get sales was no challenge to me any more, the hours were too long, and my heart wasn't in it, sitting in hospital car parks where I can remember taking his calls before or after work meetings.

I had been asked to help with the VC GC Association in the future. I am thinking about it. 'I would like to do it,' I told Didy. 'But I'm not sure I'm worthy.'

'Oh rubbish,' Didy said crisply, 'You're right for it, Swiss. But you are overdoing things at the moment and Laird comes first.'

I am still undecided as I am enjoying sorting the house out and looking after my son. I enjoy the outdoors and property and travel, and commit to doing the odd things now like the weekend of rememberance in Trafalgar Square for Armistice Day.

Oz would have loved so many of the tributes he received. But one in particular would have delighted him. He always said footballers and the like got credit these days and are seen as sexy because of the money they earn and what they look like; however, what about the values that matter? He used to say, 'That's what you find most attractive, isn't it hun?' I remember agreeing. So when the December 2010 issue of *Esquire* was published, with hot men in it, with brains and old-fashioned values and Oz's picture across a double-page spread as one of their Men of the Year, I laughed. He'd made those qualities desirable again.

The photo and the accompanying write-up were by photo-journalist David Gill, the one who sent me that now-familiar picture of Oz which was issued when he died. In the text David said:

I'd met and interviewed him [Oz] in Sangin, where he was tirelessly working to clear minefields in one of the most lethal combat zones in Afghanistan

. . . his death put the Afghanistan war in a different perspective for the whole of 2010.

He was handsome, with a beautiful wife and kid and an incredible job. He defused more than 100 IEDs, saving uncounted lives. But behind the story was a man I knew and liked. He talked to me about buying a house in Cornwall, about how he loved his job but wanted to get out of the Army. Oz wasn't there to kill people; he was there to protect them – the soldiers from his own regiment as well as many Afghan villagers who will never know the sacrifice he made. I won't forget him. No one who knew or worked with him will.

Believe it or not, Oz once said to me that he'd love to appear in a magazine like *Esquire*. I don't know why he said it; he was never vain and he wasn't that into magazines – he must have read a copy and been impressed by all the high-achieving, good-looking men in there. Or perhaps he just thought it would be fun. Either way, he got his wish, and the picture they used was brilliant. He'd have loved it.

And he'd have loved me getting together for an evening with Sam, a mad girl and great soldier, who lost a finger and part of her leg to an IED in Afghanistan. When she got back, in the summer of 2011, she said, 'Right – you, me, out on the piss.' We drank loads, cried loads and talked about Oz. She told me Oz used to say,

' "I wouldn't be me without my Chrissy." It was you two, we all knew that.'

That only made me cry harder.

Because equally, I wouldn't be me without him.

I look for him everywhere and I find him in what Laird and I call, 'Oz winks'. Little coincidences, premonitions, things that would have made him smile. One evening, last summer, I was sitting in the garden with Laird and I suddenly knew I would see two shooting stars. Oz had said in a letter that he'd seen two shooting stars and I told Laird they would be coming. We looked up, and there they were, swooping down from the heavens.

I can hear Oz laughing at me now.

I'm still restless, still thinking about moving again to Cornwall, Dorset or Jersey, to be by the sea someday soon. Somehow we don't really feel settled in the new house. I feel short-changed of the future we'd planned, and it's hard to make a different one. But, with the support of family and the unconditional friendship of my phenomenal girlfriends, who hold my hand and push me on, I can only go forward slowly, one step at a time. But I think it will be near the sea. Laird and I go there often – it's a place where we can feel carefree and remember happy times with Oz.

And every time we walk along a wide, wild beach, I know that he is with us, in our hearts.

Always.

EULOGY FOR OZ

In my eyes my husband, my son's father, was a
warrior. Warriors are unique. Our protectors, not
destroyers. Olaf and troops like him join to serve
traditional warrior values: to passionately protect the
country they love, its ideals, and especially their
families, communities and each other. In past conflicts,
where there was an immediate threat to our shores and
our existence, soldiers were never plagued with self-
doubt about the value of their role in society, and a
people and their soldiers were once close in unity. We
might disagree with a war. However, I hope through
Olaf's death, my public storytelling and appreciation,
our community display of respect here today can serve
to bridge that gap and unite us once more with our
troops.

I hope the work Olaf and others like him undertake
on our behalf is not taken for granted any more or goes
unnoticed by our leaders. For Olaf has certainly raised

the bar. From now on I expect our peacemakers to show us they are working as hard as he did to preserve life. I'd like to see them push themselves and serve us like never before. I want to see them tirelessly fight with his same spirit, dedication and integrity day in, day out for peace . . . Most of you will have known Oz the joker, always up for a giggle. However, I lived with a very different man. The last eighteen months I've stood by him as he described his toughest, darkest challenges ever. When he felt compromised, overwhelmed or threatened, I've wiped his tears, pulled him up and fought his fears for him. Becoming his proud widow is the hardest, however, best thing I have ever done for him.

I am fiercely loyal to serve him in death as I did when he was alive, however much it's breaking me. Hopefully he's watching and knows he's the only man who will always have all of me . . . Olaf lived and stood for something he believed in. And in the end he paid the ultimate sacrifice for those beliefs. We now have a duty to not just honour what he stood for but live lives which honour the sacrifice he made. Please do not allow him to die in vain.

ACKNOWLEDGEMENTS

The author and publishers would like to thank the following copyright-holders for permission to reproduce images in this book:

©David Gill; ©Michael Yon; ©Getty Images; ©Jamie Wiseman

All other images are care of the author

The author and publishers have made all reasonable efforts to contact copyright-holders for permission, and apologise for any omissions or errors in the form of credits given. Corrections may be made to future printings.

NOTES ON SOURCES

Chapter 9
'Killed in Afghanistan: My friend, the bomb disposal hero', The *Independent*, Sunday 14 September 2008, Terri Judd

Chapter 13
'His Last Lonely Walk', *The Sunday Times*, Sunday 8 November 2009, Miles Amoore © Miles Amoore / The Sunday Times / NI Syndication

Epilogue
Esquire, Men of the Year 2010, words by David Gill